D1228615

64219

HT
1581   Bolt, Christine
B63   Victorian attitudes to race

DATE DUE			
OCT 2 0 1977			
NOV 3 1977			
APR 6 1978			
MAR 9 1979			
APR 2 7 1983			
SEP 2 8 1998			

LEARNING RESOURCES CENTER
MONTGOMERY COUNTY COMMUNITY COLLEGE
BLUE BELL, PENNSYLVANIA

Victorian Attitudes to Race

STUDIES IN SOCIAL HISTORY

edited by

HAROLD PERKIN

Professor of Social History, University of Lancaster

Victorian Attitudes
to Race

Christine Bolt

LONDON: Routledge & Kegan Paul
TORONTO: University of Toronto Press

First published 1971 in Great Britain by
Routledge & Kegan Paul Limited
and in Canada and the United States of America by
University of Toronto Press
Printed in Great Britain by
Cox and Wyman Ltd, Fakenham, Norfolk
Copyright Christine Bolt 1971
No part of this book may be reproduced
in any form without permission from the
publisher, except for the quotation of brief
passages in criticism
RKP ISBN 0 7100 6926 X
UTP ISBN 0 8020 1751 7

HT
1581
B63

64219

for Ian

Contents

Preface

DURING the middle years of the nineteenth century, 'race', like 'civilization', became one of the great catchwords of those Victorians who concerned themselves with events outside Britain. Superiority of the white race justified increasing inter- vention in Africa, continuing British rule in India, the savage repression of the Jamaica revolt of 1865, and acid comments on the racial experiments of the United States during Reconstruct- ion. The innate inferiority of coloured – and especially Negro – races made such intervention and such comments not only practi- cable but excusable, in the interests of religion, progress and truth. But, as the President of the London Anthropological Society, James Hunt, complained in 1863, 'hardly two persons use such an important word as "race" in the same sense'.[1]

The word 'race' was first used in English literature as denoting a class of people, even a family. In eighteenth-century usage it was possible to speak of a race of animals or birds. By the nineteenth century this imprecision was fully recognized, and it was suggested that the term was purely subjective, and illumin- ated the 'opinion of the investigator rather than . . . the object of his investigation'.[2]

[1] *Introductory Address on the Study of Anthropology Delivered Before the Anthropological Society of London, February 24th, 1863, by James Hunt* (London, 1863), p. 13.
[2] *Encyclopaedia Britannica*, 8th Ed., IX (1855), p. 341.

ix

Such confusion was to be deplored, not merely from a scientific point of view, but because, according to Hunt, the fate of nations depended on a true appreciation of anthropology. Were not 'the causes which have overthrown the greatest of nations', he asked, 'to be resolved by the laws regulating the intermixture of the races of man'? Did not 'the success of our colonisation depend on the deductions of our science'? And was not 'the composition of harmonious nations entirely a question of race'?[3]

The question of race cropped up endlessly in Victorian speeches and writings, and all too often prejudice perverted reason, while racist and philanthropist alike described what they hoped rather than knew to be true. Many useful studies have been produced on racial attitudes in different parts of the Empire, at different times, during the nineteenth century.[4] Little has so far been done to draw this research together: to provide a comparative survey of the most characteristic Victorian opinions about coloured races.

In attempting such a work, I have taken 1850 as my approximate point of departure. The decade which followed was one of tension: improvements in medicine facilitated Britain's growing – if reluctant – involvement in the Gold Coast, Zanzibar and Central Africa; the turbulence between blacks, Boers and British in South Africa could not safely be ignored; in the United States racial animosity aggravated political and economic grievances and threatened to divide the Union; while in 1857 news of the Indian Mutiny shattered the Anglo-Indian community, the Victorian reading public, and the whole world. During the 1850s dwindling membership, shrinking funds and public indifference bore witness to the decline of the British anti-slavery movement.

Britain's industrial, financial and maritime pre-eminence at this time, associated with the triumph of free trade, rendered colonies temporarily unfashionable (as opposed to the 'interests' which were cultivated in, for instance, North Africa). Fear, the product of unhappy experiences in India, the Cape Colony and

[3] *Anniversary Address Delivered Before the Anthropological Society of London, January 5th, 1864, by James Hunt* (London, 1864), p. 16.

[4] See, for instance, P. D. Curtin, *The Image of Africa* (London, 1965); H. A. Cairns, *Prelude to Imperialism* (London, 1965).

New Zealand, undermined the Romantic view of the Noble Savage and the complacent concept of the peaceful child of Nature. A leader writer in the *Daily Telegraph* in 1866 captured this new mood exactly with his confession that 'Of all human tasks, the most hopelessly difficult is that of governing wisely, humanely, and justly a community in which unequal and antagonistic races are largely intermingled'.[5] But ironically, during a period of apparent recoil from overseas commitment, the aggressive assertion of white superiority which is such a pronounced feature of the 1850s and 1860s prepared the way for the next great phase of British expansion towards the end of the century.

This study is concerned primarily with opinion, not with establishing new historical facts or illuminating government diplomacy, and is based upon materials obtainable in Britain. The main areas here under review are Jamaica, Africa, India and the United States. To reduce the volume of material a little, in the chapter on Jamaica attention has been focused on the revolt of 1865, which crystallized Victorian thinking about the West Indian Negro. Inevitably many of those whose observations I have used had no first-hand experience of the races they described. Some were the armchair philanthropists who, as the eminent Victorian explorer Sir Richard Burton cynically put it, so loved Africa that they 'avoid it as a pestilence'. In Burton's opinion, 'ignorance, not knowledge, sentimentality not sense, sway the public mind' on racial questions.[6] But the testimony of the ignorant may be the most typical, may tell us a great deal about Victorian, if not primitive, society. British attitudes and responses to colonial and American developments, in fact, have a logic of their own, and, however inaccurate and biased it may have been, public opinion frequently influenced public policy or resulted in some sort of practical activity in the areas concerned.

The French political commentator Louis Blanc, in his *Letters on England* published in 1866 and 1867, noted that 'in this

[5] 12 September 1866.
[6] *A Mission to Galele, King of Dahome. With Notices of the So Called 'Amazons', the Grand Customs, the Yearly Customs, the Human Sacrifices, the Present State of the Slave Trade, and the Negro's Place in Nature* (London, 1864, 2 vols.), II, pp. 184–5, 183.

PREFACE

country opinion rules'. Writing at the same time, the Rev. J. Macnaught likewise commented on the importance of public opinion, which 'is, we are assured, the great force of the present day'.[7] The anti-slavery crusade in the early part of the century had served to demonstrate the power of middle-class opinion mobilized by skilful and persistent propaganda.[8]

The problems involved in measuring popular attitudes are, however, considerable (without the assistance of the statistics, polls and interviewers used by historian and sociologist equally in the present century). Such attitudes represent the reactions of particular individuals to their social environment – in other words, always have some objective reference. The ultimate proof of the existence of any attitude lies in the behaviour to which it gives rise, whether in the form of overt actions or opinion (that is, verbal or written behaviour). Opinion has the advantage over overt response in that the latter may, by its specific nature, misrepresent the attitude if it is at all complex.[9]

Then, too, there is the problem of detecting misrepresentation and insincerity, and of distinguishing a point of view independently arrived at from the 'official mind' on racial issues. Those appealing for public funds, for instance, have a powerful motive for slanting their evidence. Thus an eminent anthropologist dismissed as scientifically valueless the reports of missionaries who indulged in 'self-glorifying accounts of their own labours'. 'Some fear shocking public opinion', he remarked, 'while others indulge in exaggerations for the sake of the excitement which their narrative produces in the reading public'.[10]

The materials available for a study of public opinion in the nineteenth century are not, of course, equally representative of all sections of British society. E. D. Adams has suggested that as late as the 1860s, 'nearly all vehicles of British expression, were . . . "in the hands of the educated classes, and these educated classes corresponded with the privileged classes". The

[7] Translated by J. Hutton and L. J. Trotter (2nd Series, London, 1867, 2 vols.), II, p. 55; and *The Future: or Ten Years Hence* (London, 1867), pp. 8 and *passim*.

[8] See F. Thistlethwaite, *The Anglo-American Connection in the Early Nineteenth Century* (Philadelphia, 1959).

[9] I. D. MacCrone, *Race Attitudes in South Africa. Historical, Experimental and Psychological Studies* (Johannesburg, 1965), pp. 142–6.

[10] James Hunt, *Introductory Address, op. cit.*, p. 12.

more democratic element of British society lacked any adequate press representation of its opinions' and was forced to express itself publicly through meetings and demonstrations.[11]

By the end of Victoria's reign, as a result of changes in the franchise, the improvement of primary education, and the ending of the stamp tax and duties on paper, which encouraged the growth of a cheap Press, the 'vehicles of expression' were at last becoming available to articulate men in all walks of life. But the journals, newspapers, books and documents which have proved most vocal on the issue of race are not working-class, even though the anti-slavery and freedmen's aid movements organized workers' auxiliaries, and missionary societies published papers for 'our friends in the humbler ranks of life'.[12] Opinion as interpreted here is predominantly middle-class, referring in the main not to what the masses actually thought and believed, but to the writings of the literate minority about what *they* thought and believed their contemporaries to feel.

[11] *Great Britain and the American Civil War* (London, 1925, 2 vols.), I, pp. 40–1.

[12] *The Church Missionary Intelligencer, a Monthly Journal of Missionary Information* (London, 1850), I, 1, p. 2. (In future C.M.I.).

Notes on Press Sources

Among newspapers and periodicals frequently used in this book, the following tended to Liberalism in politics and a sympathetic approach to race questions: the *Daily News, Spectator, Economist* and *Bee-Hive* (all London); the *Freeman's Journal* (Dublin), *Northern Whig* and *Banner of Ulster* (both Belfast), *Manchester Examiner and Times* and the *North British Daily Mail* (Glasgow). The *Daily Telegraph* and *Scotsman* (London and Edinburgh respectively), though Liberal in politics, were rather conservative on matters of race. Conservative alike on these questions and in politics were the *Saturday Review*, the *Morning Post, The Times* (all London); the *Edinburgh Evening Courant, Manchester Courier, Dublin Evening Mail* and the *Irish Times*. Journals which contained a wide variety of signed articles – the *Contemporary Review, Fortnightly Review*, and *Nineteenth Century*, for instance – defy classification as far as their approach to racial issues is concerned.

The most important London journals in terms of circulation and influence were the *Daily Telegraph* (circulation 175 to 190,000 in 1870, claimed to be the largest in the world); the *Saturday Review* (its circulation rose from 10 to 20,000, 1860–70); *The Times* (circulation around 63,000 by the mid 1860s); the *Daily News* (from the 1870s a circulation of about 90,000). Of the newspapers published outside London, the *Irish Times* was Ireland's foremost journal; *The Scotsman* was supreme north of the border (circulation around 40,000 in 1871), but was strongly challenged by the *Edinburgh Evening Courant*; in the North the *Manchester Examiner and Times* was the most influential Radical paper, and the *Manchester Courier* the most noted Tory journal, a Northern counterpart of *The Economist* in its coverage.

Acknowledgments

I should like to acknowledge with gratitude the most helpful criticism of sections of this manuscript by historians at the University of Kent, Professor Roger Anstey, Mr Anthony Copley and Mr David Turley.

Abbreviations

Add. Ms. *Additional Manuscript*
A.P. *Anti-slavery Papers*
A.R. *Anthropological Review*
C.M.I. *Church Missionary Intelligencer*
J.A.I. *Journal of the Anthropological Institute of Great Britain and Ireland*
J.A.S. *Journal of the Anthropological Society of London*
J.E.S. *Journal of the Ethnological Society of London*
MS. *Manuscript*
P.M.A. *Popular Magazine of Anthropology*
P.R.C.I. *Proceedings of the Royal Colonial Institute*
P.R.G.S. *Proceedings of the Royal Geographical Society*
T.A.P.S. *Transactions of the Aborigines Protection Society*
T.E.S.L. *Transactions of the Ethnological Society of London*

I

The Scientific View

Race is everything: literature, science, art – in a word,
civilization depends on it.

ROBERT KNOX.[1]

B EATRICE WEBB once commented that 'the belief in science
and the scientific method [was] . . . certainly the most salient,
as it was the most original, element of the mid-Victorian Time-
Spirit'.[2] This scientific spirit was duly applied to the study of
man. In 1843 the English Ethnological Society was founded,
growing out of the activities of the Aborigines Protection Society,
which had been established in 1837 by Dr Thomas Hodgkin. By
1847 ethnology had been recognized as an independent discipline
by the British Association for the Advancement of Science, and
in a little over a decade the Anthropological Society of London
was formed. Philological studies were begun in 1842. All three
societies issued specialist publications. Many of those who contributed were conscious of the wide significance as well as the
difficulty of their investigations. (Part of the reason for the
London Anthropological Society's breakaway from the Ethnological Society in 1863 was a desire to popularize its discoveries,
even if this meant involvement in public controversy, though
the two associations ultimately reunited as the Anthropological
Institute of Great Britain and Ireland, in 1871.)

The first difficulty arose from 'the public indifference to man

[1] *Races of Man: a Fragment* (London, 1862 ed.), p. v.
[2] *My Apprenticeship* (London, 1946 ed.), p. 123.

1

not fully "up to date"'.[3] Travellers' books, the journals of the missionary societies and of the Royal Geographical Society (founded in 1831) enjoyed a wide readership, but the information they provided was often either unscholarly or irrelevant from the point of view of the anthropologist. But when the drama, the personalities and the discoveries were removed, the public was indifferent. The modern traveller, observed explorer and collector Augustus Pitt-Rivers, though he once wrote with care, now 'writes for a circulating library, and for the unthinking portion of mankind, who will not be bothered with details'.[4]

Even when intentions were honourable, the obstacles were great. As Sir John Lubbock testified, 'Travellers naturally find it far easier to describe the houses, boats, food, dress, weapons, and implements of savages, than to understand their thoughts and feelings. The whole mental condition of a savage is so different from ours, that it is often very difficult to understand the motives by which he is influenced.' Any judgement on matters of race would depend 'at least as much on the character of the writer as on that of the people' under discussion.[5]

Travel in remote parts of Africa and India remained hazardous to the end of the century, and language difficulties were constantly emphasized. Speaking at a British Association meeting in the early 1890s, Professor Max Müller stressed how essential it was for the individual writing of savages to have lived long among them and mastered their vernaculars, otherwise he would misinterpret what he saw; but this for long remained simply an ideal.[6] A typical criticism of anthropology, quoted by Alfred Haddon in his history of its progress during these years, was that[7]

> Anything you please . . . you may find among your useful savages. . . . You have but to skim a few books of travel, pencil in hand, and pick out what suits your case. . . . Your testimony is often

[3] *Anthropological Essays Presented to Edward Burnett Tylor in Honour of his 75th Birthday, October 2nd, 1907* (London, 1907), p. 1.
[4] A. Lane-Fox Pitt-Rivers, *The Evolution of Culture and Other Essays* (Oxford, 1906), p. 188.
[5] *The Origin of Civilization and the Primitive Condition of Man. Mental and Social Conditions of Savages* (London, 1870), pp. 3, 259–60.
[6] *Journal of the Anthropological Institute of Great Britain and Ireland* (in future J.A.I.), XXI (1892), p. 187.
[7] *History of Anthropology* (London, 1910), pp. 128–9.

derived from observers ignorant of the language of the people whom they talk about, or who are themselves prejudiced by one or other theory or bias. How can you pretend to raise a science on such foundations, especially as the savage informants wish to please or mystify inquirers, or they answer at random or deliberately conceal their most sacred institutions, or have never paid any attention to their subject ?

It was not until the 1880s that the scientist and explorer, Sir Francis Galton, pioneered anthropometric laboratories in Britain, and modern field work also developed slowly: 1898 saw the first trained experimental psychologists investigating, with laboratory equipment, people in a primitive stage of culture under their ordinary conditions of life, as part of the Cambridge Anthropological Expedition to the Torres Straits.[8] Comparative anthropology was established as the result of work by Lubbock and the self-taught Edward Tylor, and by the 1890s teaching was under way at Oxford, Cambridge and London. Even so, as Professor W. H. Flower complained, in contrast with almost every other country in Europe, Britain had no national anthropological museum (though the collections of Pitt-Rivers at Oxford and Farnham, Dorset, of the British Museum, and the College of Surgeons were extremely valuable).[9]

The Anthropological Institute operated on an inadequate financial basis and library facilities were limited. Urging the need for a State-aided Museum of Anthropology in 1907, C. H. Read, Keeper of the Department of Ethnography at the British Museum, was not hopeful that funds would be forthcoming, since 'In England, almost all great enterprises, from the possession of the Indian Empire downwards, have had their origin in the adventurous spirit of private individuals', and only very slowly forced the attention of the British Government.[10] Read also favoured the publication of scientific studies, such as those issued by the Smithsonian Institution in America. The Anthropological Society, in conjunction with the British Association, had in 1874 and 1892 put out a pamphlet called *Notes and*

[8] *Ibid.*, pp. 85–6.
[9] Address to the Department of Anthropology of the British Association, delivered at the York Meeting, September 1st, 1881, J.A.I., II (1881–2), pp. 185–93.
[10] *Anthropological Essays, op. cit.*, p. 278; also pp. 277, 279, 282–3.

Queries on Anthropology, for the Use of Travellers and Residents in Uncivilized Lands; both regularly published their proceedings, which helped to disperse public ignorance a little, but scarcity of funds ruled out more ambitious projects.[11]

Edward Tylor admitted in 1889 that 'Strict method has, . . . as yet, only been introduced over part of the anthropological field', and in fact throughout the Victorian period anthropology was compounded of the 'leavings of the historian, of the adventurer, of the missionary', and constituted the 'favourite playground of *dilettanti* of various degrees of seriousness'.[12]

But in spite of difficulties the sense of solemn purpose remained. 'Need we say', asked an article in the *Anthropological Review* in 1863, 'that the [Imperial] responsibility of British statesmen and of the British nation is most solemn? In two or three centuries a larger population than exists in the whole of Europe will curse or bless us according as we have given a bias of good or evil to their infant institutions.'[13] It was essential to understand the practical importance of race distinctions, argued James Hunt, as long as Britain possessed an Empire, because of

> the impossibility [as yet unrealized] of applying the civilization and laws of one race to another race of man essentially distinct. States-men may ignore the existence of race-antagonism; but it exists nevertheless. They may continue to plead that race-subordination forms no part of nature's laws; but this will not alter the facts.[14]

Though not sharing Hunt's racist views, Professor Flower was equally concerned about the criminal neglect of anthropology on the part of a nation whose subjects represented 'almost every known modification of the human species whose varied and often conflicting interests have to be regulated and provided for'. Addressing a British Association meeting at York, he especially deplored

> the great inconsistency [resulting from this neglect] between a favourite English theory and a too common English practice – the

[11] Testimony of James Reddie, Edinburgh University, *Anthropological Review* (in future A.R.), II (1864), p. 290.

[12] J.A.I., XVIII (1889), p. 245; and A. C. Haddon, *op. cit.*, p. 2.

[13] I (1863), p. 316.

[14] Third Annual Address of James Hunt, *Journal of the Anthropological Society of London* (in future J.A.S.), IV (1866), p. lxxviii.

former being that all men are morally and intellectually alike, the latter being that all are equally inferior to himself in all respects: both propositions egregiously fallacious. The study of race is at a low ebb indeed when we hear the same contemptuous epithet of 'nigger' applied indiscriminately by the Englishman abroad to the blacks of the West Coast of Africa, the Kaffirs of Natal, the Lascars of Bombay, the Hindoos of Calcutta, the aborigines of Australia, and even the Maoris of New Zealand![15]

It was vital, in Flower's opinion, that statesmen should not look upon human nature in the abstract and endeavour to apply universal rules, but rather consider 'the special moral, intellectual, and social capabilities, wants and aspirations of each particular race' with which they had to deal.[16]

The influential leader of the eugenics movement in Britain, Sir Francis Galton, held essentially the same views, commenting in 1885 that 'the English do not excel in winning the hearts of other nations. They have to broaden their sympathies by the study of mankind as they are, and without prejudice.' This was what anthropologists aimed to do, thus discovering unsuspected links between past and present, barbarous and civilized peoples. The latter, in consequence, came to be regarded as 'kinsmen rather than aliens', and herein lay the political value of anthropology.[17]

One of the reasons for the misconceptions entertained about race was the unfamiliarity, among the mass of the British people, with 'representatives of the many people whom we governed'. 'They seldom appeared in . . . [anthropological] meetings . . . they did not come to England. We did not see them in the streets. It was very different in ancient Rome, where the presence of foreigners from all parts of the then known world was a characteristic feature of every crowd.'[18] This remained substantially true throughout the century, in spite of the visits of ex-slaves, foreign seamen, students, and distinguished petitioners from all parts of the Empire.

Falsehood feeds upon the credulity of the ignorant. Though some narrators who were familiar with distant races confined

15 *Op. cit.*, p. 185.
16 J.A.I., XIII (1884), p. 493.
17 *Ibid.*, XV (1885), pp. 337–8.
18 J.A.I., II (1881–2), p. 353.

their more lurid revelations to discreet Latin appendices, the majority, when depicting 'a monster class of which nothing yet is known', felt free to indulge in sensational reporting – especially of Africa, 'distinguished from every country under heaven by its misery and degradation . . . [and lying] as of old, in the outer darkness'.[19] Inadequate knowledge, as we have seen, also hampered the learned societies; writing in 1910, Alfred Haddon confessed that for his history of anthropology he had been compelled to rely too much on 'the arm-chair workers, and too little . . . [on] the labourers in the field'.[20] It is therefore no surprise to find British anthropologists initially using most debatable material and involved in some unedifying controversies.

The first President of the London Anthropological Society, because of his views on 'the Negro's place in nature', was attacked as a racist, a charge which had earlier been levelled, with complete justice, against the American school of anthropology.[21] Hunt, however, was well able to defend himself, ridiculing his critics as individuals afflicted by 'rights-of-man mania', who made 'the gigantic assumption of absolute human equality', an assumption which indicated 'defective reasoning power' and should be exposed through the presentation of scientific evidence as a 'sham and a delusion'.[22] Sir Richard Burton, who put in regular appearances at anthropological meetings, supported Hunt, and testified that his own works on Africa had been attacked as prejudiced by ignorant and emotional philanthropists. Fortunately, an improved acquaintance with coloured races would still the voice of the abolitionists, for years 'a power steadily influencing national policy', and diminish the prestige of the Negro.[23]

Although Hunt was careful to disassociate himself from American racists, it is interesting to note that on his premature death in 1869 an obituary in an American newspaper – headed 'Death of the Best Man in England' – described him as achiev-

[19] Charles Dilke, *Greater Britain* (London, 1868, 2 vols.), I, p. 20; and C.M.I., V, 1 (1869), p. 53.

[20] *Op. cit.*, p. 2.

[21] *Introductory Address, op. cit.*, p. 3.

[22] *Farewell Address, Delivered at the Fourth Anniversary of the Anthropological Society of London, January 1st, 1867, by James Hunt* (London, 1867), pp. 15–17.

[23] *Op. cit.*, I, p. viii; II, pp. 177, 180, 182–3.

ing, through the brave assertion of his controversial views, more 'for humanity, for the welfare of mankind, and for the glory of God, than all the philosophers, humanitarians, philanthropists, statesmen, and, we may say, bishops and clergy of England together'.[24]

During their early years the anthropological societies encountered particularly heavy fire from the missionary Press. Controversy was sparked over the publications of William Winwood Reade, another Victorian traveller who contributed to the scientific literature of race. Having travelled widely in South-West Africa, explored the Niger and gold-mines of Bouri under the auspices of the Royal Geographical Society, and covered the Ashanti War for *The Times* from 1873, Reade was no armchair philosopher, but – like Hunt – a man of decided opinions who was not afraid of offending the conventional.[25] In his view, Christianity was doomed in Africa, since polygamy, slavery and similar practices were indispensable to the African mind. The Negro in general had no religion, and certainly no equivalents in his vocabulary of such civilized, Christian concepts as mercy, pity, fatherly love or conjugal affection.[26] Thus it was possible to assert 'the absolute futility of Christian missions' among savages. Even the culture of the much-vaunted converts of Sierra Leone remained basically unchanged, basically corrupt.[27]

This evidence was supported at a meeting in London by a ten-year resident in the colony, Mr J. M. Harris, by one R. B. Walker, who had lived for fourteen years in the Gaboon, and by Burton. Both Burton and Reade maintained that the Moslem faith won far more converts in Africa by accepting and restraining rather than trying to eradicate Negro vices. Dr R. S. Charnock added that Christian missionaries were further hampered by doctrinal divisions among themselves.[28] Sectarianism flourished, reminiscent in its narrow pride of that of Parson

[24] Quoted in A. C. Haddon, *op. cit.*, pp. 67–8.
[25] See Charles Reade's biography, *Put Yourself in His Place* (London, 1922); Winwood Reade wrote *The Outcast*, a story of a man whose religious faith was shattered by the discoveries of science, and *The Martyrdom of Man*, a work inspired by Darwinian theory.
[26] A.R., II (1864), p. 343.
[27] J.A.S., III (1865), pp. clxiv–clxvii.
[28] *Ibid.*, pp. clxviii, clxix–clxxv, ccv–ccx and ccxx.

Thwackum in *Tom Jones*, who declared: 'when I mention religion I mean the Christian religion; and not only the Christian religion, but the Protestant religion; and not only the Protestant religion, but the Church of England'.[29]

While conscious of their own shortcomings, anthropologists were even more acute in detecting the intellectual weaknesses of others. Thus the *Anthropological Review* dismissed the findings of David Livingstone as unscientific and inaccurate, though no doubt appealing to 'Nigger Worshippers, missionary exporters, and other Exeter Hallitarians'. 'A Burton may be allowed to reason', the article continued, 'but a Livingstone must only describe', and even then was likely to be in error. Elsewhere there are references to the explorer's 'poor naked mind bedaubed with the chalk and red ochre of Scotch theology, and with a threadbare, tattered waistcloth of education hanging around him'.[30] For their part, the missionaries charged such opponents with atheism, although, as T. H. Huxley pointed out, anthropology 'has nothing to do with the truth or falsehood of religion'.[31]

Nevertheless, according to the *Church Missionary Intelligencer*, the heathen of Abbeokuta were more attuned to the teachings of Christ than men like Burton and Reade. The missions they singled out for criticism were of recent origin and had scarcely had the chance to prove themselves; and it was impossible to claim any spiritual success for the Moslem faith, since it condoned practices so 'intensely revolting' and unacceptable to civilization. The sceptical failed to realize that the true purpose of European missions was 'to prepare the leaven, and introduce it into the mass'; not to convert the masses by their own unaided efforts, but to raise up those 'by which the more extended work shall be done'.[32] Some representation of such views can be found, however, in the anthropological journals, where the missionaries were also defended on the grounds that Christianity was an evangelical religion whose adherents were bound to spread the gospel throughout the world, and that only the

[29] Philadelphia and Toronto, 1948 Ed., p. 41.
[30] IV (1866), pp. 144–6.
[31] Quoted in A. C. Haddon, *op. cit.*, p. 112.
[32] July, 1865, I, 7, pp. 193, 195; and October, 1865, I, 10, New Series, p. 290.

churches of Britain had concerned themselves with the moral and educational needs of savage races.[33] To this entire acrimonious debate we shall have occasion to return in later chapters.

If all could agree that anthropology was the science of man, the proper methods of anthropologists, however, aroused considerable disagreement. Both cultural characteristics, such as language, and physical features were used to classify the different divisions of man. Ultimately the two became confused, so that something called 'race' came to be seen as the prime determinant of all the important traits of body and soul, character and personality, of human beings and nations. In other words, race became far more than a biological concept: race and culture were dangerously linked.

Before the end of the eighteenth century, when the first serious challenge to the slave traffic made the question of the status and relation of the varieties of man a subject for fierce controversy, racial theory was relatively simple. There was little speculation about the biological causes of racial differences. All interest centred round the problem of origins.

This focus gave rise to two distinct theories – those of polygenesis and monogenesis. The latter, based upon an acceptance of the literal truth of Christian revelation, was hampered by the need to derive all the races of man from a single stock within a very short period of time. (Orthodox Christians still believed that the world was only about 6,000 years old.) The monogenesists also believed in eugenesis – that is, the theory that all men were and always had been fertile with each other.

The first blow to the teachings of the Church came with the discovery of the New World, since in *De Civitate Dei* Augustine had discounted the possible existence of antipodal man as 'excessively absurd'.[34] Polygenesists gained strength steadily from the sixteenth century, especially in America and France, but also to some extent in England.

The fertility of hybrids – which we would undoubtedly accept

[33] J.A.S., III (1865), pp. clxxiv, ccxiii, ccxxiii ccxxiii, ccxxiv, ccxxxv, ccxxxvi, ccxxxvii.
[34] A. C. Haddon, *op. cit.*, pp. 51–2.

today – was denied by the polygenesists. Where sexual relations took place between races widely different from each other, it was argued, either the relationship proved barren or the offspring proved so in due time. Furthermore, such mixing, where successful, led to the deterioration of the superior race and produced a vicious type of half-breed, useless alike to himself and the world. In the opinion of the idiosyncratic French racist De Gobineau, hybrids were either 'beautiful without strength, strong without intelligence, or, if intelligent, both weak and ugly'.[35]

Language appeared to support the theory of man's descent from a plurality of races. Although the early monogenesists argued that all languages could be traced to three sources, Indo-European (or Aryan), Semitic and Malay, which in turn derived from a single parent language long vanished, the wide differences existing between the three branch languages soon made it apparent that this was a test which could be put to more effective use by their opponents.[36]

The impact of evolutionary theory on these early beliefs was, during the nineteenth century, supremely important. Although the most influential work here was produced by Charles Darwin in his *Origin of the Species*, published in 1859, and the *Descent of Man*, which appeared twelve years later, the doctrine of evolution had already been applied in astronomy and geology by men like Laplace, Hutton, Lyell, Agassiz and Buffon. The first application to biology came in 1809 with Jean Lamarck's *Philosophie Zoologique*, which presented a picture of the species of the animal world as forming a connected series, a graduated chain from monad to man. In Britain early anticipations of Darwinian theory can be found in the writings of Robert Chambers and Herbert Spencer.[37]

Darwin only hinted in the *Origin of the Species* that, by its publication, 'light will be thrown on the origin of man and his history', confessing in the introduction to the *Descent of Man* that he had no wish to 'add to the prejudices against his views'.[38]

---

[35] *The Inequality of Human Races* (London, 1915 Ed.), p. 209.

[36] A. C. Haddon, *op. cit.*, p. 53.

[37] L. J. Henkin, *Darwinianism in the English Novel, 1860–1910* (New York, 1940), pp. 24, 27, 29.

[38] *The Descent of Man, and Section in Relation to Sex* (London, 1871, 2 vols.), I, p. 1.

By the time the latter work was published, however, and influenced by less cautious individuals, including T. H. Huxley, Sir John Lubbock, Ernst Haeckel, Spencer and Lyell, Darwin had accepted the application of his findings to man.

The doctrine of natural selection, based upon the Malthusian theory of population, and assuming among men a constant multiplication and struggle for existence, in which only the best individuals out of each generation survived and passed on their desirable qualities, was taken further, in 1882, by Professor August Weissman. In his opinion, natural selection constituted the sole cause of organic evolution: the only kind of variations that could be transmitted were those defined as congenital. Lamarckian factors were thus excluded.[39] In his later writings Darwin emphasized the importance of sexual selection in human evolution.

Although he maintained that an attack upon religion was no part of his purpose, Darwin's work crucially undermined the position of the monogenesists. The theory of natural selection, as popularized by Spencer, appeared to emphasize the differences existing between human varieties, and the defenders of poly-genesis temporarily gained ground in Britain.

The old debate over language differences was reopened. Although today we should incline to the view of A. H. Sayce, Professor of Comparative Philology at Oxford, that 'language is no test of race, only of social contact', many scholars continued to apply this test.[40] Languages were divided into three basic types, isolating, agglutinative and inflectional, the last-named being the type familiar among Europeans and supposedly repre-senting the summit of linguistic achievement. As Sayce put it: 'The spirit of vanity has invaded the science of language itself. We have come to think that not only is the race to which we belong superior to all others, but that the languages we speak are equally superior.'[41] Sayce himself maintained that the isolat-ing languages were in fact superior to others in 'terseness and vividness', though he also suggested that the dialects of modern savages, which came into this category, were strictly limited –

[39] L. J. Henkin, *op. cit.*, pp. 47, 59–60.
[40] See *Saturday Review*, 3 February 1877, p. 134.
[41] *Introduction to the Science of Language* (London, 1880, 2 vols.), I, p. 75; II, pp. 66, 318, 324.

'have few words, because they have few ideas to express, and such ideas as are expressed are wonderfully simple'.[42]

However, there were those, notably Latham and Müller, who still supported classification systems based on language, which was seen to be in various stages of evolution, Latham favouring three main races, the Mongolidae, Atlantidae and Lapetidae, even though this meant grouping together, on the basis of language, peoples clearly not comparable in physical characteristics.[43] Müller's classification was sevenfold, and he began with the Australian race, ascending through the Papuan, Malayo-Polynesian, Negro, American, High Asiatic, to the Mediterranean, Semitic, Indo-German group.[44]

Writing about the same time as Sayce, E. B. Tylor was similarly reluctant to see language used as a test of race, and this was later the view of Edward Clodd. Although he accepted most of Sayce's findings, however, J. G. Romanes, as an exponent of cultural evolution, was not entirely convinced that the polysynthetic and isolating languages were little more primitive than those of the inflectional or agglutinative type.[45] This whole question was further aggravated by the arguments over polygenesis and the old Aryan controversy.

When Latham wrote the contribution on ethnology for the *Encyclopaedia Britannica* in 1855, he believed that the doctrine of the separate creation of different species of men was still worth debating, though he personally believed in monogenesis, mainly on the grounds of the common origin of all the world's languages.[46] By the time the 9th Edition of the *Encyclopaedia* appeared in 1878, the author of the ethnography section, Elie Reclus, felt that while philologists might argue from diversity of languages to the polygenesist position, ethnologists could see that the differences were not of nature, but degree.[47] In spite of the support of French writers like Pictet, Hovelacque and Chavée, the absurdities of the language test ultimately became

[42] *Ibid.*, I, pp. 375–6, 56; II, pp. 101, 270.

[43] *Natural History of the Varieties of Man* (London, 1850), p. 14.

[44] A.R., VIII (1870), pp. 93–4.

[45] E. B. Tylor, *Anthropology: an Introduction to the Study of Man and Civilization* (London, 1881), p. 152; E. Clodd, *The Story of 'Primitive' Man* (London, 1885), p. 158; J. G. Romanes, *Mental Evolution in Man – Origin of Human Faculty* (London, 1888), p. 256.

[46] IX, pp. 353–4.   [47] *Ibid.*, VIII, p. 622.

apparent. As Professor Keane remarked, when summarizing the controversy in 1896, *quod nimis probat, nihil probat*. Acknowledging the existence of at least 1,000 distinct languages (albeit divided into less than 100 basic families), was it sensible to claim for all the races which spoke them a separate creation?[48]

Nor, even, were all racists happy with the language classification. On that basis, argued James Hunt, the inhabitants of the West Indies might be grouped with Europeans rather than with Negroes. Physical characteristics and psychological differences were, in his opinion, far more important.[49] John Crawfurd, President of the London Ethnological Society, criticized the Aryan theory on similar grounds. On the basis of a number of root words common to most of the languages of Europe and Western Asia,

> and as if language were always a sure test of race, people bodily and intellectually the most incompatible – the black and the tawny, and the fair; the ever strong and enterprising, the ever weak and unenterprising – are jumbled into one undistinguishable mass, and, with extraordinary confidence, pronounced to be of one and the same blood. . . . But the Aryan is but a language of the imagination, of the existence of which no proof ever has been or can ever be adduced.[50]

As well as comments on an Aryan language, references to an Aryan race were not infrequent. Max Müller was one of the first to equate the two, but G. L. Gomme and Sayce also accepted the fact that the Aryan languages are those 'of a civilized race; the parent-speech to which we may inductively trace them back was spoken by men who stood on a relatively high level of culture, and was as fully developed, as inflectional, . . . as Sanskrit and Latin themselves'.[51] The French, British and Germans alike claimed to be the only true descendants of the original Aryans; in fact, as W. Ripley put it in 1899, 'No other scientific question, with the exception, perhaps, of the doctrine of evolution, was

[48] Quoted in A. C. Haddon, *op. cit.*, p. 54; J. G. Romanes, *op. cit.*, p. 245; and A. H. Sayce, *op. cit.*, II, p. 323.

[49] A.R., I (1863), p. 383.

[50] *Transactions of the Ethnological Society of London*, New Series (in future T.E.S.L.), I (1861), pp. 268–86, and A.R., I (1863), pp. 173–4.

[51] A. C. Haddon, *op. cit.*, pp. 144–8, on Müller, G. L. Gomme, *Ethnology in Folklore* (London, 1892), p. 18, and A. H. Sayce, *op. cit.*, I, p. 56, and II, p. 270.

ever so bitterly discussed or so infernally confounded at the hands of chauvinistic or otherwise biased writers'.[52]

Linguistic differences seemed to confirm the vast gulf which separated the various races of man. The Negro, for instance, was said not only to have invented no alphabet, but to be incapable of borrowing the letters of other nations.[53] The Aryan race, according to the Rev. F. W. Farrar, had produced all that was worthwhile in the sciences and the arts, including writing. In the opinion of H. Creswich, speaking at a London Ethnological Society meeting, 'The art of writing is held in the greatest reverence by all Africans', who did not possess it, 'and nothing elevates the European so high in their estimation as his facility in that art'.[54] The absence of numerals and abstract terms in those native languages which were grasped by Europeans was widely held to prove their inferiority. Complexity of structure was further evidence of this.[55]

However, as Tylor, Pitt-Rivers and other more detached observers admitted, the changeability of primitive languages made them very difficult to master.[56] In spite of the pioneering studies undertaken by philologists in the eighteenth and early nineteenth centuries, many of those who reported to the learned societies in Britain never surmounted the language barrier. (In his autobiography, colonial administrator and traveller Sir Harry Johnston commented that one of his main interests in Africa was a study of the huge variety of native dialects, with which most whites were unconcerned. It was partly for this reason that Johnston greatly enjoyed his meetings with Sir Richard Burton, whose linguistic abilities matched his own.[57]) Those who pointed out that the understanding of native languages often produced a new appreciation of native intelligence, or that the African could learn the languages of other nations,

[52] *The Races of Europe* (London, 1900), p. 453.

[53] J.A.S., II, pp. xxvi–xxvii; T.E.S.L., I (1861), p. 78, and IV (1866), p. 215.

[54] T.E.S.L., V (1867), p. 124, and VI (1868), p. 260.

[55] Sir J. Lubbock, *op. cit.*, pp. 3, 278, 282; W. Reade in A.R., II (1864), p. 337; G. J. Romanes, *op. cit.*, pp. 347–53; J.A.S., III (1865), p. cclxxxviii; F. W. Farrar, *Chapters on Language* (London, 1865), pp. 53–4.

[56] A. H. Sayce, *op. cit.*, I, p. 191; E. B. Tylor, *op. cit.*, p. 142; A. Lane-Fox Pitt-Rivers, *op. cit.*, p. 13.

[57] *The Story of My Life* (London, 1923), pp. 157, 213–5.

as witness the Negro in America and the West Indies, were in a tiny minority.[58]

Another aspect of Victorian racial theory which was re-examined in the light of evolutionary teaching was the classification of man according to physical features – in particular, skull measurements. Craniometry had been pioneered in Europe by Blumenbach, Camper, Retzius and Tiedemann, and in America by G. R. Gliddon, S. G. Morton and George Combe. The length and breadth of the skull, facial angle, the interior capacity of the skull and especially the dimensions of the brain were all taken into account. The work of American phrenologists in particular was thought to prove that Negroes had a smaller cranial capacity than Caucasians, and thus, it was assumed, were less intelligent. But these findings were spurious, not least because of the inadequate number of skulls examined, and as late as 1892 Professor Alexander Macalister, in a speech to the British Association, was deploring the lack of general principles underlying craniometry and the inconclusive evidence which derived from it.[59]

Even so, James Hunt was prepared to accept Gratiolet's three-fold division of man, according to skull type, into 'the Frontal (European), Parietal (Mongol), and Occipital (Negro) races – these cranial distinctions being coincident with the mental and moral characters which were solely dependent on man's physical structure'.[60] In his view, the brain of the Negro (like those of the European woman or child) closely approached that of the ape – though Hunt was prepared to admit that brain size was not the sole test of intellectual power.[61] In recent times, since it has been demonstrated that the Japanese, American Indians, Eskimoes and Polynesians all frequently have brains larger than those found among Europeans, this line of argument has lost its appeal for the racist.

Alfred Haddon and Robert Dunn, the latter a frequent contributor to British ethnological journals, both emphasized facial

[58] See, for instance, James Bonwick, reported in J.A.I., XVI (1887), p. 207; and Pliny Miles, reported in J.A.S., II (1864), p. xlii.
[59] A. C. Haddon, *op. cit.*, pp. 41–2.
[60] A.R., I (1863), pp. 382–3.
[61] *Memoirs Read Before the Anthropological Society of London* (1863–4), I, pp. 13, 16–17.

angle. The receding forehead and projecting jaws of the Negro, according to Dunn, 'speak a language which cannot be mistaken. . . . For whenever and wherever ignorance and brutality, destitution and squalor, have for a long time existed, this prognathous type invariably prevails.' By contrast, the appearance of the Saxon, the Celt or the Scandinavian was far less primitive, a broad forehead, upright jaws and symmetrical features 'clearly indicating a harmonious development of the whole brain, and a special fullness in the intellectual and moral regions'.[62] Gratiolet, Carl Vogt and Pruner Bey were all quoted in support of these views, in which man's physical structure was seen as determining his mental and moral characteristics, and we find the typical nineteenth-century confusion of race with culture.

Writing in 1898, Haddon, though doubtful about the value of craniometry and by no means a racist, believed that the prognathous jaws of the Negro were specially adapted to cope with the coarse food consumed by men in a primitive condition. A change in the shape of the jaw was generally associated with a rise in culture, greater mental activity and an increase in the volume of the brain.[63] Dunn was also convinced that brain size directly affected brain capacity, by allowing a greater structural complexity, but from the end of the nineteenth century most British anthropologists were coming to accept the view of Professor R. H. Woodworth, that, although the sensory and motor processes of the brain differed in degree from one individual to another, they were approximately the same from one race to another.[64]

Craniometry also came under fire, not simply because of its inaccuracies, but because it perpetuated the grouping together of the Indo-European races. The well-known geographer, explorer and ethnologist, John Crawfurd, complained that classification according to brain type would result in equating Hindus with Europeans, whereas he believed that the former were not only inferior in mental capacity to the latter, but also to the races inhabiting central and western Asia.[65]

Language and skull measurements were not the only aids to

[62] T.E.S.L., IV (1866), pp. 18–19, 25–6.
[63] *The Study of Man* (London, 1898), pp. 60–5.
[64] T.E.S.L., III (1865), p. 21; and A. C. Haddon, *op. cit.*, p. 86.
[65] T.E.S.L., I (1861), pp. 77, 80; also R. Mann in *ibid.*, V (1867), p. 287.

anthropologists in defining different races. The early classifiers, Bernier, Linnaeus and Blumenbach, had used skin colour, but although this was still taken into account, it was not now emphasized as a test of race in scientific circles, even though it was during the nineteenth century that the word 'racism' came to acquire its most common meaning – namely, the 'hostility that one man feels for another because of his colour alone'.[66]

William Craft, an American Negro, speaking at a London anthropological society meeting in 1863, maintained that physical characteristics were the result of climate rather than innate superiority or inferiority, something which Crawfurd denied, pointing out that Europeans could and did live and multiply in hot climates, without any marked change in physical or mental features.[67] Indian administrator Sir George Campbell was of the opinion that neither language nor colour offered the keys to an understanding of race, while Crawfurd emphasized the importance of a favourable environment. Sparse vegetation and animal life combined with aridity and isolation helped to explain the backwardness of the New Zealand or Australian aborigine, just as the 'great advantages of superior physical geography' in part, at least, explained the 'superior quality of race' which distinguished the European.[68]

Most British anthropologists accepted either the threefold classification of the Swiss, Cuvier (the three races of man being held to have descended from the three sons of Noah), or Blumenbach's earlier, fivefold grouping. Both systems were plainly hierarchical, and racialist by implication.

Following Cuvier, in 1867 C. O. Groom Napier published his own 'Table of Human Races', which consisted of the Semitic–Indo-European, the Mongolian and the Ethiopian. Various mental characteristics were associated with each group. The whole system was somewhat complex, since of the three types of mental qualities recognized – moral, intellectual and passionate – the Indo-European group combined the first two (though only the west Europeans equally) and drew strength

---

[66] R. Segal, *The Race War* (London, 1967), p. 13.
[67] T.E.S.L., I (1861), pp. 84–9.
[68] *Journal of the Ethnological Society of London* (in future J.E.S.), II (1870), p. 410; and T.E.S.L., II (1863), pp. 5, 16–17.

from the third, while the passionate family included both Mongolian and Ethiopian types. The qualities awarded to the different physical types of man by Napier clearly underlined the superiority of the European group – 'the ruling race, for they possess in a larger degree than any the qualities of all races'.[69]

Two other British anthropologists of this period, Professor Flower and James Dallas, also adapted the Cuvier classification scheme, but refrained from emphasizing the implied differences in capacity between the three groups, as did Professor T. H. Huxley. In his modified version of Blumenbach's system, Huxley described Australoids, Negroids, Xanthochroi (the fair peoples of central Europe – the term 'Caucasian' he dismissed as meaningless), Mongoloids and Melanochroi (or 'dark' whites, possibly a mixture of the first and third groups).[70] It is clear, however, that the central Europeans held pride of place, from a chance admission that some – but only some – of the Melanochroi could perhaps 'in point of physical beauty and intellectual energy be the equal of the best of the Xanthochroi'.[71]

The ancient arguments over polygenesis and monogenesis were temporarily revitalized during the 1850s and 1860s in Britain, with Robert Knox, the Scottish anatomist, and James Hunt putting forward, most strongly, the polygenesist view. Knox, like De Gobineau, based his conclusions on a denial of the doctrine of eugenesis; Hunt was more outspoken, and was particularly interested in the position of the Negro. Between 1863 and 1866, at meetings of the London Anthropological Society and the British Association, Hunt argued against the existence of 'a permanent hybrid Euro-African race', in favour of classifying the Negro as a separate species of man.[72] These views were supported by another member of the London society, C. Carter-Blake, during a debate on the subject in 1864 (though at the same meeting the Rev. J. Dingle maintained indignantly that the theory of polygenesis had, for over a century, been used

[69] J.A.S., V (1867), pp. clxi–clxii.

[70] J.E.S., II (1870), pp. 404–9.

[71] Flower, incidentally, maintained that his system of classification was arrived at on the evidence of hair type; this curious test was also applied (often along with other factors) by Bory de Saint Vincent, Saint Hilaire, Ernst Haeckel, Friedrich Müller, Paul Broca and T. H. Huxley.

[72] *Introductory Address, op. cit.*, p. 3; J.A.S., II (1864), p. xv.

to 'justify the most outrageous oppression, and to palliate the most disgusting cruelty' towards uncivilized races).[73]

Speaking on hybridity, also in 1864, and clearly influenced by the writings of French and American polygenesists, the Rev. F. W. Farrar alleged that the fertility of hybrids offered no clear proof of the unity of mankind; on another occasion, from the standpoint of a Churchman, Farrar acknowledged the common humanity and hope for redemption of all men, but denied that such would involve in addition physical or genetic identity, the descent of all races from a single pair.[74]

John Crawfurd, generally less explicit in his views, none the less concluded in an article on the 'European and Asiatic Races of Man' that between them 'there is a broad and innate differ-ence, physical, intellectual, and moral; that such difference has existed from the earliest authentic records, and is most probably coeval with the first creation of man'.[75] A contributor to the *Popular Magazine of Anthropology*, J. McGregor Allan, arguing in the light of Darwinian theory, had no reservations, for if one compared 'a low-browed, flat-nosed, woolly-headed, ebony-hued, long-headed Negro with a fair-skinned, blue-eyed, yellow-haired, large-brained Caucasian, . . . the natural conclusion would seem to be that types of humanity so opposite to and distinct from one another, were not descended from the same primitive stock'.[76]

It is noticeable that those Britons who believed in polygenesis normally took the appearance and material condition of the Negro to prove their point, although by anthropologists at least he was not cast in the role of 'the missing link' between ape and man (a theme taken up with relish by certain minor Victorian novelists).[77] There were also in Britain more opponents than supporters of the views of Hunt: Robert Dunn, for instance, who suggested that all men had basically the same animal, intellectual, moral and religious nature, even though a number of races might be exceptionally degraded, often for reasons outside their control.[78]

[73] *Ibid.*, pp. xxviii, xxx.   [74] T.E.S.L., V (1867), pp. 116, 126.
[75] *Ibid.*, p. 81. See also I (1861), p. 354.   [76] I (1866), p. 124.
[77] T.E.S.L., IV (1866), p. 221, and E. Clodd, *op. cit.*, p. 13.
[78] T.E.S.L., I (1861), pp. 186–202. See also *The Popular Magazine of Anthropology*, I (1866), pp. 128–32 (in future P.M.A.).

By 1869, in fact, the London anthropological society was able to report the decline of polygenesis, popular since Prichard's day, and the triumph of evolutionary teaching, 'which, by regarding races as divergent varieties settled into comparative permanence, meets the problem of the existence of different races more rationally than could be done by the old monogenist theory, hampered as this was by the insuperable difficulty of deriving all the races of mankind from a single stock within a very short period of time'.[79]

The decline of aboriginal populations during the nineteenth century in New Zealand, Hawaii, Tasmania, America and South Africa, with which the British Aborigines Protection Society had been struggling since 1843, was considered again in the light of popular Darwinianism. The principle of the survival of the fittest, seen to be working itself out in these regions, was proving conclusively that civilized and uncivilized races could not mix, and in a conflict situation the latter must perish. Everywhere 'the inferior organization makes room for the superior. As the Indian is killed by the approach of civilization, to which he resists in vain, so the black man perishes by that culture to which he serves as a humble instrument.'[80]

An article in the *Popular Magazine of Anthropology* stated candidly that 'to colonize and to extirpate are synonymous terms', but, like James Bonwick and Thomas Bendyshe, the latter being the author of a history of anthropology which appeared in the 1860s, it also admitted that Europeans imported liquor, disease, war (often for possession of land), and sometimes bad government into the lands they colonized, all too often making no allowance 'for the weakness and rude ideas of the aborigines', who were regarded 'only as so many butts for ridicule, insult, or practical joking; if not worse'.[81]

But if the colonizers had much to reproach themselves with, most writers on this theme believed that the destruction of the aborigine was inevitable, since 'Between the white and coloured populations . . . [involved], there are not even degrees of civilization'. The native of, say, Australia represented no material or

[79] J.A.S., VII, p. 444; and see also E. Tylor, *op. cit.*, pp. 5–6.
[80] J.A.S., II (1864), p. lxviii.
[81] I (1866), pp. 10–11. See also *ibid.*, I (1866), pp. 49–56, 75–7; Bendyshe in J.A.S., II (1864), p. ci; and Bonwick in J.A.I., XVI (1887), p. 210.

cultural tradition, and thus had to bow to the 'greater moral power' of the Anglo-Saxon, to 'a phase of humanity enlightened with intelligence, and endowed with vast intellectual superiority'.[82]

The fate of the newly emancipated American Negro aroused great interest in this context, and reports of the London Anthropological Society by the late 1860s quoted American sources as confirming the widely entertained belief that the freedmen were worse off than slaves had been before the Civil War. Their speedy extinction was predicted.[83]

From the middle of the century there is evidence of those racial interpretations of history which were to become so common by the 1890s. According to Sir Henry Bartle Frere, reported in the *Journal of the Anthropological Institute*, the history of India, Assyria, Egypt, Rome and Britain alike showed the conquest of inferior by superior peoples. The fate of aboriginal races varied, however; extermination was not always the rule. In South Africa, for instance, though the Bushmen and Bechuanas had suffered, the 'Kaffir' races had increased in numbers and improved in physique through contact with the white man, and particularly through education.[84]

Professor Flower, commenting on Frere's theories, maintained that in all temperate climates where Europeans ventured (hence suited to their permanent residence) native populations dwindled and disappeared.[85] In the opinion of J. G. Romanes, however, although inferior tribes suffered in the battle of life, the civilized races could not afford to drive the former – who fulfilled many necessary functions – off the face of the earth.[86]

An interesting new note which emerges from such discussions of racial contact is that of fear. A war of races in colonial possessions might be an unchallengeable law of nature, but some Victorians began to question whether the victory must always go to the 'superior' race. Hunt suggested in 1870 that

[82] J.A.S., II (1864), p. xcv.

[83] *Ibid.*, VII (1869), pp. clxvi–clxvii; and VIII (1879), pp. 338–58, for an opposing view.

[84] J.A.I., II (1881–2), pp. 314–15, 318–19.

[85] *Ibid.*, p. 353.

[86] *Darwin, and After Darwin. An Exposition of the Darwinian Theory and a Discussion of Post-Darwinian Questions* (London, 1892, 3 vols.), I, pp. 345–6.

ultimately, even in the New World, 'the almost exterminated savages will be amply revenged by a slow, gradual degeneracy, and perhaps final extinction, of their . . . conquerors'.[87]

Very much of the same mind, Robert Knox suggested that Europeans could only prosper in Europe – equatorial climates were lethal – and, furthermore, a permanent military establishment was necessary to bolster the colonial presence. The Negro especially was to be feared (and consequently hated). While the Chinese and Indians might be managed, wrote Knox, 'The tropical regions of the earth seem peculiarly to belong to him; his energy is considerable: aided by the sun, he repels the white invader'.[88] An article in the *Anthropological Review* in 1869 admitted reluctantly that Anglo-Saxon emigration to, and acclimatization in, the tropics was a failure; members of that race, unlike the Celt, suffered too much from nostalgia for what they had left behind.[89]

Another gloomy essay which appeared in the 1860s saw contemporary events as offering confirmation of the views of Knox. Were he still living, it inquired, might he not point to events in India, New Zealand, South Africa and Jamaica as proof of his theory of a war of races. The obvious conclusion was that 'If we are to hold places within the tropics, it can only be as military masters lording it over a sort of serf population, and under the continual fear of whose terrible vengeance we must always live. If such be really the case, then all schemes of philanthropy and of brotherhood by Act of Parliament and stump oratory, which delude us and take us off our guard, should be at once deprecated.'[90] George Gomme, the President of the Folklore Society, though less alarmist, also saw fear latent in the mind of the all-conquering white man, a natural reaction in the face of uncongenial climates, alien religions, incomprehensible languages. 'Has anyone attempted to realize', he asked feelingly, 'the effects of a permanent residence of a civilized people [usually a minority] amidst a lower civilization, the members of which are cruel, crafty, and unscrupulous?'[91]

Racial mixing and miscegenation as a possible solution aroused alarm and controversy in Britain, just as in America.

[87] A.R., VIII (1870), p. 137.
[88] *Op. cit.*, pp. 51, 243–6, 456.
[89] VII, p. 172.
[90] P.M.A., I (1866), pp. 24–6.
[91] *Op. cit.*, pp. 41–5.

According to Professor James Reddie of Edinburgh University, miscegenation was a 'filthy theory' and mongrel peoples were doomed to perish: 'The Egyptians, the Carthaginians, and now the Mexicans are historical examples of God's punishment upon those who dare to mar the works of His creation.'[92]

Emotion conquered consistency on the question of mixed breeds: those who tried, for instance, to vindicate Negro capabilities – men like the Quaker, Wilson Armistead[93] – were criticized because they could only find examples of distinguished mulattoes, yet there was a paradoxical belief in the degeneracy and ferocity of hybrids, especially when black mated with white.

Thus John Crawfurd suggested that while the Arab might breed with and improve the Negro, the Anglo-Saxon could not, because the gulf between the two races was too great: 'In a society consisting of these discordant elements, no substantial equality is possible; since, whether in a free or servile condition, the inferior race would be certain to be viewed by the superior as a degraded class, with whom it is impossible to amalgamate.' In other words, when the qualities of different races of men were equal, no harm resulted from their union; when they were unequal, the deterioration of the higher race took place, as in Mexico and Peru, or union proved impossible.[94]

Support for the view that racial intermixture only benefited primitive peoples came from Robert Dunn (as well as French and German authorities), while Henry Guppy, Fellow of the London Anthropological Society, felt convinced that, although few 'pure'-blooded Negroes could occupy positions of responsibility and trust, many of 'the mulatto and lighter-coloured classes' were equipped to do so.[95] However an article about Burton's travels in Brazil commented with dismay on the mixed breeds to be found in that part of the world, and felt that any Englishman helping to produce such hybrids should be severely punished.[96]

If evolutionary theory had given, accidentally, encouragement

[92] A.R., II (1864), pp. 287–9.
[93] See his *A Tribute for the Negro* (Manchester, 1848).
[94] T.E.S.L., I (1861), p. 81 f., III (1865), pp. 102–3, 110–11, 121, IV (1866), p. 223; A.R., I (1863), p. 405.
[95] *Ibid.*, IV (1866), pp. 26–7; and A.R. II (1864), p. ccxii.
[96] A.R., VII (1869), pp. 22–3, 30, 175, 34–5.

to the polygenesists and those who saw in the processes of history a perpetual war of races, its impact can also clearly be seen in the writings of men who cannot be categorized either as racists or philanthropists, and who probably enjoyed a majority voice in Victorian scientific societies.

Thomas Huxley, in his famous Romanes Lecture of 1893, examining *Evolution and Ethics*, confirmed that 'In every part, at every moment, the state of the cosmos is the expression of a transitory adjustment of contending forces; a scene of strife, in which all the combatants fall in turn'. Man had progressed from barbarism through the skilful use of qualities he shared with the beasts – physical strength, cunning, sociability, curiosity, imitativeness – but in proportion as he became civilized these qualities proved an embarrassment, though one which could not be shaken off. Huxley attacked the notion of the inevitability of progress, which the doctrine of the survival of the fittest had nourished (for '"fittest" has a connotation of "best"') and suggested that all too often 'what is "fittest" depends upon the conditions' or had come to mean the 'strongest' rather than ethically the best. The pleasures and pains of the world were seldom distributed according to desert; intellect and society had only succeeded in masking the savagery in modern man – in fact, 'The theory of evolution encourages no millennial anticipations'.[97]

Huxley provided simply the most lucid exposition of a widely-held view. Starting from the same premise – namely, that 'The normal state of every living thing . . . is one of conflict' – Edward Clodd likewise argued that at some high point in the development of man the action of natural selection was checked by the deliberate application of the moral and intellectual faculties. This was, however, a difficult and uncertain process. The idea of progress was a very modern, Western concept. As Henry Maine had put it, 'the entire Mohammedan world detests it. The multitude of coloured men who swarm in the continent of Africa detest it. The millions on millions who fill the Chinese Empire loathe it, and, what is more, despise it.'[98] Progress had only just begun in the Western world and was still 'too often reckoned in terms of expansion of trade and wealth, of inventions of new

[97] Published in London; pp. 4, 6, 12, 32–3, 36–7.
[98] Quoted in Clodd, *op. cit.*, p. 195.

machinery, and of discoveries of new resources of the earth'. Since it was essentially the result of education, success could be only partial, for necessarily savage races were not only opposed to the idea, but incapable of fostering it at the present time.[99]

Anthropologists were generally agreed on the conservatism of primitive peoples, especially over matters of social and religious significance, and Alfred Haddon suggested that the mingling of races, whether through commerce, immigration or even war, was an essential condition for change – a view enthusiastically endorsed by British imperialists.[100] Both Gomme and Pitt-Rivers, in addition to Tylor, accepted the survival of ancient beliefs in modern times, but generally scouted the idea of modern savages as being descended from a higher level of civilization, equating evolutionary theory with the notion of progress; though Pitt-Rivers did complain that, since

> this progressive movement is often led by men who have not made the races of mankind their study, they are perpetually falling into the error of supposing, that the work of countless ages of divergence, is to be put to rights by Act of Parliament, and by suddenly applying to the inferior races of mankind laws and institutions for which they are about as fitted as the animals in the Zoological Gardens.[101]

The most influential late nineteenth-century British anthropologist, Edward Tylor, was, with Lubbock, the best-known exponent of the theory of progress as applied to the science of man. In view of Tylor's work on survivals, this is scarcely surprising, and both men maintained that, although in common talk the words 'savage' and 'barbarous' had come to mean 'such behaviour as is most wild, rough, and cruel', 'savage and barbarous tribes often more or less fairly represent stages of culture through which our own ancestors passed long ago, and their customs and laws often explain to us, in ways we should otherwise have hardly guessed, the sense and reason of our own'.[102] Lubbock, however, was particularly insistent that the primitive

[99] *Ibid.*, pp. 16, 79, 195–6, 197–8.
[100] *Op. cit.*, pp. xx–xxi; see also E. Tylor, *op. cit.*, p. 439.
[101] Gomme, *op. cit.*, pp. 4, 19–20; Pitt-Rivers, *op. cit.*, pp. 11, 36, 44, 142; Tylor, *op. cit.*, pp. 211, 221, 345; and also A. H. Sayce, *op. cit.*, I, p. vi, and Sir J. Lubbock, *op. cit.*, pp. 1, 115.
[102] Tylor, *op. cit.*, p. 401.

condition of man was not one of attractive simplicity but unattractive barbarism, and that from this condition several races had independently and fortunately raised themselves.[103]

The Duke of Argyll and Archbishop Whately of Dublin had put a different interpretation on the evidence of savage customs and instincts surviving in modern times, Whately being emphatic in his conviction that 'Man has not emerged from the savage state'. He saw the differences between civilized and primitive man as resulting not from the progress of the former, but from the degradation of the latter.[104] Although not sharing the Archbishop's belief that no savage race had ever raised itself, Argyll similarly attacked Lubbock for trying to show that the primeval condition of man was one of barbarism. In his opinion, which also represents the last protests of the Churchmen against evolution, existing savages were mere outcasts of the human race, descendants of weak but not barbarous tribes, and, further-more, even man in his most civilized condition was capable of deterioration: knowledge might decay, religion might be lost.[105]

Lubbock repudiated these views completely, and his is the respectable, scientific voice (though Argyll took an active interest in all the scientific questions of his day); arguing that while such deterioration might be observed among individuals, it could never be true of entire races. Argyll, in defending Christian revelation, failed to understand it. To the anthropologist, Adam 'was a typical savage', naked, sensual, and imbued with a gross and anthropomorphic conception of the Deity.[106] Thus, unwittingly, was the ground prepared for the racist.

The dangers of evolutionary theory as applied to history and anthropology were great, and J. W. Burrow has demonstrated clearly the way in which such application provided for the Victorian an intellectual resting-place, a means of reconciling the need for positive conviction and the need to accommodate more social facts and interpretations than were allowed for by

[103] *Op. cit.*, p. 323.
[104] *Introductory Lectures on Political-Economy, Delivered at Oxford, etc.* (London, 1855), pp. 70–85.
[105] *Good Words*, June 1868, pp. 155–9, 249–53, 279–86, 385–92.
[106] *Op. cit.*, p. 360.

the traditional certainties.[107] And so, because a theory of progress was necessary to reassure British thinkers, its apparent absence in other cultures became a cause for their condemnation. Vestiges of barbarism might exist in civilized societies, but progress must and would eradicate these. Victorians' ethnocentrism allowed them to think in terms of a cultural hierarchy, in which Western civilizations occupied first place, followed by those of the East, and with the stagnant, technologically backward cultures of Africa and the Pacific at the bottom. The difficulties which modern scholars have experienced in attempting to establish any such hierarchy did not arise, because there was no acceptance of that degree of relativism which is essential for the study of societies as working systems.[108] The first major challenge to evolutionary theories was not to come until the First World War cast doubts on the necessary connection between technological achievement and moral improvement, and until social anthropologists ceased to be content with the inadequate results yielded by 'armchair' study in Britain, and ventured out to check their theories with the facts at first hand.

In the course of the following pages we shall be concerned with some of the components of progress and the other standards (regarding religion, appearance, attitudes to work and so on) which Victorians derived from their own culture and applied in the judgement of all others, thus arriving at their optimistic conclusions about British and Western cultural supremacy. And as we shall see, degenerationists such as Argyll and Whately were in a minority, not only among British anthropologists, but among Victorian observers in general. Hence there was very little support for the theory that the Africans encountered in the nineteenth century had fallen away from an earlier level of civilized attainment, due largely to the disruptive influence of European invaders on the African continent. Rather, they were seen as in an infantile condition, likely to progress to maturity only with the aid of superior white races.[109] In the same way,

[107] *Evolution and Society. A Study in Victorian Social Theory* (Cambridge, 1966), pp. 263–77.

[108] See, for instance, M. Leiris, *Race and Culture* (Paris, 1952, U.N.E.S.C.O.), pp. 35–9.

[109] See H. A. Cairns, *op. cit.*, p. 88.

with regard to India, there was a decline of interest in Oriental studies and respect for native institutions, and an increase in intolerant chauvinism, as everything was measured in the light of British technology, law, religion and philosophy.[110]

[110] G. D. Bearce, *British Attitudes towards India, 1784–1858* (London, 1961).

II

America:

the slave made free

He has been called the 'irrepressible nigger' and he is irrepressible. No one pretending to be a statesman, still more
no one pretending to be a ruler, can venture to overlook him.
In fact, just now, the first question which has to be settled
is the position of the 'freedman' in the great republic.
Manchester Courier, 1866.[1]

T HE British and Foreign Anti-slavery Society, founded in 1839,
was dedicated, with characteristic Victorian optimism, to the
abolition of slavery and the slave trade throughout the world.
Among the countries upholding these institutions, of which
Britain had with difficulty rid herself, the United States was the
most important, with some two and a half million slaves in 1842.
(By the outbreak of Civil War, in 1861, this figure had risen to
approaching four million.)

The Quaker-dominated B.F.A.S.S. assiduously cultivated its
contacts in the American anti-slavery movement through the
exchange of propaganda and personnel, but prejudices as well
as confidences were shared. Abhorrence of slavery did not always
imply sympathy for the Negro, in either American or Englishman.[2] In a curious way, the British anti-slavery campaign

[1] 7 March 1866.
[2] E. Berwanger's *The Frontier against Slavery*, for instance, establishes
that many in America's north-west who condemned slavery opposed its
extension for economic rather than humanitarian reasons, sharing current

29

became a commitment to abstract principles, like justice and equality, in which the Negro was overshadowed. The slave was idealized and, in consequence, de-humanized.

In addition, Britons who viewed race problems – whether in America, Africa or the West Indies – from a distance, might respond as Christians, but found solutions difficult, perhaps not their concern. The automatically charitable far outnumbered, by mid-century, the practical abolitionists. Clearly not even active philanthropists in Britain could hope to influence directly the policy of the United States towards the black population of the South. But as regards the colonies, throughout the 1850s and 1860s, there was a similar reluctance to interfere in internal-policy matters – as witness the refusal of the British Government to reconsider its withdrawal of troops from New Zealand, in spite of settler agitation, during the Maori Wars of these decades.

At a time when a substantial body of British opinion questioned the value of colonial possessions, it was understandable that coercive measures against the slave trade and thus, indirectly, slavery itself (retained by some of Britain's most important trading partners) should come under attack.[3] Middle-class and Government support, both vital to the initial success of the abolitionists, became less than wholehearted when it seemed that Britain alone was prepared to discharge her duty to the slave, and when commercial and humanitarian interests came into conflict. It should be remembered, however, that ultimately neither official nor abolitionist policy on the slave trade changed materially, in spite of adverse criticism, even though the fight to prevent the admission of foreign, slave-grown sugar was lost in the 1840s.

None the less, the British cruiser system offended the United States, traditionally touchy on the question of maritime rights, as well as disturbing the pacifist wing of the British anti-slavery movement, whose funds and personnel were depressingly diminished by the 1850s. It is therefore, at first, surprising to find that

[3] This hostile attitude was regularly deplored in the columns of the Royal Colonial Institute's journal.

---

prejudices against the Negro, while many leading Republicans played down their commitment to the black race (published Urbana, Chicago and London, 1967).

the attacks on Southern slavery in British journals, newspapers and popular travel books show no sign of abating. But, judging from authorship, it seems that many such were animated by a general hostility towards American institutions masquerading as respectable concern for the American Negro.

Part, at least, of the enormous popularity in Britain of Harriet Beecher Stowe's *Uncle Tom's Cabin* – which presented the Northern stereotype of slavery as an institution permitting no kindness in the master, no evil in the slave – resulted from the feelings of self-satisfaction which its exposures provoked. As one contemporary observer admitted, it was acclaimed out of 'national jealousy and national vanity. We have long been smarting under the conceit of America – we are tired of hearing her boast that she is the freest and most enlightened country that the world has ever seen. . . . All parties hailed Mrs. Stowe as a revolter from the enemy.'[4]

While critics of American political or economic practices advocated abolition out of malice, many genuine admirers of the young republic attacked slavery as the one institution which shadowed both past achievements and future promise.[5] But though at odds as regards motives, Conservatives and Radicals were united by their weakness for oversimplification, each projecting an America subtly adapted to suit British political and religious beliefs. This same tendency can be seen at work influencing British interpretations of the American Civil War.

To Radical friends of the North like John Bright, here was a grand collision between the forces of good and evil, with the minority South striving to 'found a slave state, freed from the influence and opinion of freedom. The free states of the North now stand before the world the advocates and defenders of freedom and civilization.'[6] At the opposite end of the political spectrum were many London and North Country newspapers which maintained that the contest would go against the tyrannical North, deservedly, for – as *John Bull* put it – 'Nothing can

---

[4] N. W. Senior, *American Slavery* (London, 1856), pp. 38–9.

[5] See G. D. Lillibridge, *Beacon of Freedom* (New York, 1961), pp. 111–13.

[6] *Rochdale Spectator*, 7 December 1871. See also *Reynolds's Weekly*, 2 June 1861.

be clearer than this, that black slavery has nothing to do with this Civil War in America'.[7]

There were those, however, capable of grasping the complexity of events in America, notably the abolitionists and the stricken cotton operatives of Lancashire. Although, as has been suggested, the anti-slavery movement became an impersonal religious crusade, dictated by 'a law above all the enactments of human codes . . . a law written by the finger of God in the hearts of men', those actively involved in the work (as opposed to those who deemed themselves abolitionists on the strength of occasional speeches and donations) had a better acquaintance with the United States than almost any other group in Britain.[8]

Consequently, there was a long period of silence from the B.F.A.S.S. at a time when all other organs of public opinion in Britain were competing to explain the war; it was impossible to vindicate a mere contest for the preservation of the Union. Only in 1863, with the final promulgation of Lincoln's Emancipation Proclamation, did the British philanthropist feel free to speak. It was in any case difficult for the Quaker members of the anti-slavery movement to justify the war, whatever its aims. We may also see here relics of that addiction to 'moderation, compromise, and delay' of which Joseph Sturge had once complained, somewhat unfairly, since a less moderate course might, without proportionate gain, have brought to British abolitionists a share of the odium heaped upon their American counterparts.[9]

The recent researches of Mary Jones and others have demonstrated that the Northern working men, long seen as solidly for Lincoln, thinking in abstract terms of democracy and the freedom of labour the world over, may also be identified as practical individuals, influenced by economic and regional circumstance. Accordingly in the weaving areas of north-east Lancashire, quickly affected by the disruption of the Southern cotton supply, the economic causes and effects of the war were emphasized, whereas in the south-east of the county, which did not feel the impact of the cotton famine for some time, there was an

[7] 14 September 1861. See also *Saturday Review*, 14 September 1861; *Economist*, 17 August 1861.

[8] *An Epitome of Anti-slavery Information, or A Condensed View of Slavery and the Slave Trade, etc.* (London, 1842), p. 16.

[9] H. Richard, *Memoirs of Joseph Sturge* (London, 1864), p. 78.

additional concern for the fate of the slaves. The role of Non-conformists and Radicals in mobilizing support for the Union has been greatly exaggerated. Altogether sixty-two cotton towns at different times during the war petitioned the British Government for recognition of the South or mediation between the belligerents, at the expense of the official policy of neutrality.[10] Such complexity of attitude was, however, the exception, not the rule.

Americans of both sections, unconsciously avenging the over-simplified accounts of their Civil War, displayed a similar willingness to misrepresent British attitudes. With the victory of the Union ensured in 1865, the aggrieved generalizations of the North became particularly important, and, in spite of the avowals of sympathizers like Goldwin Smith, the Oxford history professor who ultimately made his home in America, that the Federal cause had attracted 'a strong party of friends in Britain', many dwelt indignantly on the numerous 'excellent and intelligent people in England [who had] sympathized with the South in their attempt to establish a new nation upon slavery as its corner-stone'.[11] And indeed there is much truth here.

British newspapers friendly to the Union remained in a minority throughout the war; Lincoln's administration was ridiculed until his death; while Southern Independence societies flourished – with at least eighteen in Lancashire alone.[12] Supporters of the Confederacy could be found among all Church groups, the Nonconformists not excepted, and a Manchester paper unkindly but truthfully drew attention to the 'few surviving chiefs of the great anti-slavery struggle in England'.[13] Furthermore, with the end of the conflict there came other potential sources of friction.

Friends and critics of the North alike, on both sides of the Atlantic, agreed that the Negro had been inadequately prepared

[10] 'Lancashire and the American Civil War' (London Ph.D., read in manuscript), pp. 67–73, 95, 320.

[11] G. Smith to C. E. Norton, Oxford, 7 November 1863, Goldwin Smith Papers, No. 14/17, 134, Cornell University Library, Ithaca, New York; and Neal Dow – American abolitionist – to Henry Wilson of Mansfield, Notts., 12 March 1865, English MS. Collection 741 (28), John Rylands Library, Manchester.

[12] *Manchester Guardian*, 30 January 1864.   [13] *Ibid.*, 20 February 1863.

for freedom. In recognition of this fact, help was offered in the later stages of the war by the Federal army, the Freedmen's Bureau, and a host of voluntary (often Church-sponsored) organizations.[14] From 1863 onwards freedmen's aid societies, composed largely of veteran abolitionists, were established throughout Britain, where they constituted the last great Victorian protest against slavery and its aftermath, and helped to keep interest in American affairs extraordinarily high for at least another decade.

Unfortunately for racial harmony, the combined efforts of these charitable agencies brought little comfort to the ex-slave-owners, deemed too numerous to receive compensation, as had the West Indian planters in 1833, even if this had been practic-able in the strained circumstances of 1865. Further, by making slavery a mortal sin – and ignoring its economic ramifications – the American abolitionists had ruled compensation out of court.

British observers were gloomy about the Negro's prospects when the war ended. The old suspicion of Northern motives and attitudes – which had led John Ruskin to describe the Civil War as fought 'partly for money, partly for vanity, partly for wild anarchy and the Devil's cause and crown' – reasserted itself during the Reconstruction, the postwar restoration of the Southern economy and political system.[15]

The *Daily Telegraph* stigmatized the Northern leaders as cynics 'who desire to use the Negroes as instruments for the furtherance of political power, but care not a whit for their true interests!'[16] Even the *Spectator* – with the *Daily News*, one of the few consistent British supporters of the Union – complained of the violence of Radical Republicans like Stevens and Sumner, who appeared to be animated as much, or even more, by 'aversion, not to say hatred, to the late rebels of the South, as by a sense of justice to the loyal freedmen of the South'.[17]

[14] See, for details of American efforts, H. L. Swint, *The Northern Teacher in the South, 1862–70* (Nashville, 1941); H. Donald, *The Negro Freedman* (New York, 1952); G. R. Bentley, *A History of the Freedmen's Bureau* (Philadelphia, 1955).

[15] *Letters of John Ruskin to Charles Eliot Norton* (Boston, 1905, 2 vols.), I, pp. 134–5.

[16] 27 June 1865, correspondent.

[17] 10 March 1866, p. 261.

Everyone knew, according to Liverpool merchant William Rathbone, that 'In the Northern States of America previous to the War, the antipathy to the black skin was far more rabid than in the South'. The Negro had been regarded as 'an irresponsible and inferior order of creation', and Rathbone predicted, in the light of past attitudes, that there was much suffering in store for black and white in the United States 'before a healthy beneficial system can be adopted'.[18]

The corruptibility and indifferent calibre of American politicians had long proved an attractive theme to British moralists. Reconstruction was presented as the fulfilment of generations of Tory prophecies. 'During General Grant's term of office [as President]', observed the *Irish Times*, 'the United States were delivered over into the hands of Philistines and robbers.' The Federal Government became simply a 'den of thieves', a 'wholesale nest of corruption and sin', an 'Augean stable of all things foul and demoralizing'.[19] Press opinion was complemented by the observations of British travellers, whose outspokenness during Reconstruction took little account of American sensibilities.

According to journalist W. H. Dixon, in his enormously popular *New America*, during the postwar period of Northern intervention in the South white citizens could not cast their votes, while crime and poverty, and rates on property increased beyond endurance.[20] In the opinion of economist Robert Somers, a generally more restrained commentator, Reconstruction was characterized by 'a delirium of folly and corruption'.[21] Comparable views were expressed by the judicious Sir George Campbell, by George Sala, a journalist of similarly liberal outlook,

[18] William to Elizabeth Rathbone, 9 February 1866, Rathbone Papers, Liverpool Public Library.

[19] 9 November 1876. See also, for a jaundiced view of Northern motives, *Irish Times*, 4 July 1865; *Manchester Courier*, 22 March 1862, 10, 12 January, 1 August 1863; *Manchester Guardian*, 2, 7, 9 January 1863, 22 August 1864; *Birmingham Daily Gazette*, 5 May, 1, 7 July, 29 December 1864, 23 February, 12 June 1865.

[20] London, 1869 (8th ed., 2 vols.), I, pp. 340–1. Dixon was Editor of the *Athenaeum* and the writer of popular travel and history books. His book was first published 1867, and went through nine editions in England, three in America, and several in France, Italy, Russia, Holland and Germany.

[21] *The Southern States Since the War, 1870–1* (London, 1871), pp. 51, 41–3, 227, 269–70.

by James Bryce and many others.[22] That this corruption was not the monopoly of one race or section during these turbulent years was invariably overlooked. The Northern politician, whether he remained at home or went south, became the scapegoat.

Often it was the element of force employed by the North to implement its Reconstruction policies which made outsiders uneasy. Many Britons held that gradual emancipation would have been better for the Negro, since, as a speaker in Bolton put it in 1863, 'freedom obtained by the sword could not rest on a solid foundation but would eventually produce . . . sad and degenerating results'.[23]

This argument was taken up and urged repeatedly by the historian J. A. Froude. In punishing the South for slavery, he commented, the North was

> playing once again on a new stage the old game of Philip the Second and Alva. You cannot be more persuaded of the wickedness of slavery than they were of the wickedness of heresy. The universe does not allow one section of mankind to inflict its views upon another at the point of the sword. If the sword is pressed into service beyond the common sense of mankind, it will kill the man that uses it.[24]

The recent history of Poland and centuries of conflict with Ireland convinced many Victorians that if Radical policies were pursued, 'for centuries to come the South will be to the North, as Ireland . . . still is to England, a source not of strength, but of weakness, in time of danger'.[25] Although he deplored such sentiments, John Stuart Mill was forced to admit privately that in Britain 'Every one is vaguely inculcating gentleness'.[26]

[22] G. Campbell, *White and Black* (New York, 1879), p. 180; G. Sala *America Revisited* (London, 1882, 2 vols.), I, p. 232, II, p. 49; J. Bryce *The American Commonwealth* (New York, 1895, 2 vols.), II, pp. 377–448, 476–8.

[23] *Bolton Chronicle*, 4 July 1863.

[24] W. H. Dunn, *James Anthony Froude. A Biography* (Oxford, 1962–3, 2 vols.), II, p. 342.

[25] *Scotsman*, 12 March 1866; for similar comparisons between the South and Poland/Ireland see *Saturday Review*, 22 August 1868, p. 983; *Spectator*, 27 June 1868, p. 760, and 16 November 1867, p. 1,281; *Daily News*, 10 June 1865; *Dublin Evening Mail*, 12 May 1865; *Freeman's Journal*, 27 July 1865; *Irish Times*, 2 May 1865.

[26] Mill to Parke Godwin, Avignon, 13 May 1865, *The Letters of John Stuart Mill* (London, 1910, 2 vols.), II, p. 32.

A new element was added to the argument by the *Manchester Guardian* when it suggested that coercion of the South was futile as well as dangerous, since even four bloody years of war had not been able to 'induce several millions of people of English race to acknowledge that they have finally lost all which free men value'.[27] Pride of race was stirred in those Britons who sympathized with the white planter, facing simultaneously military defeat, economic ruin and loss of personal prestige. Commentators as different as Roebuck, Thackeray and Disraeli had already publicized the notions of Anglo-Saxon solidarity and the nobility of the 'English race' in the South. The *Daily Telegraph* ultimately justified its support of President Johnson's Reconstruction policies on the grounds that 'While his opponents denounce, he conciliates; and it has never yet been found, at least among an Anglo-Saxon race, that brute threats were effectual to quell distrust or antagonism when gentle measures had failed to soothe'.[28]

The reports of those best placed to judge, though not necessarily impartially – the British consuls in the South – show the similarity between Victorian public and private opinion on American politics.[29] Since an important part of their function was to advise the Foreign Office about the state of trade, the consuls generally had connections with just those sections of Southern society which most resented the postwar political and economic changes. Consular views were clearly coloured by the complaints of the planter class. In Charleston, H. P. Walker (echoing the *Guardian*), though full of grievances about Radical rule, predicted that not 'even the military power of the United

[27] 20 April 1866.

[28] 19 September 1866. For other pleas for a generous peace see *Daily News*, 9 December 1865; *Saturday Review*, 1 July 1865, pp. 4, 37, 26 August 1865, pp. 255–6; *Edinburgh Evening Courant*, 15 May 1865; *Northern Whig* (Belfast), 13 June 1865; *Freeman's Journal* (Dublin), 25 May, 27 July 1865; *Dublin Evening Mail*, 12, 26 May 1865; *Irish Times*, 27 May, 12 June 1865; *North British Daily Mail* (Glasgow), 15 May 1865; *Birmingham Daily Gazette*, 9, 16 May 1865.

[29] Cridland in Mobile, Walker in Charleston, and Tasker Smith in Savannah were definitely English by birth; it is less easy to establish the antecedents of the other consuls, but it is likely they too were English. See E. Lonn, *Foreigners in the Confederacy* (Chapel Hill, 1940), p. 412, and M. L. Bonham, *The British Consuls in the Confederacy* (New York, 1911), pp. 16–17, 256–7.

States can for any lengthened period compel the silence of a naturally high-spirited [white] race'.[30]

The heightened suspicion of Northern politicians, resulting in part from the truly extraordinary political experiments of Reconstruction and from a sentimental sympathy for a gallantly defeated people, served to encourage such views. The sense of racial kinship was easily transformed into a belief in Anglo-Saxon superiority, even in those professing concern for other races. Thus David Macrae, a Scottish traveller and one-time missionary, who visited America in the late 1860s, sympathized with the freedmen, but thought that fears of the Negro ruling in the South were preposterous, since Anglo-Saxon ideas were dominating and moulding the length and breadth of the republic.[31] In similar, though sarcastic vein, the journal of the London Freed-men's Aid Society inquired of 'those who raise the cry of negro supremacy, on what grounds are the Freed-men themselves to be blamed in this matter. We always understood that the Southern planter prided himself on his superior intelligence, and on the extent of his influence. Is all this superiority gone?'[32] A seemingly unanswerable question, surprisingly not often asked, either in Britain or the United States.

Anglo-Saxonism was in vogue, like civilization and science, free trade and progress. Thus Sir George Campbell stressed the ties of affection which bound Englishmen to Americans, regarding the latter as 'really and truly our kin', and in his very successful book, *Greater Britain*, the Liberal M.P. Charles Dilke, though at pains to defend the potential of the Southern Negro, enthused over the demonstrated grandeur of the Anglo-Saxon race, 'already girdling the earth, which it is destined, perhaps, eventually to overspread'.[33]

[30] Walker to Lord Stanley, 10 November 1866, F.O. 5, 1,078, No. 56, Foreign Office records, Public Record Office, London. Walker had settled in the U.S. in 1839, practising law in Charleston until the war, when he became first Vice-consul, then Consul, and was accused of Southern bias.

[31] *The Americans at Home* (Edinburgh, 1870, 2 vols.), II, p. 18.

[32] *Freed-man*, 1 January 1868, p. 7 (published monthly from August 1865 to September 1868).

[33] Campbell, *op. cit.*, p. 2; Dilke, *op. cit.*, I, pp. ix–x. See also L. Oliphant, *On The Present State of Political Parties in America* (Edinburgh and London, 1866), pp. 27–30; F. B. Zincke, *Last Winter in the United States*

Many of those who lent their support to the British freedmen's aid movement did so out of sympathy for the United States, rebuilding after a bitter war, and a desire to improve Anglo-American relations badly strained as a result of that war. Self-interest as well as sympathy dictated a conciliatory approach: the tremendous power of America, both real and potential, was widely recognized even in the 1860s.[34] Men like Jacob and John Bright, Thomas Hughes, J. S. Mill and W. E. Forster, and others less well known, readily endorsed the official aim of the movement – that of drawing 'into closer friendship . . . the two great branches of the Anglo-Saxon race'.[35]

This belief in Anglo-Saxon solidarity and supremacy gave strength to theories about the extermination of native races and race war which were to influence British attitudes to Reconstruction. In 1876, departing from the relative moderation of his earlier work, W. H. Dixon published one of the most curious Victorian treatises on this theme, the *White Conquest*, at once a tribute to the supremacy of the Anglo-Saxon in North America and a warning against the threat offered by the Negro and Indian on that continent. Here we have an exact reproduction of Knox's 'war of races' theory, in which racial arrogance and insecurity are both essential elements.

In confident mood, Dixon compared the British and American Civil Wars, with the Roundheads represented in the latter struggle by the North and the Cavaliers by the South. The whites of both sides won praise, but the South was most favoured, for in this semi-tropical region, with its master–servant society, the traditions of chivalry had been preserved; even lawlessness could be excused, for the Southerner was 'a mounted man – a knight, who rides and carries arms. The air is hot and swells in mortal veins.' The preservation of white values in a racially

[34] See, for instance, *Saturday Review*, 15 June 1867, p. 743; *Times*, 13 February 1866; *Spectator*, 17 February 1866, pp. 177–8.

[35] *Freedmen's Aid Reporter* (London, published monthly from May 1866 to December 1867; in future simply *Reporter*), June 1866, p. 1; also April 1866, pp. 12–13, December 1866, p. 84; *Freed-Man*, 1 March 1866, p. 168, 1 June 1866, p. 263.

(London, 1868), p. 151; Sir J. Kennaway, *On Sherman's Track* (London, 1876), p. viii; *Daily Telegraph*, 11 April 1866; *Spectator*, 11 August 1866, p. 880, 8 September 1866, pp. 993–5; *Times*, 30 July 1866, 5 May 1868.

diverse society was, however, essential 'if we wish to see order and freedom, science and civilisation preserved'. But Dixon was not, apparently, entirely confident that this would be the case: it was necessary to appeal for white solidarity, even while it was taken for granted that 'The lower forms of life give way in presence of a higher type'. The Englishman was forced to admit that the Negro–Indian mixing which he saw at Caddo, a small Southern town, was producing a new race known as Zambos, and 'these ugly creatures are said to be prolific. Every cabin in Caddo shows a brood of imps; and if the new school of ethnologists are right, they may increase more rapidly than the ordinary Blacks. What sort of mongrels shall we find at Caddo in a hundred years?'[36]

The debate over whether the Negro would survive in the Southern states, now that he was exposed, without protection, to competition with whites, interested many other British writers, as we would expect. A strong element of wishful thinking seems to have been present in the discussions on this issue: certainly little statistical proof was offered of a declining Negro population in America. Like the earlier colonization schemes, the doctrine of the survival of the fittest as applied to the South offered hope to those barren of practical solutions for the racial problems of that section, as well as being in line with popular anthropology. The harrowing accounts of suffering and deaths among the freedmen during 1865, given by the British Press in order to rouse middle-class consciences, no doubt encouraged the extermination theory. And, of course, British colonial experience seemed further proof, though few appeared to notice the remarkable staying power of the West Indian Negro, for whom a similarly brief existence had been predicted in 1833.

The British Ambassador in Washington reported privately to Lord Stanley that the superintendence and 'care of the white man is essential to the increase if not the permanence of the [black] Race'.[37] Although such a view confirmed the supposed superiority of the white American, it also implied responsibility on his part as well as rights. The well-known journalist William Rathbone Greg – a firm believer in the doctrine that 'the negroes

[36] London, 1876, 2 vols.; I, pp. 273–4, 325, II, pp. 138–43, 372.
[37] Sir Frederick Bruce to Lord Stanley, 22 December 1866, F.O. 5, 1,068, No. 383.

are made on purpose to serve the whites, just as the black ants are made on purpose to serve the red' – put the normal conservative viewpoint when he argued that the choice of the freedmen was between 'enforced labour . . . or ultimate extermination', and was thus able to make out an ostensibly high-minded case for the former.[38] These views were frequently repeated by British travellers and in the Press, but there were those who, for various reasons, questioned their validity. David Macrae, for instance, maintained that the common assumption 'that the negro is dying out is, to say the least of it, premature'.[39] Speaking after his 1866 tour of America, the Rev. Dr McCosh of Queen's College, Belfast, likewise sympathetic towards the Negro, confessed: 'Any fear that I may have of the coloured people dying out in America, does not arise from any native incapacity in the race, but from the prejudice of the whites, which may lead them to neglect their duty.' It was an unpalatable fact that 'The Anglo-Saxons, ever ready to advance themselves, have not been so successful in advancing other races. In this country we cannot boast of what we have done in the West Indies, at the Cape of Good Hope, in Australia and New Zealand, or even among the Celtic Irish. . . . The Americans have certainly made little progress in raising the condition of the Red Indians.'[40]

The fate of the original inhabitants of the United States was perhaps the most obvious precedent – sometimes encouragement – for those writers, whether British or American, who predicted the disappearance of the Negro. (The Church of England mission to North American Indians was just one source of information about their desolate condition at this time.[41]) But an additional prejudice, as regards the Negro, reinforced the doctrines of Social Darwinianism and the evidence of history. The freedmen were characterized, according to Victorians – and here is the European racist's most persistent obsession – by their uninhibited sensuality. This was expressed in a passion for eating and drinking, sleeping, dressing up, dancing and sex. Such

[38] *Pall Mall Gazette*, 21 April 1865, pp. 3–4, and *Spectator*, 16 September 1865, p. 1,035.
[39] *Op. cit.*, II, p. 16.
[40] *Banner of Ulster*, 8 November 1866.
[41] Details given regularly in the *Church Missionary Intelligencer*.

qualities repelled the Anglo-Saxon, publicly, at least, and British writers confidently predicted that no fusion of races could be brought about under conditions of freedom.

Some radical spirits thought intermarriage might be desirable – Macrae, for instance, and Goldwin Smith, who believed that without it, 'there can hardly be social equality; [and] without social equality there can hardly be real political equality or a genuine commonwealth, let the franchise be distributed as it may'.[42] But it was generally concluded, in the words of F. B. Zincke, a clergyman and Radical in politics, that 'History assures us . . . nothing of the kind has ever been accomplished and that it is physically impossible'.[43] *The Times* went further, arguing that miscegenation was not merely unlikely, because of Southern prejudices, but a prospect infinitely degrading and proof of the degeneracy of those American Radicals who condoned it.[44]

Before turning to a detailed examination of Victorian attitudes to American race problems, it is necessary to say a word about those who do not fit in with the general alignment of British sympathies. As we have seen, the basic approach to Reconstruction was conservative, compassion going out to the planter and suspicion being aroused by the radical programme of the North. In particular, alarm was expressed at the deteriorating relations between black and white in the South.[45]

This gloomy and reactionary view was strenuously rejected by the British freedmen's aid movement, although it was ostensibly pledged to avoid political comment. This is not to say that philanthropic Victorians were either men in advance of their age or utterly one-sided in their sympathies. But, in the words of a leading Quaker journal, it was vital to hold a 'moral balance, . . . [not] suffering our hatred of slavery to degenerate

[42] G. Smith, *The Moral Crusader, William Lloyd Garrison: a Biographical Essay* (Toronto, 1892), p. 182.

[43] *Op. cit.*, p. 107.

[44] 18 February 1864.

[45] *Saturday Review*, 7 October 1865, p. 442; *Times*, 13 January 1866; *Scotsman*, 12 March 1866; *Daily Telegraph*, 12 September 1866, 30 November 1876; *Dublin Evening Mail*, 11 November 1876; F.O. 5, 1,132 and 1,484, Sir Edward Thornton's and R. G. Watson's reports from Washington.

into hate of the slaveholder', and an address to the freedmen issued in 1868 by the London Meeting for Sufferings urged the Negro, in very conservative terms, 'to obey the laws, to be subject to those in authority, to maintain order, to fulfil your bargains, ... to labour diligently ... for ... your wives and children' and for America, and if oppressed by the Southern whites to be patient in the knowledge that '"All things work together for good to them that love God"'.[46]

In order to secure the widest appeal in Britain, divided as men had been over the Civil War, and in America, where memories of British conduct during that war still rankled, such caution was, in theory, quite vital. But in practice it proved impossible to maintain. A movement devoted to the welfare of the freedmen was bound ultimately to favour whichever party in America seemed to promise them the best opportunities of advancement. And in this connection the attitudes of the ex-slaveowners were regarded with increasing suspicion – there was no admiration of the 'Southern oligarchs', but rather a belief that the latter 'seem determined to annoy and discourage those who are endeavouring to instruct and elevate the Freedmen'.[47]

There was also a small section of the British Press which, though sympathetic towards the widespread demands for a generous peace, shared this aversion for the white South. Thus the *Daily News* depicted the planters as 'reckless and ambitious men [who] ... had no career except that of political intrigue and piratical adventure', and the major part of the Southern population as being 'known all the world over for their pride of race and poverty of purse, and for their mingled ignorance and violence'.[48] The *Spectator*, though less outspoken, noted with critical concern that 'All over the South the ... [former] absolute contempt for the civil rights of the negro is shown'. Once more the old conflict 'between the aristocratic and demo-cratic constitution of society' was disturbing America, the old struggle 'between ideas which cannot be equally triumphant,

[46] *Friend*, 1 March 1863, p. 58; *Extracts from the Minutes and Proceedings of the Yearly Meeting, Held in London ... 1868* (in future M. & P.), pp. 55–6.

[47] *Friend*, 1 September 1866, pp. 189–90; *Reporter*, May 1866, pp. 7, 9, January 1867, p. 93; *Freed-Man*, 1 June 1866, pp. 260–2, 1 January 1868, pp. 2–3.

[48] 10 June 1865, 18 August 1866, 9 December 1865.

slavery and freedom, privilege and equality, caste and Christianity'. Under these circumstances, the *Spectator* – like the *News* – was prepared to condone even military rule in the South, since the 'only thing in which [that section] . . . is at present prepared to obey the North is in doing whatever the North supports by an army'.[49]

For the same reasons Edward Dicey (Editor of the Liberal *Observer*, and at one time of the *Daily News*), writing in the *Fortnightly Review*, suggested that the policy 'of concession to the South is a fatal error', and that the best plan would be to impose Federal and military rule until 'a generation had sprung up to whom slavery was unknown, except as a tradition'.[50] After some initial doubts, *The Economist* also argued that local autonomy was impossible in a society 'divided into two internecine sections, . . . except by one section at the expense of the other'; the obvious remedy was 'to dispense with self-government [in the South], to keep strict order, to form and protect institutions administering impartial justice *and imparting impartial education*', and to trust to the healing influence of time for the restoration of a more normal state of affairs.[51]

From a realistic standpoint, however, these British observers were forced to admit that their proposals were probably valueless: even the North had shown an 'almost nervous horror of open military occupation' of the defeated states, despite mounting racial tension in, for instance, Louisiana and Georgia.[52] One sees in this debate a reflection of the conflicting American approaches to Reconstruction, with the Radical Republicans favouring immediate action as regards the freedmen, and, if necessary, some years elapsing before the South was restored to its former position in the Union, while the conservatives urged an immediate return to the prewar political situation, followed by a gradual elevation of the Negro. Writers like Bagehot were, in fact, more insistent even than the Radicals on

[49] 12 January 1867, p. 34; 11 August 1866, pp. 881, 25 August 1866, p. 932, 2 February 1867, p. 121; *Daily News*, 21, 28 March 1867.

[50] July–December 1874, XVI, p. 827.

[51] 21 December 1867, p. 143; see also 16 March 1867, pp. 293–4, 3 October 1868, pp. 1,131–2, 5 December 1874, pp. 1,450–1, 21, 28 March 1867.

[52] *Spectator*, 7 November 1868, p. 1,302.

the need to reduce Southern independence, and clearly British colonial experience was a factor here.[53]

In a case where a large element of society was deemed unfit for political privileges, as were the American freedmen, government should be conducted, according to *The Economist*, 'on principles like those applied to our great Indian dependency'.[54] But the United States was unable to learn from Britain, it was alleged, not because of tenderness for the Negro, but from an aversion to such dependencies and a 'superstitious faith' in a Constitution and Declaration of Independence dedicated to the principles of freedom, equality and popular participation in politics. It was always much easier for the Englishman than the American to point out that this Constitution had been radically altered by the war, and had never in fact guaranteed the civil rights of all inhabitants of the Republic.[55]

However, those who criticized the actions of white Southerners and supported at least some aspects of Republican policy always remained in a minority.[56] As the *Daily Telegraph* affirmed, public opinion among Englishmen was almost unanimously in favour of Presidential Reconstruction, in spite of the occasional professions of neutrality, and the aspect of Reconstruction which provoked the most comment was 'the Negro problem'.[57]

This was not simply a question of academic interest. There was a strong feeling that the United States should be warned by British experiences with West Indian freedmen over the past

[53] The Conservatives, who, as we have seen, opposed the use of force during Reconstruction, did so because it applied to both races in the South and not just the Negro.

[54] 21 December 1867, p. 1,443.

[55] See, on this fixation with the Constitution, *Saturday Review*, 23 March 1867, p. 355, 10 March 1866, p. 283; W. H. Dixon, *New America*, p. 439; *Hansard's Parliamentary Debates*, Third Series (in future simply *Hansard*), *Daily Telegraph*, 5 December 1876; C. Dilke, *op. cit.*, 1, p. 288; *Times*, 19 March 1869, 1 August 1867, correspondent.

[56] In addition to the *Daily News*, *Spectator* and *Economist*, we may include in this group the *Manchester Examiner and Times*, *Northern Whig*, *Banner of Ulster* and *North British Daily Mail*.

[57] *Daily Telegraph*, 31 August 1866; see also *Manchester Guardian*, 6 March 1866, *Manchester Courier*, 5 March, 28 May 1868, *Edinburgh Evening Courant*, 14 March 1867, supporting this view of British public opinion during Reconstruction; and for professions of neutrality *Daily News*, 5 March 1866.

thirty years, and that Britain in turn had something to learn from Americans about the handling of coloured races. The Victorian freedmen's aid societies divided their time equally between the Negroes of Jamaica and the South – though I am here only concerned with their activities as regards the latter – and co-operated closely with the American voluntary societies in the field.[58] They effectively translated attitudes into action, which until the abolition of slavery by the Federal Government between 1863 and 1865 had been denied them, raising money, collecting clothes, endowing and maintaining schools in the South, even sending out teachers.

The ensuing pages examine the response to the American Negro – as citizen, voter, student and labourer – among British philanthropists and those less kindly disposed. In the conditioning of this response, it will be seen that American advice, along with the prevailing notions of Anglo-Saxonism and scientific theories of race, played an important part.

The British attitude towards the American freedman was, on the whole, lofty, paternalistic and narrow, coloured – as the *Spectator* remarked – by the old 'ferocity of prejudice on the side of the South'.[59] The abstract, religious nature of the anti-slavery crusade, combined with the prevailing ignorance of Negro culture, encouraged even philanthropists to think of the latter as of a white man enslaved. Hence the suggestions for improving the position of the freedmen made by Britons might equally well have been offered for the elevation of the Victorian working man. In brief, there was approval for Negro civil rights and education, a desire to see physical distress alleviated and steady labour exacted, if necessary by force, and hostility towards plans for the redistribution of planters' land among the freedmen and for Negro suffrage. Missionary work was acceptable in the South; the remaking of the section's political and economic system was not.

Present-day charities appeal to the emotions and thence the purse by jolting pictures of human degradation in distant places;

[58] Chapter III deals specifically with Britain and the West Indian, especially the Jamaican, freedmen.
[59] 25 August 1866, p. 93.

the Victorian Press, if it could not rely on photographs, was at least not short of sentiment, and produced regular reports of Negro suffering during and after the Civil War to stir up interest in freedmen's aid, or to expose the shortcomings of the Federal Government, or both. Thus the *Birmingham Daily Gazette*, a Conservative journal sympathetic towards the South, complained of 'old men and children, the infirm and suffering, and the women, . . . left to rot and die in thousands'.[60] Similarly critical of Federal policy, a correspondent of that paper none the less urged Britons to help 'alleviate the privations and distress of freed negroes', though it seemed 'bitter mockery' to call them freed when appalling destitution existed among them – 'the poor victims of bondage [left] to nearly starve under shelter of the star-spangled banner of freedom'.[61] The *Preston Guardian*, publicizing the valiant work of the freedmen's aid societies, noted that 'diseases arising from hunger, exposure, and other causes incident to poor humanity, have thrown thousands into helpless suffering, which it is the duty of Christianity to pity and relieve'.[62]

The abolitionists, as they had always done, held up the Negro as an object of pity – as a pamphlet published in 1865 put it, 'No such absolutely pauper population has probably ever been known in modern times'.[63] Even more affecting was the appeal of the National Committee of British Freedmen's Aid Associations, declaring that 'self-adjustment [by the blacks] to the duties and privileges of their new position, independently of friendly guidance and special help from without is an absolute impossibility'. The Negroes were 'as a whole, in a position of absolute helplessness, beset with immense perils; their very freedom being a powerful temptation to idleness, disaffection, and violence. Children without recognized parents; mothers and fathers without the ties of marriage; the diseased, the maimed, and the aged; all unlettered, and untrained to habits of self-support; what a field for philanthropy!'[64] The truth of such accounts was

[60] 29 December 1864.   [61] 30 January 1865.
[62] 11 March 1865.
[63] *A Plea for the Perishing;* pamphlet of the Leeds Freedmen's Aid Society (Leeds, 1865), John Rylands Library pamphlets, Manchester.
[64] *Four Millions of Emancipated Slaves in the United States*, pamphlet in John Rylands Library Collection, p. 1.

E   47

confirmed by American correspondents of the British freedmen's aid movement. The Birmingham society quoted a Cincinatti worker as saying in 1865 that there was and would be during the coming winter a mighty effort on the part of the whites of the South to render 'the condition of the Coloured People as miserable as they possibly can, in order to demonstrate the necessity of holding them in bondage'.[65]

As we have seen, many Britons felt that action on the part of the Federal Government could have averted such a crisis, and various counter-suggestions and explanations had to be offered by the freedmen's societies. Here was an opportunity to rise above wartime animosities. It was 'a universal duty to feed the hungry and clothe the naked', and even those who thought the war 'as carried on by the North, purely evil in its motives, in its conduct, and its chief consequences', must see in the liberation of millions of Negro slaves that 'the sable cloud has a silver lining'. Observers who, like 'some Southern *savants* and their English disciples of the Anthropological Society', regarded the Negro 'as a highly endowed species of ape' must recognize the immediate material needs of the freedmen; must acknowledge that 'it will be cruel to let them perish when the war is no fault of theirs'.[66]

It was emphatically pointed out that the Federal Government and the Northern people were grappling manfully with this tremendous difficulty, but that 'the demands for help are so large, sudden, and unforeseen that they exhaust the resources and the strength of their American benefactors'.[67] Suggestions that there was no further need for intervention in the South were dismissed as absurd – the troubles of Jamaica after 1838 stemmed directly from the fact that 'the British people, thinking their work was done, left the arrangements for . . . [the black] people in the hands of their former oppressors'.[68]

Furthermore, Britain had played an important part in the

[65] Circular No. 10 of the Birmingham Freedmen's Aid Society, John Rylands Library Collection.

[66] *Birmingham Daily Gazette*, 20 December 1864, and *Belfast Northern Whig*, 23 December 1864.

[67] *Plea for the Perishing, op. cit.*, pp. 4, 6.

[68] *Annual Report of the Edinburgh Ladies' Emancipation Society, and Sketch of . . . the Condition of the Freedmen During the Year Ending 15th February 1866* (Edinburgh, 1866), pp. 21–6.

slave trade which took the Negro to America, and since then had helped to perpetuate slavery by importing Southern cotton. As a Birmingham appeal concluded, since 'we have had so much to do, from first to last, in the causes of the distress, so it is our duty to take a large share in relieving it'.[69] It was also necessary not to 'overlook the bearing of this good work, on the general interests of the world'. In the first place, emancipation of the American Negro could be seen as the prelude to the downfall of slavery elsewhere: it was therefore vital, in the interest of slaves in Cuba and Brazil especially, that the experiment of freedom should prove a success. Furthermore, once 'Let the African race in America be well cared for, and duly raised to the full dignity of citizenship, and many of them, of their own accord, will prove the best pioneers in the future civilization of the Continent from which, in the days of the slave-trade, they were so cruelly torn'.[70]

As it happens, this prophecy has remained unfulfilled, though the Liberian experiment was watched with interest by Victorian philanthropists. The above proposal, of course, envisages voluntary return to exile, while the colonization schemes of the nineteenth century paid minimal attention to the wishes of those transported to West Africa and elsewhere; the American Negro rightly regarded himself as an American citizen, and dismissed colonizing as 'a product of slavery. Nobody proposes to colonize any other class.'[71] In typically cynical vein, however, the *Saturday Review* enquired whether it might not be better to reverse the trend, for 'In his native seats the negro is still everywhere a degraded savage', whereas under the influence of the white race in America the African had certainly prospered. Those 'silly philanthropists' who asserted that the freedman was in fact fit to share in the government of the United States were

[69] *Why Should Birmingham Workmen Help the Freed Refugees from Slavery in America? Who are in Great Distress*, John Rylands Library Collection pamphlet.

[70] *Help For the Freed Slaves. Large Public Meeting in Derby*, John Rylands Library pamphlet, and *An appeal to the People of England, from the National Committee of the British Freedmen's-Aid Associations*, in *ibid.*, p. 2.

[71] *Cincinatti Colored Citizen*, 1865; Negro newspaper, reported in H. Aptheker, *A Documentary History of the Negro People in the United States* (New York, 1951, 2 vols.), I, p. 550.

furnishing 'an unanswerable apology, not only for the system in which he was trained, but for the slave-trade on which the institution was originally founded. . . . experience has shown that neither missionaries nor traders can make a perceptible impression on . . . [African] barbarism', and therefore a scrupulous conscience would feel the duty of kidnapping the remaining population of central Africa, 'to pass them through the process which has refined and sublimated their happier kinsmen beyond the Atlantic'.[72]

The British freedmen's aid societies were also at pains to assure prospective donors that the Negro would work efficiently in the South. The question of free labour – like that of Negro franchise – touched Britons on the raw. For all the high hopes of abolitionists, the experience of the West Indian planters after emancipation had proved an unhappy one. Stress was therefore laid upon the freedman's willingness to accept work for reasonable wages. (American correspondents confirmed this view.[73]) 'When Slavery no longer exists in the South to affix the stamp of degradation to honest labour,' argued a Birmingham circular in 1864, 'there is nothing to prevent an extensive cultivation of cotton by the same arrangement of labour and capital which have given such preponderance to the productive industry of the Northern States.'[74]

But the commercial interests of the North of England were even more important to British observers, as the freedmen's aid movement recognized. Cotton was intimately bound up with 'the commercial greatness of our country', it was argued, and there could not be 'a single inhabitant' who had not worn the end-product of Negro labour. A free and educated peasantry in the South, with money to spend, would not only increase output of the vital fibre and render Lancashire even more prosperous, but would also help to increase the orders for consumer goods from every industrial region in Britain. This prospect,

[72] *Saturday Review*, 9 April 1870, p. 468, and 30 September 1865, pp. 4–11.

[73] *The Twenty-Fourth Annual Report of the British and Foreign Anti-Slavery Society* (London, 1863), p. 13; for American confirmation see Circulars No. 11, 13 and 14 of the Birmingham Society, John Rylands Library Collection.

[74] *Considerations on the Transition State of the Freed Coloured People in America*, Birmingham Public Library.

after the difficulties experienced during the Civil War, was infinitely attractive.[75]

According to a *Times* estimate in 1861, approximately one-fifth of the entire population of England lived directly or indirectly by the cotton industry, and the South provided four-fifths of the raw material. As a result of the wartime blockade, by 1862, many hundreds of thousands in Lancashire and the North had been forced to accept relief and perhaps a third of those employed in the cotton trade had been pauperized. The magnificent aid of the Federal Government during this crisis was repeatedly emphasized by the freedmen's societies (British aid to the American Negro was to be a *quid pro quo*), and, of course, existing stockpiles of cotton in Britain, combined with supplies smuggled out of the South, prevented a total disaster. In due time new sources of supply in India and Egypt were developed. But in 1865 American cotton was still vital – and unusually expensive. Thus far all Britons were agreed, but many were unable to share the abolitionists' optimism about Negro labour.

It was universally assumed that the freedmen would continue to provide the agricultural labour of the South. The arguments of American Radicals – white and black – that true emancipation for the Negroes would follow only if they acquired land of their own were received with disfavour, bearing in mind the labour needs of the cotton plantations, and because Britons believed confiscation of planter holdings was the only way to achieve this. Consuls in the South complained that the freedmen imagined they must have 'a proportion of the white man's property', and the British Ambassador felt that if the Southern economy were ever to recover, 'vague threats of confiscation of property cannot be kept hanging over the heads of the proprietors in general'.[76]

---

[75] *Birmingham and Midland Association for the Help of Refugees from Slavery in America, By a Vessel to be Freighted With Stores*, John Rylands Library pamphlet; *Why Should Birmingham Workmen Help the Freed Refugees From Slavery in America?* etc., *op. cit.*; and Bradford appeal found in the papers of the Anti-Slavery Society, Rhodes House, Oxford (in future simply A.P.), d. 12 November 1867, A.P. C40/51.

[76] W. Barnes to Lord Stanley, 27 May 1867, F.O. 5, 1,113, No. 10; F. J. Cridland to Lord Stanley, 16 May 1867, F.O. 5, 1,111, No. 19; Sir Frederick Bruce to Lord Russell, 26 May 1865, F.O. 5, 1,018, No. 313.

Some writers believed that President Johnson's early proposals to exclude from amnesty those Southerners with property worth more than $20,000 heralded widespread forfeiture – would, as the *Freeman's Journal* dramatically put it, 'extirpate the whole propertied race'.[77] But the *Saturday Review*, though similarly critical of such attempts to create a 'social' or 'Socialist revolution', shrewdly pointed out that though the President 'proposed to plunder the rich for the benefit of the poor, his system of redistribution never included the negroes'.[78] The Freedmen's Bureau, however, did just that, hence the British opposition to its renewal.

According to the *Irish Times* the Bureau was unconstitutional and unprecedented, in that it sought to 'confiscate and divide among the manumitted slaves the property of the planters'.[79] The London *Times* was equally critical of proposals involving the 'forcible dispossession of Southern landowners', though confident that the Americans would never endure such a sacrifice.[80]

Instinctive sympathy for the white Southerners and a predictable dread of disturbing property rights do not alone account for the opposition of Britons to the Bureau, however. In the climate of the nineteenth century, even in view of the extraordinary situation of the Southern freedmen, impartial legislation was held to be essential. Thus the *Spectator*, though friendly towards the Negro, felt he should expect no special favours, therefore approving an imaginary situation where President Grant might veto 'a Bill to give negroes land for nothing while hanging whites who robbed them of land purchased with their own savings'. In a multi-racial state, it was felt, colour should be no recommendation, but also no disqualification.[81] What was so objectionable about Radical Reconstruction legislation was that it conferred unprecedented and exclusive benefits on the freedmen while treating the Southern whites as inhabitants of conquered territories, whose rights

[77] 27 July 1865; See also *Irish Times*, 9 May 1865.
[78] 26 August 1865, p. 256, 5 August 1865, p. 163, 23 March 1867, p. 356, and 16 September 1865, p. 349.
[79] 9 March 1866.
[80] 2, 31 January 1866.
[81] 14 November 1868, p. 1,330.

depended entirely upon the dubious clemency of the North.[82]

It was not widely recognized in Britain that the Negroes had already been settled on confiscated land during the war, and that provision might have been made for them under the terms of the Southern Homestead Act, without recourse to confiscation at all. The freedmen's aid societies, advised by workers in America, were anxious to see the ex-slaves obtain land (and the machinery necessary to cultivate it) under the homestead law, but devoted most of their somewhat limited funds to educational work, as being more acceptable in the South.[83] Abolitionists had to be content with registering a protest at the ejection of the 'coloured people . . . from lands which they had cultivated for . . . years, in favour of the old proprietors restored by the President [Johnson] to place and power'.[84]

British hostility to Negro land-ownership also sprang from two other considerations. First, such ownership would undoubtedly strengthen the case for Negro suffrage, on the 'no taxation without representation' principle. There is a cynical inconsistency in the favourite conservative argument that the freedmen exercised political rights though they possessed 'no property whatever', when those same conservatives opposed any measures which might have helped them acquire it.[85] But, more important than this factor was the conviction that Negroes who owned land would allow it to deteriorate. As a result, the planter would be deprived of his labour force and Southern agriculture would become steadily more primitive. At this point it was generally believed that the white labourer, even had he wished to compete with the freedman, could not do so on account of the Southern climate.[86]

---

[82] *Freeman's Journal*, 7 March 1866; *Manchester Guardian*, 20 April 1866; and see also F. B. Zincke, *op. cit.*, pp. 121–2; *Manchester Courier*, 8 March 1866; *Saturday Review*, 17 February 1866, pp. 191–2; *Manchester Guardian*, 6 March 1866; *Irish Times*, 9 March 1866.

[83] See *Friend*, 1 January 1866, pp. 8–9, *Reporter*, August 1866, p. 27; and *Annual Report of the Birmingham and Midland Freedmen's-Aid Association to May 19, 1865* (Birmingham, 1865), pp. 7–8.

[84] *Annual Report of the Edinburgh Ladies' Emancipation Society . . . 1867* (Edinburgh, 1867), p. 11.

[85] H. P. Walker to Lord Granville, 22 July 1870, F.O. 5, 1,202, No. 25.

[86] For a typical expression of this view see *Daily Telegraph*, 23 June 1865.

The freedmen's societies were almost alone in praising, without reservation, free Negro labour. Tasker Smith, the British Consul in Georgia, reported his conviction that the efforts of the blacks would 'be confined to the minimum which will suffice to procure the simplest of food . . . and the coarsest of clothing'; already disposed to find faults with the contracts offered them, they were unlikely 'for years to come, [to] settle down to labour, as they were formerly constrained to do, when under the yoke'. Echoing the views of the Southern whites, Smith concluded that the Negroes evidently failed to realize that 'their freedom entails duties, as well as enjoyments'.[87] In Texas, according to Consul Barnes, the industry of the freedmen was reduced fully one-half by emancipation and must continue to deteriorate; he predicted that the cotton crop for 1867, 'in consequence of the general lazyness [sic] of the negro, . . . will be much smaller than the last'.[88] Similar reports came in from South Carolina, Alabama and Louisiana, and Sir Frederick Bruce also commented that there was difficulty in persuading the freedmen 'to settle down to continuous and steady labour', though he added that it was only the 'worthless part' of the Negro population 'who prefer hanging about the towns and . . . Freedmen's bureaux to hiring themselves out'.[89]

English travellers also drew attention to the indolence of the freedmen. Since in most cases they went with introductions to the 'respectable' elements of the white Southern population, and on average stayed only a short while, the comments of such men, like those of the British consuls, were strongly influenced by the views of conservative opponents of Reconstruction. The result of emancipation, according to the unpleasantly prejudiced George Rose, writing from Virginia, had been to fill the streets of Richmond and other Southern cities with 'crowds of great, hulking, idle black men, with their tattered and filthy women, and more than half naked, neglected children, all waiting for the eleemosynary meal with which the freedman's bureau supplies

[87] W. Tasker Smith to Lord Russell, 5 July 1865, F.O. 5, 1,131, No. 14.

[88] W. Barnes to Lord Stanley, 4 April 1867, F.O. 5, 1,113, No. 9

[89] See dispatches from South Carolina, F.O. 5, 1,030, No. 40, 1,114, No. 59, 1,078, No. 56, 1,136, No. 49, 1,030, No. 44; from Alabama, F.O. 5, 1,029, Nos. 8 and 11; from Louisiana, F.O. 5, 1,137, 1,509, No. 13, 1,545, No 1; and Sir Frederick Bruce to Lord Clarendon, 25 June 1866, F.O. 5, 1,065.

hundreds of them daily, and thereby encourages them in their darling vices of idleness and want of thought for the future'. W. A. Dixon argued, not without satisfaction, that a combination of 'laziness and sauciness' was threatening to deprive the freedman of his daily bread. To the Negro mind, the chief distinction of a white Southerner was immunity from labour.[90]

The more sympathetic Bryce, who visited America with A. V. Dicey in 1870, was, in outlook, similar to Southern moderates like Wade Hampton. Generally concerned about the fate of the Negroes, he suggested that they could not indiscriminately be charged with sloth, but argued the case for white supervision, concluding that 'anyone who knows the laborious ryot or coolie of the East Indies is struck by the difference between a race on which ages of patient industry have left their stamp and the volatile children of Africa'. However, unlike most Britons, Bryce did acknowledge that, innate qualities apart, the Negro's economic apprenticeship had not been ideal, since slavery tended to produce 'labour whose aim was to accomplish not the best possible but the least that would suffice'. Colonization projects were discounted, not only on the grounds that the Negro was unwilling to leave America, but also because he was 'essential to the material prosperity of the South, and his departure would mean ruin to it'. Bryce even accepted that the difference in efficiency between white and black workmen might some day be overcome.[91]

After touring the South, Henry Latham, though fairly optimistic about the future, concluded that up to 1867 free labour had proved less productive than slavery; he also had grave reservations about the share-cropping system, which would result 'in the master having to make advances, after which the negro will be greatly tempted to decline to work'.[92] Another Englishman, Robert Somers, whose observations received wide notice, was even more vehement in his condemnation of a system which has since been described by economists and historians as disastrous

[90] Rose, *op. cit.*, pp. 152–3, and Dixon, *The White Conquest, op. cit.*, II, p. 166, I, p. 344.

[91] *The American Commonwealth, op. cit.*, II, pp. 493–4, 497, 501, 515–16.

[92] *Black and White* (London, 1867), pp. 138, 128–9.

for the South. Somers maintained, like most Englishmen, that the planters recognized the need to conciliate their ex-slaves, and acknowledged that some progress had been made by the latter as free labourers, where free from political interference. But the share-cropping system he regarded as primitive, 'more like a half-way slavery than any relation of capital and labour of an advanced type', and destined to retard future progress by the confusion it introduced 'as regards right and duty', the uncertainty and fluctuation of reward for labour involved being 'more likely to be adverse than favourable to the formation of steady industrious habits among a race so lately freed from the most absolute dependence'.[93]

Clergyman and Liberal F. Barham Zincke, although careful, during his visit to the South, to stress the different conditions prevailing from state to state, and among different groups of white Southerners, tended to fall into the Victorian habit of generalizing about 'inferior' races. 'It was not in the nature of the black', he confidently declared, 'that he should ever work hard enough to cultivate the soil, where the climate is such that the European is capable of labouring in it', while the Freedmen's Bureau in the South had drawn to the cities 'multitudes of negroes loafing about, doing nothing'. (Zincke was unusual in accepting that whites could perform heavy labours in the South.) Reacting to the punitive Radical programme, whites were in turn attempting to drive the freedmen out of industrial occupations, and would ultimately, Zincke predicted, force them from the plantations which they were already disposed to leave.[94] This lack of sympathy for the restlessness of a people once tied by law to the land, sprang from too much sympathy for the undoubted labour problems of the planters. Like Somers and Zincke, Arthur Graville Bradley, writing in 1878, deplored the drift of the Negroes to the towns of the South, their indifference to the terms of the new labour contracts, and their minimal wants, which made it 'difficult . . . to control labour as it ought to be controlled for the prosperity of the country'.[95]

An Englishwoman who had lived in Georgia for many years,

[93] *Op. cit.*, pp. 65, 84, 128–31, 147–8, 281.
[94] *Op. cit.*, pp. 58, 60, 105–6.
[95] *Macmillan's Magazine*, 39, November 1878, pp. 61–2, 65–6.

but ultimately returned with her husband to Britain, Frances Butler Leigh, confirmed the gloomy prognostications of these temporary observers. Again and again Mrs Leigh returned to the labour problem; subscribing to the generally sentimental picture of master and ex-slave united by a sense of duty on the one side, love and respect on the other, she none the less felt that the freedmen's 'idea of work, unaided by the stern law of necessity, is very vague. . . . I don't think one does a really honest full day's work, and so of course not half the necessary amount is done and I am afraid never will be again . . . they are affectionate and often trustworthy and honest, but so hopelessly lazy as to be almost worthless as labourers.'[96]

Economic self-interest, ignorance, and a different set of standards for the two races in the South prevented many Victorian writers from acknowledging the relative social mobility which prevailed in America, by which the Negro was at last influenced, and thus from accepting the migrations of the freedmen to the Northern states and the West. Some believed that anti-Negro prejudice in those areas would in fact keep the freedmen in the South.[97] Little allowance was made for the lingering stigma which attached to labour on the plantations in a society where such labour had traditionally been performed by slaves. It is no surprise to find the notion of apprenticeship regarded with approval; although they had fought formal schemes for this in the West Indies, even British abolitionists saw themselves as easing the freedmen through an apprenticeship between slavery and true freedom.

The American Radicals, consequently, by insisting on unconditional emancipation, were thought to have 'simply ruined the object of their sympathy', still a slave to his own passions, who would have to be taught that 'if he will not work [on the plantation] neither shall he eat'. The *Daily Telegraph* and the *Irish Times* would also have preferred some scheme of gradual liberation, having strong views on the 'duties as well as the rights of freedom', while *The Economist* approved in theory the Democrats' desire to see some system of apprenticeship or supervised labour in the South, though acknowledging that in

[96] *Ten Years on a Georgia Plantation Since the War* (London, 1883), pp. 24–7, 56–7, 71, 124.
[97] *Times*, 2 September 1867, 2 January 1866.

practice 'honest agents for such a task may not be readily found, or found at all'.[98]

Often British fears about the inefficiency of Negro labour sprang not so much from a reading of the evidence on this point as from strongly ingrained prejudices about the Negro temperament, held to be the same the world over. The freedmen of the West Indies, according to conservative observers, had not worked; therefore it was certain that in similar circumstances the freedmen of America would decline to do so. Few acknowledged that the well-known effects of slavery on labour efficiency must last for some time after emancipation. Instead, reference was made to innate qualities for an explanation of postwar difficulties – to the 'innate laziness of the blacks'.[99] Thus the most vehement exponent of this approach, *The Times*, argued that the services of the Negro would have been enhanced in value by freedom, on the grounds that 'One volunteer is worth two pressed men', only if he had resembled the European in his wants or disposition. But 'the black when he ceases to be a pressed man, does not become a volunteer. He will work for nothing but the necessary satisfaction of his bodily wants, and as these wants are on the smallest possible scale, it follows that of his own free will he will hardly work at all.'[100]

Yet in spite of his supposedly unconquerable laziness the freedman was generally expected to embrace Anglo-Saxon mores, to acknowledge the dignity of labour, which until so recently had been exacted forcibly by a class which despised it. Self-help was at once expected from those traditionally regarded as children.[101] The initiative-sapping paternalism of the Freedmen's Bureau was rejected, the recipients of its aid being regarded as better off than the average British working man, but planter supervision was acceptable. This was because such paternalism did not degenerate into 'immoral benevolence' – the

[98] *Edinburgh Evening Courant*, 16 February 1866; *Daily Telegraph*, 14, 21 April 1865; *Irish Times*, 4 July 1865; *Economist*, 17 June 1865, pp. 719–20.

[99] *Freeman's Journal*, 10, 24 June 1865; see also F. B. Leigh, *op. cit.*, pp. 70, 147–8.

[100] 31 January 1866; see also *Birmingham Daily Gazette*, 25 July 1865; *Daily Telegraph*, 23 June 1865.

[101] *Daily Telegraph*, 8 August 1865; *Economist*, 23 September 1865, pp. 1,143–5; *Freeman's Journal*, 18 April 1866.

philanthropic section of the American and British public alike, it was objected, appeared 'to be constantly waiting for an opportunity to give something to somebody'.[102]

There were a few British observers, however – the active opponents of slavery, the Liberal sympathizers with the Northern cause, and one or two whose favourable comments were made with obvious reluctance – who managed to rise above contemporary prejudices.[103] David Macrae suggested that though the freedmen were working as well as they could, some of the planters wanted emancipation to be a failure 'and in many cases, by withholding their land and refusing to employ negro labour, did something to make it a failure'.[104] The Marquis of Lorne, who visited the South in 1866 after a trip to the West Indies, was, by comparison, favourably impressed with the progress the American freedmen were making, while by the end of the 1870s several travellers, including Campbell, Sala and Saunders, confirming the earlier impressions of Sir Samuel Morton Peto and W. H. Dixon, reported that the Negroes 'thrive and thrive wondrously, all things considered'.[105]

In fact, as the *Daily News* put it, those 'who complain of the negroes, and dread them, and despair of them and their fate, are still in the slave-holding state of mind, utterly unable to conceive of negroes as men and citizens and to believe that they can appear as such in the Free States'.[106] Other Liberal journals also made some allowance for the initial postwar restlessness of the Southern freedmen, took an optimistic view of the labour situation, and noted with disapproval the Black Codes enacted by the Johnson governments, which had sought to enslave 'the labour of coloured men, while they were left nominally free'.[107]

[102] *Saturday Review*, 20 January 1866, pp. 75–6.

[103] Sala and Dixon acknowledge progress reluctantly, as Southern sympathizers.

[104] *Op. cit.*, II, pp. 49–54.

[105] Lorne, *op. cit.*, pp. 253–4; G. Campbell, *op. cit.*, pp. 142–3, 159–60; G. Sala, *op. cit.*, 1, pp. 294–5; W. Saunders, *op. cit.*, pp. 75–6; Sir S. Morton Peto, *Resources and Prospects of America* (London, 1866), pp. 347, 407–8; W. H. Dixon, *New America, op. cit.*, pp. 433–5.

[106] 26 December 1865; see also 20 June 1865.

[107] *Banner of Ulster*, 25 February 1868; *Spectator*, 22 August 1868, p. 982; see also 27 July 1872, pp. 937–8; *North British Daily Mail*, 11 April 1867; *Northern Whig*, 6 May and 10 June 1865, in favour of helping Negroes to acquire land.

But even these few British supporters of Radical Reconstruction could not completely accept the assumptions of men like Phillips, Sumner and Stevens. Although envisaging Negro land-ownership in the future, Campbell, for instance, believed that the Negro was so much at his best in the role of hired labourer that he should be encouraged to remain as such.[108] And the *Spectator*, in spite of its Northern sympathies, was only in favour of the freedmen acquiring land which was useless to the whites, and felt able to generalize about Negroes who, 'like all the dark races except the Chinese, like the natives of India, and the Italian peasantry, . . . are extremely industrious when working for themselves, and grossly negligent when working for hire'.[109]

The inability of most Victorians to grasp the crucial importance of the Freedmen's Bureau made it inevitable that the significance of the later Civil Rights Act should often be overlooked. Discussions of this issue in the conservative section of the British Press were distinguished by those arguments over constitutionality which one finds advanced by Southerners themselves. Accordingly, *The Scotsman* reported in April 1866 that 'as was expected, and as it deserved, the President has vetoed the Civil Rights Bill – another pet but mischievous measure of the Radicals'; what the British journal objected to was not so much protection for the Negroes as the offence given to Southern whites, so that true reconstruction was rendered impossible.[110] The *Edinburgh Evening Courant* managed to discuss the Civil Rights Bill and Johnson's veto of it strictly with reference to the Constitution, without once mentioning the content of the Bill.[111] We see again here the strong British sympathies for the South and for state rights, and the violent objections to punitive legislation.[112]

There was, however, considerably more support for the Radicals over the extension of civil rights to the Negroes than

---

[108] *Op. cit.*, pp. 159–61.

[109] 13 July 1861, p. 750.

[110] 12 March and 9 April 1866.

[111] 11 April 1866.

[112] See *Manchester Guardian*, 20 April 1866; *Manchester Courier*, 19 April 1866.

there had been for redistributing Southern land or reorganizing the Southern labour force. Since the freedmen were not guaranteed the franchise under the legislation of 1866, the liberal-minded could support it without qualms.

> The Civil Rights Bill [declared the *Manchester Examiner and Times*] is a measure of pure and simple justice. As its title suggests, it . . . merely deals with those rights which in civilized societies are held to appertain equally to all men. . . . If the negro is not to be permitted to make contracts, or to sue in courts of law, or to give evidence in suits affecting his personal interests, he may not be a chattel, but he is assuredly not a man. . . . The President is courageous and honest, but freedom as he understands it is not a boon worth having.[113]

An identical line was taken by the *Banner of Ulster* and the *Northern Whig*, the latter maintaining that by the Civil Rights Act the Republican Party, quite rightly, wished 'to make the negro a free man, not merely in name, but in reality. They wish him to be emancipated, not only according to the letter but the spirit of the Constitution.'[114] The *North British Daily Mail*, while concerned that the Radical legislation involved a complete disregard for state rights, acknowledged that it 'has all the breadth of principle which antecedes the institution of the civil order altogether'.[115] Both of the major London journals which took an enlightened view on the subject of race, the *Spectator* and the *Daily News*, welcomed the decision to admit Negroes to the full 'rights of republican citizenship', and even the generally hostile *Saturday Review* recognized the Federal Government's duty 'to secure its clients against injustice and persecution'.[116]

Those British Radicals who kept in the closest touch with developments in America, Mill, Bright and the Argylls, all felt equally strongly that – as Mill put it – 'the Federal authorities . . . are bound by every consideration both of duty and interest,

[113] 17 April 1866.
[114] *Banner of Ulster*, 2, 22 October 1866; *Northern Whig*, 12 June, 13, 29 September 1866.
[115] 16 April 1866, 11 April and 5 December 1867.
[116] *Spectator*, 27 June 1868, pp. 760–1, 23 February 1867, pp. 206–7; *Daily News*, 18 November 1865, 10, 11 April and 30 June 1866; *Saturday Review*, 26 January 1867, p. 97.

to secure [civil rights] to the freed race'.[117] As one would expect, the British freedmen's aid workers, those most directly concerned to see that the Negro benefited from his new condition, argued emphatically that the only true policy was that which offered the races 'equal religious, political, commercial and social rights recognized and secured'. The Civil Rights Bill was consequently seen as preserving from destruction by President Johnson the 'essential principles of citizenship', and inaugurating an 'era of justice . . . alike for white and black'. Those who opposed this legislation, according to the journal of the London society, were those who, in the past, wronged the Negro most deeply.[118]

However, once the Fourteenth Amendment, ratified despite Presidential and Southern opposition, went some way towards guaranteeing the suffrage to both races in the South, Victorian attitudes hardened. It is important to recall that outside the Reform organizations, their own and labour journals, and certain extreme Radicals, there was no support for universal suffrage in Britain. American proposals seemed little short of revolutionary. Nor was their effect likely to be confined to the States. From the moment Republicans took an interest in the Negro vote, British writers became aware of the impatience which might be generated among the disfranchised classes at home.

The *Saturday Review* noted in 1867 that, as 'Mr. Bright and his followers sometimes complain, the negro in the United States may possibly obtain the franchise before the English workman', and indeed the Lancashire statesman constantly argued from the American example during Reconstruction, using the black vote as a precedent for manhood suffrage in Britain.[119] Nor was he the only reformer to do

[117] J. S. Mill to Judge Dickson of Ohio, Blackheath Park, Kent, 1 September 1865, *Friend*, 1 November 1865, pp. 231–2; Bright to Charles Sumner, Rochdale, September, 20 October 1865, *Proceedings of the Massachusetts Historical Society*, 1912–13, XLVI (in future simply *Proceedings*), p. 147; Elizabeth Argyll to Charles Sumner, 20 March 1866, in *ibid.*, XLVII, p. 106.

[118] William Collins, Northampton, to T. Phillips, 31 January 1868, in A.P. C39/85; *Freed-Man*, 1 June 1866, pp. 260–2; *Reporter*, August 1866, pp. 37–8.

[119] 30 December 1865, p. 410, and 19 January 1867, p. 69; see Bright in

so.[120] But the British Press – with the exception of a few radical journals, such as the *Daily News* – was nervously hostile, campaigning against the adoption of 'uncontrolled and irresponsible democracy' on the American pattern. 'Let the democratic steed rush off with the bit between its teeth', warned the *Dublin Evening Mail*, 'and there is no knowing where its headlong career will end.'[121] In the view of a prominent Edinburgh journal, the American Radicals wished to annihilate the rights of the South 'just as our Radicals seek to destroy in the House of Commons the influence of the landed interest and the Conservative classes. The American Radicals make the negro their stalking-horse, just as our Radicals . . . use the working man.'[122]

Suspicions of the American political system can be found even in journals like *The Scotsman*, *The Economist* and the *Daily Telegraph*, which admitted a Liberal affiliation, and moderate members of both parties held to the view that while democracy might flourish in a land where property and educational opportunities were unlimited, it was probably unsuited to the needs of the Old World.[123] And to function properly in America itself, democracy 'implies an approximate equality among the electors, and a common interest in the measures which ultimately express popular opinion', whereas the whites and blacks in the South 'are not in any sense equal'.[124] As Sir Frederick Bruce observed in 1866:

It is very desirable that political speculators in England should understand . . . that the wisest men in the United States consider

[120] George Howell to W. F. Johnston, 21 December 1866, Reform League Letter Books, Bishopsgate Institute, London.

[121] *Daily News*, 28 March 1867, 27 February 1868; for different viewpoints, *Manchester Courier*, 29 April 1867, 5, 10 March 1868, 25 April 1871; *Times*, 21 August 1865; *Dublin Evening Mail*, 9 April 1866, 8, 11 January, 8, 22 February, 2 April, 7 December 1867.

[122] 2 June 1866; see also 11, 17 April 1866, 8 April 1867.

[123] *Scotsman*, 25 August 1866; *Economist*, 23 March 1867, pp. 324–5; *Daily Telegraph*, 18 December 1865, leader, and Mr Seymour Fitzgerald in *ibid.*, 16 December 1865; Goldwin Smith in *Daily News*, 10 September 1866; Disraeli in *Hansard*, CLXXXIII, p. 103 f., 27 April 1866; Sir S. Morton Peto, *op. cit.*, pp. 389–91.

[124] *Saturday Review*, 13 January 1866, p. 38.

Hansard, CLXXXII, 1,900 f. (23 April 1866); *Speeches of John Bright . . . in Birmingham . . . 1868, etc.* (London, 1868), pp. 2–3, 8; *Times*, 23 May 1866, 28 August 1868.

the conservative influence attached to the possession of land, as being an essential element in the successful working of the present . . . suffrage and that they should not be misled by the false notion that the experiment if successful here is considered by them as . . . proof of what the result would be were universal suffrage placed in the hands of a majority without this guarantee for its temperate use.[125]

It is against this background of domestic political ferment that one must judge the almost unanimously hostile reaction of Victorians to the enfranchisement of Southern Negroes, with British conservatism formidably strengthening British racism. 'To nearly all Europeans,' wrote Bryce, 'such a step seemed and still seems monstrous.'[126] Those who sympathized primarily with the ex-slaveowners saw how humiliating this Radical measure would be to men who might themselves be disfranchised, awaiting pardon from the Federal Government. 'The power of a lower race over a higher', it was said, 'must be essentially tyrannical,' and such a 'perfectly unnatural reversal of the proper order of society can only be maintained by force.' As Robert Somers expressed it: 'The exclusion of the superior part of the population from all influence in public affairs must of itself tend to magnify the enormity of everything enormous, and to distort everything not quite square that is done.'[127] In other words, the Negro vote was unacceptable, like the Freedman's Bureau, because it further alienated the sections and the races, thus postponing a proper reconstruction of the South.[128] This was the view of Froude and Carlyle, as expressed to Northern abolitionist Moncure D. Conway, who, though initially impatient with his English friends, later 'often had to reflect on the greater foresight with which [Froude] . . . apprehended some of the sequelae of a reform secured, however inevitably, by force'. Carlyle mainly emphasized the absurdity, as he saw it, of freedmen voting, but Froude, more shrewdly, predicted that the Southern whites

[125] Sir Frederick Bruce to Lord Clarendon, 9 January 1866, F.O. 5, 1,062.

[126] Bryce, *op. cit.*, II, p. 481.

[127] *Saturday Review*, 17 February 1866, p. 191, 9 March 1867, p. 291, 23 March 1867, p. 355; H. P. Walker to Lord Stanley, F.O. 5, 1,136, No. 32, 6 April 1868; *Times*, 22 February 1877; *Scotsman*, 12 March 1866; *Manchester Courier*, 7 March 1866; Somers, *op. cit.*, pp. 41–2.

[128] *Manchester Guardian*, 16 December 1865.

would 'never forgive New England and will watch for the time to be revenged'. 'Do what you will,' he warned, 'the whole South will be Democrat.' But at least the historian was prepared to acknowledge that if the Negroes were not to vote, they ought not to count for the purpose of Congressional representation.[129]

The extent of Negro voting during Reconstruction was in fact greatly exaggerated by British and American conservatives, just as it was exaggerated in the West Indies, as we shall see; little distinction was made between states like South Carolina, where the freedmen after the war were in a position of political power, and those such as Florida, where they were not. Nor was it acknowledged that the disfranchised white element in the South dwindled rapidly during the 1870s. Instead, we find repeated references to Negro rule.[130] (Though the most ardent British exponents of white supremacy rejected, as one would expect, the notion of black dominating white: no matter how long it took, the latter would ultimately control the votes of their ex-slaves.[131])

Furthermore, as the *Daily Telegraph* put it, Englishmen were unanimously opposed to conferring 'not only self-government, but the government of others, on such a class as the African, at the very moment of his emancipation from a slavery which has endured for generations'.[132] Again we see the British preference for gradual solutions to the problems of Reconstruction, and failure to realize that had the suffrage not been conferred during these years, it would never have been granted at all, as the history of the past 100 years demonstrates. Thus *The Scotsman* argued that the freedmen would get the vote 'in course of time' if they had 'all the good qualities that their friends assign them'.[133]

[129] *Autobiography. Memories and Experiences of Moncure D. Conway* (London, 1904, 2 vols.), II, pp. 184–7; W. H. Dunn, *op. cit.*, II, p. 341.

[130] *North British Daily Mail*, 13 March, 5 December 1867; *Glasgow Daily Herald*, 14 March 1867; *Edinburgh Evening Courant*, 2 June 1866; *Freeman's Journal*, 18 April 1866; *Times*, 8 August, 2 September 1867.

[131] *Saturday Review*, 19 August 1865, p. 233, 23 December 1865, p. 775, and 2 February 1867, pp. 126–7; *Scotsman*, 23 March 1867; F. B. Zincke, *op. cit.*, p. 102; W. Saunders, *op. cit.*, p. 78.

[132] 11 April 1866.

[133] 12 March 1866.

In the meantime a variety of safeguards was suggested, the most common being an educational qualification.[134]

Since the most common condemnation of the Negroes was on the grounds of ignorance, such suggestions were perfectly logical. 'The numerous statements which purport to prove the moral and intellectual aptitude of the emancipated slaves may be dismissed as simply incredible,' said the *Saturday Review* bluntly. In *The Economist's* view, 'There never was in the history of democracy so dangerous an experiment as that of entrusting full electoral power to nearly four millions of persons, but just emancipated from actual slavery, totally uneducated, and hungry for material advantages.'[135]

British consuls in the South privately confirmed these typical Press comments. Tasker Smith referred to the freedmen as 'uneducated and inferior people . . . foisted into offices demanding qualities which neither by nature, habit nor instruction, do the coloured race exhibit or possess'. In Charleston, H. P. Walker likewise emphasized the ignorance of the Negro voters, and Sir Edward Thornton's deputy in Washington suggested that the freedman was not fitted for political duties 'either by natural instinct, education, principle or self-restraint'. The result of their efforts, not surprisingly, was 'outrageous legislation', a system productive of 'nothing but discord, anxiety and crime'.[136] The political privileges granted to the Negro were, as *The Economist* put it, 'shamefully and disastrously abused'.[137]

Very seldom was it perceived in Britain that a qualified suffrage for the freedmen, in the face of white hostility, would be tantamount to no suffrage at all. However, Charles Dilke was one of the few who did recognize that if the Negroes were to vote as

[134] *Saturday Review*, 28 October 1865, p. 536, suggested a property qualification; also F. B. Zincke, *op. cit.*, p. 123; *Daily Telegraph*, 30 November 1876, preferred an education test; also J. S. Mill, *Friend*, 1 November 1865, p. 231, provided it was required from both races; *The Times*, 22 February 1877 and Bryce, *op. cit.*, II, pp. 511–12.

[135] *Saturday Review*, 30 September 1865, p. 411; *Economist*, 9 November 1872, p. 1,367.

[136] W. Tasker Smith to Lord Stanley, 24 April 1869, F.O. 5, 1,169, No. 7; H. P. Walker to Lord Stanley, F.O. 5, 1,136, No. 32, 6 April 1868, to Lord Clarendon, 6 April 1869, F.O. 5, 1,166, No. 9, and to Lord Granville, 22 July 1870, F.O. 5, 1,202, No. 25; Mr Watson to Lord Derby, 4 September 1874, F.O. 5, 1,484, No. 91.

[137] 19 September 1874, p. 1,132.

soon as they could read, it was certain that the planters would take care that they never should be taught. In this opinion Dilke was supported only by David Macrae (who suggested that 'perhaps . . . the speediest way of preparing a negro or any other man to exercise the suffrage, is to give it to him'), and among Victorian newspapers by the *Daily News* and *Spectator*, which acknowledged that while President Johnson and his supporters would make the education of the Negroes the condition of giving them any political security for justice, 'political security for justice is properly the only conceivable condition of their education'.[138]

Apart from sympathy for the disfranchised whites and opposition to the rapid enfranchisement of any poorly educated and propertyless class, British conservatives were critical of Radical proposals because of their old suspicions of the ulterior political motives of the Northern leadership, and because it was believed, as already indicated, that the South was being asked to make concessions to Negroes which the North itself would not countenance.

The Times pointed out triumphantly that the repugnance which all classes in the North felt towards accepting the Negro franchise was 'notorious and undeniable'.[139] 'Your lordship will not fail to remark,' wrote Clare Ford from the Washington Embassy to Lord Stanley, 'the inconsistency, which can only be excused on the score of expediency, of forcing negro suffrage on the Southern portion of this Continent whilst its adoption is so strenuously opposed in some of the Northern States.'[140] British supporters of Radical Reconstruction, particularly Bright and the Argylls, were acutely embarrassed by this difficulty, and the Duke predicted shrewdly that while the North opposed Negro 'political rights . . . the forcing of them upon the South will make them the hated badge of *white* servitude, and the coloured race will suffer'.[141]

If the Radicals did not from conviction accept racial equality,

138 Dilke, *op. cit.*, I, pp. 29–30; Macrae, *op. cit.*, I, pp. 360–1, II, pp. 69–70; *Daily News*, 30 June 1865; *Spectator*, 23 February 1867, p. 206.

139 31 January 1866; see also 2 January 1866 and 3 April 1868; and *Saturday Review*, 3 March 1866, p. 252.

140 15 October 1867, F.O. 5, 1,108, No. 22.

141 See Bright in *Proceedings*, *op. cit.*, pp. 145–6, and the Argylls in *ibid.*, pp. 89–90, 106.

it could be argued that they advanced it in the South simply to increase Republican strength in that section. In the words of F. B. Zincke, 'no man who knows anything of the capacity of the black race . . . thinks they are qualified for taking part in the government of the country', but all 'consideration of the fitness of the late slave is . . . dismissed, and nothing insisted on but what is needed by the necessities of the dominant party'. It followed from this that the votes of the freedmen would be manipulated by Northern politicians. British consular reports were emphatic on this point, William Barnes predicting that the 'partizans who gave them votes will be sure to instruct them how to use this privilege according to their dictation'; the least difficulty between black and white would be exaggerated into a riot, and would lead to the former receiving further advantages.[142]

As a result of this cynical reading of Radical motives –nothing, interestingly, is said of the Northern Negro vote, ultimately secured, for very mixed reasons, by the passage of the Fifteenth Amendment – some observers saw the freedmen as getting no real benefit from the vote, and even using it against the Republican Party.[143] Consul Cridland reported from Alabama that the Negroes were beginning to see how completely the Radicals had used them at the polls, in order to be elected and then get control of the public offices, giving them nothing in return, or merely the poorest offices, which they themselves did not want.[144] The *Saturday Review*, with its usual cold shrewdness, predicted as early as 1867 what was indeed to occur ten years later – namely, that 'in some political crisis the whole fabric of present [Reconstruction] legislation will be eagerly thrown down by rival candidates for Southern support. The negroes and their privileges will form a convenient medium of exchange, when their patrons have become weary of their cause.'[145]

The 'anti-slavery philanthropists in England', whom the *Review* described as anxious to see Negro suffrage, are very hard to find.[146] The *Daily News* felt that the black vote was necessary

142 William Barnes to Lord Stanley, F.O. 5, 1,113, No. 9, 4 April 1867.
143 *Irish Times*, 6 November 1876.
144 F. J. Cridland to Earl Granville, F.O. 5, 1,198, 15 September 1870.
145 23 March 1867, p. 357.
146 8 July 1865, p. 37, 30 September 1865, p. 410.

to secure 'in any of the states a majority really faithful to the Union', and the *Spectator*, in spite of a certain reluctance about admitting hosts 'of ignorant, and often, perhaps, half-savage negroes, to equal electoral rights with all the present electors', was obliged to note that freedmen understood the value of their suffrage and cast their votes persistently for the Republican Party.[147] However, there is no Press support for the franchise experiment outside these two journals, though Dilke was a staunch advocate, and Mill, Bright, Macrae and the Argylls gave qualified support.

The British freedmen's aid movement was, of course, as we have seen, little concerned with politics, emphasizing the supreme importance to the Negroes of educational advance. Relief alone was not enough, for, as a Birmingham circular stated, 'Their education relieves the immortal part, while the sufferings of the body are temporal and transient'.[148]

There was in fact unanimity among British observers about the need to establish schools for the freedmen, since the majority in the South had been deliberately kept illiterate. As to how far the Negroes themselves aspired to knowledge or could benefit from it, there was considerable disagreement.

The freedmen's aid movement was directly influenced by its American advisers – particularly in Philadelphia, New York and Baltimore – on this point. But at a time when there was mounting pressure in England for educational reform and the extension of educational opportunity, it was natural for Victorians, unable to effect political or economic changes in the South, to see schooling as a panacea for the problems of American Negroes. It was hoped that education would help the freedmen to defend their civil rights and advance their economic interests, while at the same time assuaging the resentments of Southern whites over the sudden advancement of their former slaves. (Negro suffrage was even accepted by the British societies as a

[147] *Daily News*, 26 June 1865; *Spectator*, 9 March 1867, p. 263, and 24 August 1867, p. 939.

[148] *Birmingham and Midland Association for the Help of the Refugees from Slavery in America, by a Vessel to be Freighted with Stores*, Circular No. 2 (1864).

means of securing educational opportunity to black and white alike.[149])

From America there came regular assurances that the Negroes – even to the oldest – expressed a desire to learn, and many thousands had been successfully instructed. And it was pointed out that not only were the educational needs of the freedmen great, but 'The Southern people have neither the means nor the will to help them'.[150] Northern and British aid was therefore vital, and the work of establishing normal schools was felt to be particularly valuable with the passage of time.

British reports reflected this advice. Freedmen's societies in London, Edinburgh, Birmingham and elsewhere emphasized the Negroes' desire to acquire education and their ability to learn, as did the journals of the British movement.[151] Normal schools were urged as 'the great want', since American observers as early as 1865 warned that public interest in and generosity to the cause was waning. Establishments which trained black teachers would ensure at least some Negro educators in the South – cheaper than whites, and more acceptable to that region than outsiders – when the freedmen's aid societies finally disbanded.[152] American friends testified that 'one [Negro] graduate of a Normal school . . . will do more than five ordinary teachers'.[153] There was also a tacit recognition here that the early hopes of providing integrated schools in the South had been over-optimistic. British philanthropists noted the trend towards segregation with alarm, but naturally could do nothing to prevent it.[154]

Perhaps not entirely free from a sense of white superiority, and

[149] *Reporter*, December 1867, p. 21.

[150] *A Plea for the Perishing, op. cit.*, p. 5, Levi Coffin quoted; Circulars 11, 13 and 15 of the Birmingham Society; M. C. Cooper of Baltimore to A. Albright, 2 January 1868, C121/43.

[151] *The Second Annual Report of the Ladies' London Emancipation Society, op. cit.*, p. 24; *Annual Report of the Birmingham and Midland Freedmen's-Aid Association, op. cit.*, p. 12; *Annual Report of the Edinburgh Ladies' Emancipation Society, and Sketch of Anti-Slavery Events and the Condition of the Freedmen During the Year Ending 1867, op. cit.*, pp. 13, 15, 16–17; *Reporter*, May 1866, pp. 4, 10, 13; *Freedman*, 1 September 1866, pp. 22–4.

[152] E. W. Clark, Philadelphia, to J. Simpson, 25 September 1865, C120/27; letter from J. Simpson, 23 October 1865, C120/21.

[153] F. King, Baltimore, to A. Albright, 10 December 1867, C121/88.

[154] *Freed-Man*, 1 January 1868, p. 2.

because of its special wish to avoid political controversy, the British movement also placed particular emphasis on the need for industrial or vocational education for the Negroes.[155] The difficulties Britain was experiencing with an educational policy in India, which, according to some critics, turned out too many aspiring clerks and lawyers and too few skilled labourers and craftsmen, may well have exercised some influence here. Furthermore, conservative Britons, like the Southern planters, recognized that educating a peasant population might release it from bondage to the soil and deference to the ruling *élite*.

The attitude of British philanthropists was summed up at the annual conference of the freedmen's aid movement in 1867, at which it was reported that the 'freshness of novelty as to schooling having passed away, steady application proves that it was no mere transient impulse which induced attendance, but a healthy abiding thirst for knowledge . . . [and] the capacity of coloured teachers to impart instruction . . . is becoming daily more and more satisfactorily developed'.[156] No gloomy accounts of Negro capabilities were allowed to find their way into the two journals of the British movement, though the Quakers involved sometimes permitted themselves to be critical or despondent in their publications. Victorian abolitionists and missionaries both faced the difficulty of having to prove the necessity for British aid, as well as the immediate benefit of that assistance. Travellers were often more sceptical.

By insisting on mixed schools, the North was, in the opinion of Robert Somers, forcing a change desired by neither race in the South, and, as in so many matters, 'putting the fool's cap on Republican principle'. To F. B. Zincke, the schools of the Freedmen's Bureau could only be mischievous in their effects by inculcating the notion in the mind of the Negro that during the time education was being carried on labour must be suspended. 'And what is the use and value of education in the eyes of the negro?' he inquired. 'Just this – that it will fit him for the situation of a clerk or for keeping a shop. At all events it is no preparation for field labour.' Since Zincke saw this as the

155 See letters in A.P. C118/29–35; *Reporter*, November 1866, p. 74, and December 1867, pp. 31–2.
156 *Reporter*, December 1867, p. 21; for a similar American view, F. King, Baltimore, to J. Taylor, 7 January 1868, C121/87.

inevitable function of the freedmen, the Bureau's programme was necessarily 'false and mischievous'.[157]

There is some credence given to the theory, fully elaborated somewhat later and still in currency today, that the Negro youth was subject to arrested development: in other words, could be educated well enough up to the age of puberty, but not thereafter, the passionate side of his nature, reluctantly curbed, being then in the ascendant. The freedman's intelligence 'is rather quick than solid', said Bryce; 'he shows the childishness as well as the lack of self-control which belongs to the primitive peoples'. According to Dixon, the Negro's desire to learn was 'a spark – a flash – and it is gone'. Campbell quoted American opinion that 'while the younger children are as bright and quick as white children, they do on average fall off in some degree as they get older'.[158]

However, even where there were doubts about whether Negro enthusiasm for education would last, black schools were welcomed. (British travellers, like British philanthropists, were prepared to accept segregated establishments.) Thus Dixon in his *New America*, urging the planters and Southern whites to unite, noted that some freedmen were founding their own schools and, in spite of great difficulties, beginning 'the work of emancipating themselves from the thraldom of ignorance and vice'. Campbell felt that, under adverse conditions, Negro education had none the less made great strides. Praise for the schools established by the Freedmen's Bureau came from the Marquis of Lorne, and David Macrae was extremely impressed by the eagerness for schooling which he saw among Negroes of all ages.[159] It might be, he wrote, that to date 'the white race has shown more energy, more grasp of thought, and more power of command than the black race', but, given the same opportunities for development, no one could predict how far the freedmen might develop. George Sala was of the same mind, and particularly optimistic about 'the coloured man with only a slight admixture of black blood in his veins', who, he predicted, 'if he

[157] Somers, *op. cit.*, p. 228; Zincke, *op. cit.*, p. 103.

[158] Bryce, *op. cit.*, II, p. 496; Dixon, *White Conquest*, *op. cit.*, II, p. 169; Campbell, *op. cit.*, p. 136. See also F. B. Leigh, *op. cit.*, p. 179.

[159] See for similar testimony, Dilke, *op. cit.*, I, pp. 23–4; Saunders, *op. cit.*, p. 85; Campbell, *op. cit.*, p. 131.

avail himself of the facilities for culture now open to him . . . [might] become as intellectually distinguished as Alexander Dumas'.[160]

After the end of Reconstruction, and with the settlement of the Alabama claims question arising from the Civil War, British interest in American domestic politics declined, and these turbulent years became the preserve of the historian. Then, at the end of the century, a complex of factors – including a mutual interest in imperialism – drew the governments of Britain and the United States into a closer relationship. Victorian travellers, during this quiet period, do not exhibit the same degree of chauvinism as their compatriots who had crossed the Atlantic in the early part of the century. Consciousness of American power produced not only envy, but respect, even though the late Victorian might continue, in Emerson's words, to hate not only the Negro, but also 'the French, as frivolous; . . . the Irish, as aimless; [and] . . . the Germans, as professors'. Indeed, while the British were 'very conscious of their advantageous position in History', they could not fail to see that they might have to share it with their 'kin across the sea'.[161]

This growing sense of identity is well illustrated by two articles which appeared in the *Contemporary Review* at the turn of the century, comparing the South African Wars with the American Civil War. In each case the author argued that the British, like the North during the latter conflict, were fighting for free institutions, political democracy and racial equality. Both struggles were said to demonstrate 'the dogged Anglo-Saxon spirit confident in the justice of its country's cause, *because the cause is its country's*, refusing to be beaten, and gradually but surely wearing down its opponent'.[162] We have observed, however, that, in spite of such pride in Anglo-Saxon virtues, British and American racial opinions during Reconstruction were often similarly bitter and conservative.

A Virginian, P. A. Bruce, visiting England in 1900, after

[160] Dixon, *op. cit.*, p. 425; Campbell, *op. cit.*, p. 136; Lorne, *op. cit.*, pp. 309, 335; Macrae, *op. cit.*, II, pp. 57–66; Sala, *op. cit.*, II, pp. 54–5.

[161] R. W. Emerson, *English Traits* (London, 1856), pp. 69, 77.

[162] W. H. Sands, January–June 1901, LXXIX, pp. 665–6; S. Wilkinson, January–June 1900, LXXVII, p. 804.

recounting the miseries and mistakes of the postwar period in America, concluded that[163] 'Until the English people have had a long experience in trying to solve a perplexing negro problem of their own in Africa, I venture to beg that they will not condemn too severely the general policy towards the same race which the South has felt compelled to pursue.' There was, in fact, little evidence of such condemnation on the part of Britain, even during Reconstruction; rather – and certainly by the time Bruce wrote – Victorian attitudes in matters of race were basically in sympathy with the Burgess–Fleming racialist interpretation of Reconstruction, which had just been established and was to dominate American historiography in this area for over thirty years.

Furthermore, hostility was directed not merely against the American freedman, but against the African generally, the peoples of India (to a lesser degree), and towards the black population of the West Indies. It is to a consideration of the problems of the freedmen of Jamaica that we must now turn.

[163] *Ibid.*, January–June 1900, LXXVII, p. 297.

III

Jamaica, 1865:
the turning point

> On the one hand stands the cause of personal liberty, the
> inviolability of law, just procedure, official responsibility,
> equal justice, and ancient precedent. On the other, that of
> arbitrary rule, military jurisdiction, wild injustice, martial
> licence, race prejudice, and strange prerogative. Let us see
> on which side the English public will be.
>
> Frederic Harrison on the debate in
> Britain over the Jamaica Revolt.[1]

W ITHIN the last few years Eric Williams' book, *British Historians and the West Indies*, Bernard Semmel's *The Governor
Eyre Controversy* and others have served to reveal the virulence
of race prejudice in mid-nineteenth-century Britain.[2] After an
examination of Victorian attitudes to American racial problems,
these findings are not startling, though the temper of Dr
Williams's brief study will doubtless offend some, and does tend
to overlook the opinions of British philanthropists.

The anti-slavery movement, which had worked so long for
abolition in America, found in freedmen's aid its last great
challenge. Events in Jamaica split the movement, just as they
divided the Victorian political and literary world, and the prejudice aroused contributed in no small degree to the success of the

[1] *Jamaica Papers No. 5, Martial Law. Six Letters to 'The Daily News'*
(London, 1867), p. 42.
[2] Published, respectively, London, 1966, and London, 1962.

75

theories of British anthropologists like Hunt. Furthermore, just at a time when knowledge of the diversity of African life was being increased through the combined efforts of missionaries, traders and explorers, the Jamaica revolt increased the vulgar tendency to see all black men as alike and inferior, and all white men, by dint of their colour alone, as superior. As *The Times* put it in November 1865:

> It seems . . . impossible to eradicate the original savageness of the African blood. As long as the black man has a strong white Government and a numerous white population to control him he is capable of living as a respectable member of society. He can be made quiet and even industrious by the fear of the supreme power, and by the example of those to whom he necessarily looks up. But wherever he attains to a certain degree of independence there is the fear that he will resume the barbarous life and fierce habits of his African ancestors.[3]

Even Negroes outside Africa were simply seen as Africans: not as Fanti or Ashanti, Ebos or Mandingoes, but as savages about whom it was possible to generalize, aliens who resisted all efforts to civilize them – that is, convert them to Western ways – in the United States or the West Indies. The race situation in these two areas was endlessly compared by Britons during the 1860s, and indeed the fate of the black population of the Caribbean had been interesting to Southern planters since the Emancipation Act of 1833, and before.

Americans had been fascinated and appalled by the long Negro revolt in St Domingo, resulting by 1804 in the formation of the new Republic of Haiti and nothing less than Negro rule. Free blacks from the French West Indies were denied entry to the United States as potential agitators. Those who saw a solution to slavery in colonization projects often looked to the Caribbean islands as an asylum for the troublesome Negro.[4] This is not to say that slavery and race problems shaped identically the development of the American South and the West Indies. In the latter whites were in a minority (outnumbered ten to one in Jamaica), in the Southern States a majority: consequently the West Indian colonies operated more stringent

[3] 13 November 1865.
[4] W. Jordan, *White Over Black. American Attitudes Toward the Negro, 1550–1812* (Chapel Hill, 1968), pp. 377–84, 547, 562, 564, 566.

control over the lives of their slaves, but perforce recognized their importance, while the American planters, confident of their numerical and cultural supremacy, violently rejected any trespass upon their society by a people so alien as the Negroes.[5]

However, in spite of the assumptions of white superiority, it is clear that in both regions the black inhabitants, slave and free, were feared. The South went in dread of a large-scale servile revolt, especially during the Civil War, and of a war of races after it. The Jamaica revolt was seen as encouraging and presaging such a conflict.

In January 1866 the American correspondent of *The Times* reported that the outbreak in Jamaica had helped to create 'widespread alarm' in the South and fears of a 'general insurrection' among the freedmen.[6] The introduction of the Radical reconstruction plans of Sumner and Stevens was, in view of these fears, seen by *The Times*' own reporter to show a 'singular want of skill'. 'The insurrection in Jamaica,' he argued, 'little as that event seems to have been thought of in some quarters in England, has had the effect of deepening the belief that the negro is not fit for the possession of political power.' (The writer hastened to add that such a belief might well be erroneous, but its existence in America was undoubted and was proving an embarrassment to the Radicals in Congress.[7])

But the rebellion of 1865 was an even greater shock for British sensibilities. *The Times* explained, it

comes very home to the national soul. Though a fleabite compared with the Indian mutiny, it touches our pride more and is more in the nature of a disappointment. . . . Jamaica is our pet institution, and its inhabitants are our spoilt children. We had it always in our eye when we talked to America and all the slaveholding Powers. It seemed to be proved in Jamaica that the negro could become fit for self-government. . . . Alas for grand triumphs of humanity, and the improvement of races, and the removal of primeval curses, and the expenditure of twenty millions sterling, Jamaica herself gainsays the fact and belies herself, as we see to-day. It is that which vexes us more than even the Sepoy revolt.[8]

[5] *Ibid.*, pp. 140–2.
[6] 13 January 1866.
[7] 31 January 1866.
[8] 18 November 1865.

The Duchess of Argyll, writing to Sumner about her son's visit to the West Indies, referred to Jamaica as 'that place of bitter humiliation for us'.[9] How had this humiliation come about – how could the Negro, 'protected and elevated' by England 'when every other Power neglected him or trampled on him', have betrayed his supposed saviours?[10]

In August 1833 an Act was passed for the abolition of slavery in the British colonies. But the West Indian Negro was not completely free, for the Act imposed a transitional apprenticeship system on the islands, with the exception of Antigua and the Bermudas, for six more years.[11] This partial achievement was made possible by the formal ending of the British slave trade in 1808, through the decline of the West India interest in Parliament, the increasing political effectiveness and public appeal of the anti-slavery movement, and as a result of pressure in the islands themselves.

But though the planters had been financially compensated for the loss of their property, they did not receive more than half the current market value of the slaves, and were reluctant to accept the social revolution which emancipation brought. Apprenticeship, being – like slavery – based on coercion, encouraged this attitude, appearing rather the last phase of bondage than the first stage of freedom. Furthermore, the power of the planter-dominated island Assemblies (everywhere except Trinidad) was not checked, in spite of the fact that they had led the opposition to emancipation.

In Jamaica, of course, the disgruntled planters faced real problems, the majority being in debt and capital scarce. Labour relations were strained to breaking-point as many Negroes, taking advantage of their freedom, moved off the sugar estates to obtain small plots of ground in the backlands or hilly country.

---

[9] 20 March 1866; letter in *Proceedings, op. cit.*, p. 106.

[10] *Times*, 4 November 1865,

[11] In the pages that follow I have drawn on M. Ayearst, *The British West Indies: The Search For Self-government* (London, 1960), P. Sherlock, *West Indies* (London, 1966); W. L. Burn, *The British West Indies* (London, 1951), P. D. Curtin, *Two Jamaicas, 1830–65* (Harvard, 1955), M. G. Smith, *The Plural Society in the British West Indies* (California, 1965), and D. Hall, *Free Jamaica, 1838–65. An Economic History* (New Haven, 1959).

(The number of freehold properties increased from 2,014 in 1832 to 7,848 in 1840, and it has been estimated that up to 50% of the effective labour force left the plantations.) Many planters were forced, for want of labour, to give up growing provisions, and although the freedmen on their new land cultivated root crops for home consumption, the island became increasingly dependent for food on the United States. In the early 1860s years of drought brought great hardship as food crops perished.

Under the apprenticeship system, racial tension mounted, particularly over vagrancy laws and legislation confining the freedmen to their former masters' estates or to specific localities, and permitting severe corporal punishment, as well as fixing hours of work and allowances for food, clothing, medicine and lodgings. Although the experiment came to an end in 1838, ahead of schedule, largely as a result of abolitionist pressure, resentments remained, and the efforts of the planter class to ease their labour problem through importing indentured labourers, mainly from India, were seen as tending to introduce a disguised form of slavery. Furthermore, relations between the newcomers and the Negro population were not especially harmonious.

The planters related the beginning of their decline to the Emancipation Act of 1833, though this decline was apparent even by the end of the eighteenth century; the removal of protection for West Indian sugar in the British market in 1846 was believed to have completed the ruin of Jamaica. And indeed the Act was followed by an immediate decline in island sugar prices, and the gradual loss of a privileged position in the British sugar market. By 1851 over one-third of the sugar retained for use by Britain was of foreign origin. However, it should be noted that sugar exports from Jamaica, after dropping slightly during the early 1830s, almost halved between 1838 and 1840, to the embarrassment of British philanthropists who had campaigned against apprenticeship. But although the West Indian planters lost to the East India interests and the free traders over the sugar equalization duties, as did the abolitionists who opposed equal treatment for free and slave-grown sugar, the British Government was not totally indifferent to the former, who declined steadily in numbers as planters went bankrupt and estates were abandoned or sold. Relief and development grants were paid out, and the freedmen discouraged from acquiring land which took them away from the sugar and coffee estates.

In Jamaica these measures were not effective. The sugar-planters, despite labour difficulties and soil exhaustion, proved reluctant to diversify, and such attempts as were made to establish new capital enterprises enjoyed little success. They made their resentments felt in the island's Assembly. Since the Negroes were generally blamed for economic stagnation, it was predictable that this body, of indifferent calibre, and often deadlocked by disputes between its town and country factions, or at odds with the Governor and his ineffectual executive council, should decline to take over from the estates the obligation to provide public services. The interests of the majority of the freedmen were scarcely considered. An ostensibly representative system of government rested upon a tiny electorate: by 1861 the voters were considerably under 1 in 200 of the population. Schools, roads, sanitation, and the administration of justice were all neglected. The decline in the numbers of stipendiary magistrates was particularly unfortunate, since the Negroes increasingly found themselves charged before petty sessional courts almost exclusively composed of laymen and planters. It should be noted here that the role of the coloured population of Jamaica was virtually ignored by Victorian observers, both before 1865 and during the revolt. This is a typical example of the British tendency to oversimplify when racial matters were under review. The careful distinctions which sociologists of the twentieth century have made between black, white, and coloured, in terms of religious beliefs, education, legal and political rights, land tenure, occupations, family organization and value-systems were understandably beyond most Victorians, at a time when race prejudice was well developed, but the social sciences were rudimentary.[12] Instead, a picture was presented in terms of black and white, and the articulate urban coloured class was largely ignored, perhaps partly out of fear of its political influence,

[12] See, for instance, M. G. Smith, *op. cit.* G. Roberts, *The Population of Jamaica* (Cambridge, 1957), pp. 64, 66, shows that the black population between 1844 and 1911 composed over 75% of the total; the coloured population was most numerous in 1871 (19·8% of the total) and smallest in 1943 (17·5%). The white population of the island did not expand after 1844. The numbers of East Indians and Chinese grew steadily once miscegenation became common.

perhaps partly because of a greater fear of the less 'civilized' black majority.

In spite of the early enthusiasm of the freedmen to acquire education, the task of combating large-scale illiteracy was immense, as American abolitionists were to find during Reconstruction, and the results of missionary effort on the island somewhat meagre. Attendance at Christian churches in time also became disappointing, as from the 1840s revivalism, obeahism and myalism fed the development of an indigenous religion and culture, which helped further to undermine the existing economic and political system. These changes were far more important than a comparable cultural renaissance would have been in the Southern States of America. As more and more substantial planters returned to England, the dwindling white population of poor planters, attorneys, overseers, bookkeepers and merchants was bitterly aware of lost influence as well as numbers, as the black population continued to grow.

During the early 1860s a tense situation in Jamaica was aggravated by the arrival of a new Governor, Edward Eyre. Drought for three successive years had resulted in a severe shortage of food, and imports were highly priced. This factor was probably more important than the position of sugar, which had improved somewhat. But distress, according to the testimony of the sympathetic Baptist missionary, Edward B. Underhill, being inadequately eased by poor relief, had led to a disturbing increase in crime. Underhill recommended the development of new crops, an emphasis on local food production, and the recognition of the importance of the small native freeholds. This could only be done if the island's entire administration – especially of justice and taxation – were reformed. Edward Eyre, sent to Jamaica in 1862, and confirmed as Governor two years later, proved unable to cope.

Before his appointment to Jamaica, Eyre had served as a Protector of Aborigines in Australia, Lieutenant-Governor of New Zealand, Protector of Indian indentured immigrants in Trinidad, Lieutenant-Governor of St Vincent, and Governor of the Leeward Islands: an administrator of wide experience, it would appear, but also a weak and intolerant man. The Governor failed to win the respect of the Assembly, and made an open enemy of one of its members, the wealthy mulatto, George

William Gordon, whose dismissal from the magistracy he secured, and whose complaints about island discontent he was inclined to ignore. The inadequacy of Eyre and the demagogy of Gordon created in 1865 an explosive situation, the spark to which was given by the rejection on behalf of the Queen of an appeal from her Jamaican subjects of St Ann's Parish for land, with a reminder that the prosperity 'of the labouring classes, as well as of all other classes, depends, in Jamaica, and in other countries, upon their working for wages, not uncertainly, or capriciously, but steadily and continuously, at the times when their labour is wanted, and for so long as it is wanted'. The reply concluded that it was 'from their own industry and prudence, in availing themselves of the means of prospering that are before them, and not from any such schemes as have been suggested to them, that they must look for an improvement in their conditions'. Special treatment for the freedmen, even under special circumstances, was therefore rejected.

In October 1865 frustration was translated into violence at Morant Bay, St Thomas-in-the-East. The local disturbance soon spread to several parishes, and in the course of the pacification of the island by the Army, nearly 500 Negroes were killed and many more savagely punished. Governor Eyre also secured the execution of Gordon on the charge of having stirred up the black population to revolt. The commission appointed by the British Government in December to investigate the rebellion was critical of Eyre's action regarding Gordon, condemned the unnecessary bloodshed and uncivilized treatment of rebels, and recognized the genuine grievances of the black population. The Governor defended his actions vigorously and found a number of distinguished supporters in England, among them Ruskin, Tennyson, Kingsley, Dickens, Carlyle, Tyndall and Murchison, while critical British Radicals formed themselves into an opposing Jamaica Committee, which included John and Jacob Bright, J. S. Mill, Edward Forster, Edmond Beales, Goldwin Smith, A. V. Dicey, Henry Fawcett, T. H. Green, Darwin, Huxley, Spencer and Lyell.[13]

Investigation into the causes of the revolt apparently added

[13] In addition to Semmel and Williams, see, for background, W. L. Mathieson, *The Sugar Colonies and Governor Eyre, 1849–1866* (London, 1936), and S. Olivier, *The Myth of Governor Eyre* (London, 1933).

little to British understanding of West Indian Negroes, serving only to offend the pride, arouse the fear, and encourage the hostility of whites far removed from the scene of violence. By the mid-nineteenth century the West Indies had ceased to be of real importance – or even interest – for Britain, but the race prejudice aroused in 1865 was to be of incalculable importance, not just for the former, but for the whole world.

It is all too clear that even among the members of the Jamaica Committee and among the Liberal Press this prejudice was not lacking. Eyre was attacked because it was felt he represented conservatism, planter opinion, indifference to the rule of law. Defence of the rights of Negroes was equated with defence of the rights of British working men, and of labour the world over.

Various articles contributed to the London labour journal, the *Bee Hive*, were most explicit on this point, and the paper's leader writer was quick to maintain that 'The working classes of the United Kingdom have never subjected themselves to the charge of what is mockingly styled "negro worship"'.[14] Professor E. S. Beesly emphasized in a critical letter on the handling of the revolt

> I protest I am no negro-worshipper. I don't consider a black man a beautiful object, and I daresay he sings psalms more than is good for him. Some negroes may be men of ability and elevated character, but there can be no doubt that they belong to a lower type of the human race than we do, and I should not like to live in a country where they formed a considerable part of the population.

But, continued Beesly, 'there is no reason why the negro should work cheaper for us because he is ugly. . . . when the upper classes see how . . . injustice to labour, even in a distant colony, is resented by the working men of England, they will be careful how they trifle with similar interests at home.'[15]

As Royden Harrison has pointed out, Beesly and others aroused considerable alarm by linking up, in the workers' Press, martial law abroad and police violence at home.[16] Frederic

[14] 10 February 1866.
[15] 25 November 1865.
[16] *Before the Socialists: Studies in Labour and Politics, 1861–1881* (London, 1965), p. 85.

Harrison took up a variation of the same theme, also in the *Bee Hive*, declaring that

> This is a question far deeper than sect or colour. It does not concern Baptists, or black men, or merely the character of a public servant. I have no more liking for black men than for Baptists, and very little liking for Governor Eyre's past history. . . . The question is, whether *legality* is to be co-extensive with the Queen's rule, or whether our vast foreign dominions are to be governed by the irresponsible will of able, absolute, and iron-willed satraps. It is on this ground that it so peculiarly concerns the working classes. They alone are as yet untainted by the reckless injustice with which our empire has been won and kept.[17]

A leader in the *Bee Hive* found it ironical and alarming that just when American Negroes had won their freedom Jamaican working men 'have yet to be assured that their very lives are not at the capricious and absolute disposal of a man styling himself Governor, and actually bearing Queen Victoria's commission'.[18]

At a reform meeting in the summer of 1866, the popular speaker, Henry Vincent, emphasizing the political significance of the revolt for British conservatives, noted that

> The Tories are the same now as they were thirty years ago, and as they were last year in the Jamaica business. (*Cheers.*) I will, with regard to Jamaica, give you a rule-of-three sum. As the latitude of Jamaica is to the latitude of Hyde Park, so is the fate of George William Gordon to that of John Bright. (*Cheers.*) The battle has yet to be fought . . . but I tell the aristocracy this . . . if they dare to cross arms with the people in this great struggle, why the measures of radical Reform will tumble in faster than we dared to hope. (*Loud cheers.*)[19]

Most of the membership of the Jamaica Committee had been involved with the principal pro-Northern emancipation societies during the American Civil War, as well as still being involved in the struggle for extension of the franchise in Britain. In both these crusades fundamental principles rather than the fate of human beings were felt to be primarily at stake, though there were some abolitionists whose concern was more personal and practical than theoretical, as we shall see. The typical Radical

[17] 9 December 1865.
[18] 10 February 1866.
[19] Reported in the *Daily Telegraph*, 31 July 1866.

view, however, was expressed by J. S. Mill when he wrote: 'There was much more at stake than only justice to the negroes, imperative as was that consideration. The question was, whether the British dependencies, and eventually, perhaps, Great Britain itself, were to be under the government of law or of military licence.'[20]

The defence of the black rebels in sections of the Liberal Press reveals a similarly implicit sympathy for the Negro cause and indifference or aversion for the Negro. A critical article in the *Spectator* noted that by defending Eyre 'the literary aristocracy of England are contracting one of the worst vices of aristocracies of all kinds, the entire loss of reverence for inferiors . . . those whose character as well as fate lies more or less in your own power, which is one of the deepest principles of Christianity', and at the present time recognized only by 'working men's open-air meetings, the Anti-Slavery Society, and . . . the *Bee Hive*'.[21] The inferiority as well as the defencelessness of the Jamaican Negroes was not questioned. Though complaining that some Britons believed 'that ignorance, and squalor, and savagery *increase* the moral responsibility for crime', the *Spectator* took it for granted that these qualities distinguished its protégés.[22]

In the course of a long examination of the causes of the revolt, the *Pall Mall Gazette* was highly critical of British handling of the island, but referred to 'the poor deluded negro[es]' as 'the most inflammable and unreasoning population on earth', which Britain had falsely assumed 'would need no more guidance, no more control, than an Anglo-Saxon people'.[23] Writing in the *Gazette*, Huxley admitted that he had been drawn into the Jamaica Committee primarily as a protest against the introduction of martial law on the island and not by any particular love for or admiration of the Negro. *The Economist* argued against Eyre not so much out of a conviction of the equality of black and white, but in the interests of the economic expansion of the British Empire and the rule of law.[24]

[20] *Autobiography* (London, 1908), pp. 169–70.
[21] 15 September 1866, pp. 1,024–5.
[22] 24 March 1866, pp. 321–2.
[23] 13 February 1866.
[24] See B. Semmel, *op. cit.*, p. 120; E. Williams, *op. cit.*, pp. 143, 151.

These wider considerations also influenced the British freedmen's aid movement, which between 1865 and 1866 debated whether or not to take up the cause of the Jamaican as well as the American Negroes. This was to be expected, since the London freedmen's society enjoyed the support of a number of prominent Jamaica Committee men, including Jacob Bright, F. W. Chesson, Thomas Hughes, J. M. Ludlow, Lord Alfred Spencer Churchill, John Hart Estcourt, and Peter Taylor. In time the London association broke away from the other freedmen's aid groups and adopted the title of 'British and Foreign Freed-man's Aid Society', and in the *Freed-Man*, the society's journal, attention was indignantly drawn to Governor Eyre's illegal use of martial law.[25] Most freedmen's associations, however, believed that since involvement in Jamaican affairs would raise 'many questions of a religious and political nature' not contemplated in their original 'purely *philanthropic* aim', it was best avoided.[26] In addition, there was some feeling that members of the London society were not simply motivated by genuine humanitarianism, but distinguished rather by 'self seeking and clap trap'.[27]

This emphasis on the legal and democratic implications of the Jamaica rebellion unfortunately had the effect of discrediting the existing system of government and the notion of Negro suffrage – largely because of misconceptions about the extent to which it was exercised. As Wesleyan missionary the Rev. William Arthur complained: 'Jamaica is exhibited as a specimen of a country under negro ascendancy, as the pet, model government of philanthropists and Missionaries, as brought to ruin in spite of great advantages by the natural tendency of the negro, when free, to sink and drag down those who try to save him.'[28]

Thus a Tory M.P., G. M. W. Peacocke, at a gathering in Essex, declared quite seriously that the Jamaican Negroes, in spite of having been 'placed in a position of perfect political equality with their white brethren' had 'absolutely organized for

[25] 1 December 1865, p. 110; 1 January 1866, pp. 131–2.
[26] J. Gallaway to A. Hampson, C118/71.
[27] J. H. Tuke to A. Hampson, 9 September 1865, C120/70.
[28] *The Outbreak in Jamaica. A Speech by the Rev. William Arthur, M.A., Delivered at the Anniversary of the Folkestone Auxiliary to the Wesleyan Missionary Society, November 21st, 1865* (London, 1865), pp. 3–4.

next Christmas Day the massacre of every white inhabitant upon the island', a totally unfounded charge.[29] The *Saturday Review* was at pains to point out that such senseless ingratitude, as it was thought, might have been anticipated. Political rights 'presuppose on the part of those who exercise them a previous preparation such as the negro never underwent'. Doctrines of equality when applied in the West Indies, among freedmen 'endowed with no power of reflection, but gifted with an amount of self-conceit which no other race of human beings ever possessed', had made 'the negroes fanatical democrats of the socialist type'.[30] The only remedy in the tropics was a strong, if necessary despotic, government.

In its coverage of the Jamaica revolt, *The Times* frequently implied[31] that there was a large and pampered black electorate, arguing from this premise the base ingratitude of the ex-slave,

> he, who has come in as the favoured heir of a civilization in which he had no previous share – he, petted by philanthropists and statesmen and preachers into the precocious enjoyment of rights and immunities which other races have been too glad to acquire by centuries of struggles, of repulses, and of endurance – he, dandled into legislative and official grandeur by the commiseration of England, – that he should have chosen . . . to revolt . . . this is a thing so incredible that we will not venture to believe it now.[32]

The paper then went on to stress repeatedly that the United States Government should take note of events in Jamaica and frame a policy for its own freedmen which would avoid the pitfalls into which the British had fallen. A leader in November 1865 concluded that 'Though we should be sorry to see this event [the revolt] made use of as an argument against giving the [American] coloured man due political rights, and even the suffrage, on such conditions as a well-devised property qualification would impose, yet we are convinced that the latter should remain essentially under the tutelage of the former'.[33]

In an article which appeared a few months later *The Times* leader-writer was arguing, more forcibly, that given Negroes everywhere were 'careless, credulous, and dependent; easily

---

[29] Reported in the *Daily Telegraph*, 7 December 1865.
[30] 3 February 1866, pp. 134–5, and 20 January 1866, pp. 73–4.
[31] See, for instance, 3 November 1865, 31 January 1866.
[32] 4 November 1865.   [33] 13 November 1865.

excited, easily duped, easily frightened', once invested 'with full political rights, the race must be a magazine of mischief', whether in Jamaica or America.[34] The *Daily Telegraph* was equally critical of the performance of the Jamaica Assembly, which was seen as composed of 'unscrupulous demagogues placed there by negro vote' and bringing the island to ruin, just as the so-called Negro governments of Reconstruction were later seen as ruining the South.[35]

It is quite apparent that the Jamaica experiment coloured the comments of Britons on the Radical Reconstruction programme, and that both in turn were influenced by the knowledge that some whites in the U.S. and Britain remained without the suffrage. As *The Times* pointed out, the full rights of citizenship were not granted to most American immigrants until they had been in the country for five years, while nobody thought it necessary to enfranchise British agricultural labourers, let alone illiterate rural Negroes, just released from slavery.[36]

Opposition to Negro suffrage in the West Indies had, of course, been building up well before 1865. Carlyle's views on black indolence and unfitness for civil and political rights had been expressed with enormous venom in his *Occasional Discourse Upon the Nigger Question*, and were merely reinforced by the pamphlet, *Shooting Niagara: and After*, published in 1867.[37] After a visit to Jamaica in 1859, the novelist Trollope complained that the Assembly was dominated by coloureds and even Negroes who were not able to secure the respect of the island's 'white aristocracy'. Democracy could not work in a predominantly black country, for while a handful of white men could not hope to rule it was hard to find even 'three or four [Negroes] of the class who are fit to enact laws for their own guidance and the guidance of others'. Five years before the Jamaica revolt made such defeatist action possible, Trollope was prepared to see the suspension of democratic institutions and the institution of Crown Colony rule.[38]

Even commentators who did not talk of black rule in Jamaica

---

[34] 10 April 1866.   [35] 1 January 1866.

[36] 10 April 1866.

[37] London, 1853, pp. 5–14, 37–41; London, 1867, pp. 13–14, 19–21.

[38] A Trollope, *The West Indies and the Spanish Main* (London, 1859), pp. 55-100, especially pp. 82, 85, 97; and pp. 121–30, especially pp. 123–4.

– in the same exaggerated way that white Southerners came to talk of Negro supremacy in the South – were quick to point out the dangers inherent in treating the ex-slave as though 'we believed him as fit to take care of himself, to guide himself, to judge for himself . . . as any other British subject in short'. Britons had no right to be surprised at what happened in Jamaica, had only themselves to blame in giving the island a parliamentary government and its inhabitants equal political rights, but must learn once for all that 'securing civil rights to a people is one thing, and conferring on them political privileges is another; that all races and all classes are entitled to justice, but that all are not fit or ready for self-government; that to many, and notably to the West Indian negroes, giving them to themselves, as we have done, is simply the cruellest and laziest neglect'.[39] This view was supported by a correspondent of the *Pall Mall Gazette*, who complained that equal suffrage was not the panacea which the *Spectator* (almost alone among British journals) believed it to be, both for Jamaica and America.[40] This was because, in Jamaica, very few Negroes had bothered to avail themselves of the franchise, either out of indolence or indifference. The conclusion was predictable: 'If . . . the negro is oppressed and maltreated in Jamaica, it is not for the want of the "right of suffrage", and if the suffrage has failed in the West Indies, why should it work wonders [for the black population] in the United States?'[41]

Genuine friends of the Negro admitted doubts about the suffrage experiment. Liberal M.P. Sir John Kennaway, for instance, argued against political rights for the American freedmen because of their failure in Jamaica. 'All races and all classes are entitled to justice,' he wrote, echoing the *Gazette* almost verbatim, 'but all are not ready for self-government.'[42] After a visit to a number of West Indian islands in 1866, the Marquis of Lorne, in some ways a sympathetic observer, argued in favour of abolishing the House of Assembly and the vestries, on the

[39] *Pall Mall Gazette*, 13 February 1866.

[40] See *Spectator*, 11 November 1865, p. 1,248, 16 February 1866, pp. 152–3.

[41] *Pall Mall Gazette*, 17 February 1866, p. 5.

[42] *On Sherman's Track; or, the South After the War* (London, 1867), pp. 76–7.

grounds of local rivalries which elections to the latter provoked. 'All appointments in a community like this,' declared Lorne, 'ought to come from above, not from below; from the Government, not from the people.' He also quoted in full some contemporary verses entitled 'A Planter's Lament', which reproached 'those who, not content with their votes, had schemed to cut all our civilized throats!'[43] Lorne's mother, the Duchess of Argyll, considered British efforts in Jamaica since emancipation to have been a 'total failure', even though political rights were given.[44]

When, therefore, the frightened island Assembly accepted the advice of Governor Eyre and voted to surrender its powers to the Crown, Parliament, without raising any public opposition, authorized an Order in Council which made Jamaica a Crown Colony, abolishing elections and instituting a legislative Council consisting of the Governor, six *ex officio* officials, and any other unofficial members the Governor might nominate.[45] In the course of the next half-century, other West Indian colonies followed suit, until only Barbados, always fairly prosperous, retained its all-elected representative assembly (somewhat modified in 1881).

This was an enormously important development: just at a time when America was trying to implement human equality in the South, and agitation for suffrage reform and white colonial self-determination was moving forward successfully in Britain, the latter was deciding in favour of semi-despotic government over millions of coloured colonial subjects. The ineffectual Radicals of the Jamaica Committee had failed in their effort to change the character of the Empire, and in time this failure was to be conveniently rationalized in terms of the inevitable. In 1878 Gladstone, comparing developments in the Southern states of America and the British colonies, noted ruefully that[46] 'the South enjoys all its franchises, but we have, *pro pudor*, found no better method of providing for peace and order in Jamaica,

[43] *Op. cit.*, pp. 109–10, 147.
[44] Letter to Charles Sumner, 23 July 1866, *op. cit.*, p. 107.
[45] For the view that the Assembly's record was not so bad as to justify such drastic action, see D. Hall, *op. cit.*, p. 262.
[46] 'Kin Beyond Sea,' *North American Review*, September 1878, 127, p. 187.

the chief of our islands, than by the hard and vulgar, where needful, expedient of abolishing entirely its representative institutions'. Commenting on this decision some six years later, by which time it was, in fact, about to be reversed, the *Saturday Review* was in approval, on the grounds that a wide extension of the franchise would have reversed the roles of the two races, and that the vote should not be given to 'an ignorant and irresponsible rabble'. (However, this High Tory journal did have the grace to add that in Jamaica 'station and property afford no sufficient guarantee for impartial justice'.[47]) Writing shortly afterwards, the historian J. A. Froude, not surprisingly in view of his attitude to Negro suffrage in America, strongly criticized the Gladstone Administration for restoring a representative government and easily obtainable suffrage to Jamaica in 1884, arguing that no one in Britain wanted the change.[48]

Strong government had become the ideal: this might well be compatible, for some liberals, with the notion of trusteeship; certainly it was argued not only as essential for the safety of whites but also as in the best interests of blacks. An article published by the *Contemporary Review* put forward the view that only the 'preponderance of an Anglo-Saxon element guarantees an inherent capacity for freedom'; Jamaica had proved what had earlier been suspected in Britain's other tropical dependencies – namely, that 'among the stationary races . . . of which the negro is the most conspicuous example', there were no materials for self-government.[49] A correspondent of *The Times*, Rear-Admiral J. L. Stokes, compared the Jamaica insurrection with Fenianism, which – like the latter – required a strong hand to put it down: 'Of the risk, failure, and subsequent expense often attending conciliatory measures we have an example before us in the New Zealand war.'[50]

The Times itself, together with the *Daily Telegraph*, led the clamour for the smack of firm government in the colonies, well representing the views of Jamaica whites, as expressed by the Rev. J. Radcliffe (a Scottish minister living in Kingston) in the columns of the former newspaper in November 1865. 'We want

[47] 1 March 1884, pp. 271–2.
[48] *The English in the West Indies* (London, 1888), pp. 202–3.
[49] II, 1869 (May–August), p. 230.
[50] 8 December 1865.

no tentative or blundering legislation,' wrote Radcliffe. 'We want protection. We want to be ruled with a strong hand, or we shall not be in existence to be ruled at all.'[51] *The Times* stressed the necessity of keeping ever displayed before the eyes of 'barbarians', in their own interest, the 'signs and symbols of civilized authority'.[52] The *Telegraph*, similarly gloomy, concluded that 'we must rule the African with a strong hand, since we are bound to continue the thankless task of ruling him at all'.[53]

Among the members and supporters of the Eyre Defence Fund similar views were forcefully expressed. Carlyle hoped that, since Britons had never loved anarchy, 'miserable mad seditions' of the Jamaica variety would be dealt with firmly. Dickens, Ruskin, Hooker, Tennyson, and Tyndall felt the same, the last-named arguing that in governing Jamaica the only fatal error would be the error of weakness.[54]

The notion of trusteeship, of duties as well as rights regarding colonized peoples, was not abandoned, but the abolitionist and missionary attempt to demonstrate the essential equality of all men before God seemed disproved by this supposed example of the innate savagery of the Negro – a savagery which permitted, even made essential, savage counter-measures on the part of the superior white race. 'It has been in later years too much the fashion to rely on phrases,' wrote the Oxford don, Herman Merivale, four years before the revolt, 'to imagine that by proclaiming that all fellow-subjects of whatever race are equal in the eye of the law, we really make them so. There cannot be a greater error, nor one more calculated to inflict evil on those classes whom it is intended to benefit.' Merivale went on to preach the doctrine of 'separate but equal' some thirty years before this principle was to be sanctified by the Supreme Court of the United States. The alternative policies, he believed, were extermination of native races or racial mixing, with the whites inevitably in a position of supremacy.[55]

Such views were made the more dangerous because they

[51] 18 November 1865.
[52] 4, 13 November 1865.
[53] Quoted in *Jamaica; Who is to Blame?* (London, 1866), p. viii.
[54] Williams, *op. cit.*, pp. 128–40.
[55] *Lectures on Colonization and Colonies Delivered Before the University of Oxford in 1839, 1840 and 1841* (1861 Ed., London), pp. 509–10, 522–3.

received support from the professional exponents of racial theory, the ethnologists and anthropologists. As we have seen, men as different in outlook as James Hunt and Professor Flower had complained of the tendency to look at humanity in the abstract, had stressed the impossibility of 'applying the civilization and laws of one race to another race of man essentially distinct'.[56] Equally clearly, such statements might be taken at their face value, as a plea for more sophisticated studies of race, or they might be directed – as in the case of Hunt – against the gigantic assumption of absolute human equality, which was in fact a 'sham and a delusion'.[57]

Thus, in his Third Annual Address to the London Anthropological Society in 1866, Hunt, after a few sharp words about the pernicious doctrines of pseudo-philanthropists, remarked that 'we anthropologists have looked on, with intense admiration, at the conduct of Governor Eyre. . . . The merest novice in the study of race-characteristics ought to know that we English can only successfully rule either Jamaica, New Zealand, the Cape, China, or India, by such men as Governor Eyre. Such revolutions [as that in Jamaica] will occur whenever the Negro is placed in unnatural relations with Europeans.'[58] The *Popular Magazine of Anthropology* endorsed this view with vigour. The Negro, it maintained, belonged to that race which was least understood by Europe. For the last half century he had been 'an idol to the masses of the British public, and all classes of society have refused to listen to any depreciation of this chosen race. . . . Nearly all . . . have . . . agreed that the negro is a being very little (if at all) inferior, either mentally or morally, to the European.' Even men of science had supported this popular delusion – but with the events of 1865 the reaction had been absolute. The bitterest enemy of the Negro was seen to be the man 'who persistently shuts his eyes to his faults, and never ceases to thrust his time-honoured grievance [slavery] before us'.[59]

This article was written with reference to Knox's theory of the war of races, and reveals a clear undercurrent of fear,

[56] See above, pp. 4–5.   [57] See above, p. 6.
[58] J.A.S., IV (1866), lxxviii.
[59] Captain Bedford Pim, letter to *The Times*, 13 December 1865, and P.M.A., I (1866), pp. 14–15, 26.

disguised by bravado. Such fear is apparent in the agitated reporting of the Press. The *Bee Hive* quoted the warning of an English writer that it was too late for whites to draw their line in the West Indies: 'Without doubt the [Jamaica] insurrection will be crushed, and a proper example made of the leaders; but in these regions the white man must sooner or later give place to the black.'[60]

The *Daily Telegraph* noted with gloom that in her dependencies all over the world England stood confronting hostile races; large powers such as those assumed by Eyre were essential in lands where 'the British are looked upon as intruders, and are constantly exposed to extreme peril'.[61] *The Times* urged its readers to visualize the terrors facing a minority threatened by a numerous and barbarous enemy.[62]

While abolitionists looked with pleasure upon the results of the American Civil War, conservatives took alarm at the coincidence of black agitation in America, Haiti and Jamaica.[63] The Negro might contemptuously be referred to as a savage, but, as the botanist Hooker apprehensively expressed it, 'he is a most dangerous savage'.[64]

Inevitably, during the three-year debate over the Jamaica revolt, attempt was made to lay blame for its outbreak as well as for the nature of its suppression, and the scapegoats were not all black. Of all the white groups on the island, the missionaries – who alone accepted the now derided principle of racial equality – received the most abuse. The anthropologists' contempt for the attitudes of such men, which we have already observed, no doubt contributed to the bitterness of this criticism. Part of the irritation shown stems from the impatience with the operations, in Britain, of the Dissenting sects of Exeter Hall, who were apparently more concerned with evils at a distance than problems at home. The planters in particular, and some sections of the Press, resented the defence of the Jamaican Negro undertaken by Exeter Hall, and also the missionaries of these

60 18 November 1865; for an earlier prediction of a war of races, see Earl Grey, quoted in D. Hall, *op. cit.*, p. 257.

61 14 December 1865.

62 27, 30 January 1866.

63 *Daily Telegraph*, 1 August 1866, *Times*, 10, 20 November 1865.

64 Quoted in Williams, *op. cit.*, p. 137.

sects – notably the Baptists and the Wesleyan Methodists – who had been the Negroes' chief allies on the island.

An anonymous pamphlet put out in 1867 by the planter interest purported to expose the evil intentions, not only of the London Freedmen's Aid Society, but also of the Baptist mission-aries. The latter, regarded as 'a political as well as a religious sect', were held responsible for fomenting the 1830–1 Negro rebellion, bringing undeserved odium on the planters, and pre-cipitating the 1865 revolt through the irresponsible actions of Underhill.[65] The *Daily Telegraph* was similarly critical of the operations of these two groups, alike noticeable in the Jamaica crisis for their 'fanaticism', 'sectarian prejudice', and 'lack of Christian charity'.[66] The tenderheartedness of philanthropists towards barbarous races, argued *The Times*, was no recommen-dation when it was seen to rule out any sympathy for 'persons of our own', and to encourage the blacks to assert social equality with the whites.[67]

In the Britain of 1865 philanthropy in general, and missionary work in particular, were unfashionable, notwithstanding the enormous expansion of missionary effort which was about to begin. This was ominous, not because the Victorian philan-thropist was free from cultural arrogance or colour prejudice, but because he was the least prejudiced, the least dangerous to the material and spiritual possessions of the so-called inferior races. British humanitarianism had been accepted without question by Victorians themselves and by outside observers: during the American Civil War it seemed to falter; by the time of the Jamaica revolt, the efforts of the Jamaica Committee not-withstanding, it was a comparatively negligible force.

Fears about Negro ferocity and fears about entrusting ex-slaves with political privileges were combined with serious mis-givings about the effectiveness of Negro labour.[68] The depth of these misgivings bears witness to the strength of the planter

[65] *Jamaica: Its State and Prospects. With an Exposure of the Proceedings of the Freed-Man's Aid Society, and the Baptist Missionary Society* (London, 1867), p. 2.
[66] 9, 11 December 1865.
[67] 12 December and 4 November 1865.
[68] For a background to labour questions, see A. W. Lewis, *Labour in the West Indies* (London, 1939).

influence in Britain even at this late date, for the West Indies, staple exports had long since ceased to be crucial to the British economy. If little could be done to redeem the islands, however, at least the Southern States of America might be persuaded to take a warning from British errors.

Disillusioned abolitionists like Elizabeth Argyll suggested that 'Our West Indian mistakes ought to be very carefully studied. If it had been as well carried out a good work, as it was well begun, there would have been a tiny model farm for your great continent.' After looking at the economic situation with a fair degree of dispassion, the Rev. David Macrae concluded that the results of emancipation had fallen short of what was anticipated, and 'this is the aspect of the case which was constantly looked at by the people of the Southern States'.[69] As Charles Dilke summed it up: 'The negro question in America is briefly this: is there . . . reason to fear that, dollars applied to land decreasing while black mouths to be fed increase, the Southern States will become an American Jamaica?'[70]

Those who made such comparisons were, however, generally the conservatives and the racists. *The Times* never tired of pointing out that at a time when Americans were coping with the aftermath of slavery 'it must be poor encouragement to them to observe the actual condition to which thirty years of a similar trial have brought Jamaica'. The problems of the island were different only in degree from those of the Southern States.[71] The *Daily Telegraph* reported that while Britons might regret the 1865 revolt, 'there was one country, at all events, which would derive a seasonable and salutary lesson from it' – namely, the United States.[72] (And as we have already seen, the problems both countries faced with regard to black suffrage formed a common bond between them.)

It is curious to come across evidence during the 1860s, in the dispatches of the British Ambassador in Washington, that the emigration of American Negroes to the British West Indies was

[69] Argyll to Sumner, *Proceedings, op. cit.*, p. 105, and Macrae, *op. cit.*, I, p. 303.

[70] *Op. cit.*, p. 25.

[71] 31 January and 20 June 1866; see also 3, 4, 13 November 1865, 10 April 1866.

[72] 7 December 1865; 12 September 1866.

envisaged on the part of the Government in London. Bruce, however, interestingly advised that Negro labour and votes were too valuable to North and South alike to be spared, and that any proposal to benefit 'Her Majesty's Colonial possessions' would be rejected by the American Government so soon after the Civil War.[73] Since the West Indian planters, in Jamaica at least, were short of labour, colonization schemes were not seriously entertained by British observers as a means of ridding the islands of their troublesome blacks, nor was black immigrant labour favoured, though not a few hoped to see the Negro population dwindle away, to be replaced by a mixture of Indians and Chinese, acceptable to the Victorians by their willingness to 'trade, . . . speculate, and endeavour in other modes to emulate the wealth and prosperity of their fellow citizens'.[74] The *Spectator* caustically suggested that, given the contemporary climate of opinion in Britain on race matters, it might be helpful to import the masters, rather than the slaves, from the Southern states of America (and of great benefit to that region), so that the West Indian planters could be instructed in reimposing Black Codes and even slavery.[75]

The *Manchester Courier*, a staunch supporter of the South during the war, felt that in fact Americans would handle their freedmen more successfully than Britain, not only because both political parties had an interest in voting and therefore educating the blacks, but because by the postwar reconstruction the Negroes had been kept from idleness, 'which is a synonym for mischief'.[76] A similar line was taken by the equally pro-Confederate *Edinburgh Evening Courant*, which saw in Southern efforts to obtain European labour evidence that the planters had learned, from British hard experience, that simply to free the Negro was to abandon him to the worse slavery of 'his own brute laziness', and to risk the ruin of the land on which he was with difficulty employed.[77] Another conservative journal, however, the *Irish Times*, observed maliciously that the people of Jamaica, as they traced the end of their prosperity to the

[73] Sir Frederick Bruce to Lord Clarendon, 25 June 1866, F.O. 5, 1,065.
[74] A.R., II (1864), p. ccxi.
[75] 2 December 1865.
[76] 7 March 1866.
[77] 16 February 1866.

Emancipation Act of 1833, looked for its revival to the emancipation of American Negroes thirty years later, since their experiences had not convinced the West Indian planters 'that free labour is cheaper than the task-work of slaves'.[78]

This debate had, of course, long been waged between philanthropists and their enemies. The former argued that the freedmen were grossly maligned, that the planters wanted coolie labour, not because labourers were scarce, but because of a hankering after slavery;[79] the latter maintained that in a tropical climate the only labour which could be exacted from the black population (alone presumed suited to perform it, hence the irritation) was forced labour, or otherwise there was 'ever the same vegetating of brute animal life', with even the Creole Negroes too indolent to advance.[80] To accept such a situation, according to *The Times*, it seemed that Britons had been mesmerized by years of humanitarian cant into believing that 'the world was made for Sambo, and that the sole use of sugar is to sweeten Sambo's existence'.[81]

With the American situation in mind, British observers after 1865 emphasized the land question. A few Radicals in Congress, with the aid of the Freedmen's Bureau, were committed to distributing certain confiscated Southern property among the Negroes; this was seen as highly undesirable by conservatives on both sides of the Atlantic. According to the Marquis of Lorne, the prosperity of the islands of the West Indies was in direct proportion to the amount of land the black population had been able to secure for squatting, since a 'great amount of squatting is sure to involve a great want of labour'. The fact that the freedman in America could not, as in Jamaica, 'fatten upon a small piece of land', was regarded as an advantage.[82]

---

[78] 4 July 1865.

[79] *The West India Labour Question, etc.* (London, 1858); Glasgow Emancipation Society Minute Book 3 (8th, 9th and 10th Annual Meetings, 1842, 1843, 1844); *Emancipation In the West Indies. Two Addresses by E. B. Underhill, Esq., and the Rev. J. T. Brown, etc.* (London, 1861).

[80] H. B. Evans, *Our West Indian Colonies. Jamaica, a Source of National Wealth and Honour* (London, 1855), pp. 12, 17, 21, 27.

[81] 6 January 1860. See also, for planter views, E. Thompson, W. Smith, W. Girod, *Statement of Facts Relative to the Island of Jamaica* (London, 1852), pp. 3–7, 24–7.

[82] *Op. cit.*, pp. 33, 264.

This was also the view of the *Daily Telegraph*, which did, however, acknowledge some months after the revolt that squatting was often the fault of the resentful planters, who had failed to pay their workers sufficient wages.[83] In the excitement of November 1865 this journal had been more unsympathetic, maintaining that the Jamaica freedmen were indolent and unambitious, unable to understand the motives that stimulated white men into strenuous activity, and declining to work even for high wages.[84] *The Times*, predictably, was full of warnings about the impossibility of persuading the free Negro to work for more than the bare satisfaction of his bodily wants; about the freedman's desire to appropriate the white man's property; about the duties as well as rights of freedom.[85]

British anthropologists did little to dispel the notion that the West Indian Negro, when free, was promptly enslaved by his own passions and could never be converted to the gospel of work – thus Henry Guppy, at a meeting of the London society in 1864, described the blacks of Haiti as shiftless, idle and indifferent to the outside world and to all forms of knowledge; even when provoked to rebellion, 'the object is generally one of lust or ease, and not one caused by ambitious and domineering ideas'. Consequently, Guppy predicted that the Negro race – though not the mixed races – would soon die out in the West Indies.[86] However, a few voices were raised at society meetings in defence of Negro diligence in Jamaica and Barbados, and, of course, the abolitionists present, though under heavy fire, put up a spirited defence of the notion of human equality.[87]

The London Freedmen's Aid Association also condemned the Jamaican planters for keeping down wages in order to reduce the independence of their black labourers, and were fearful that the Southern planters might attempt to do likewise.[88] (The planters retaliated by arguing that the freedmen's movements of Britain and America were united in a conspiracy to ruin the

[83] 23 June 1866.
[84] 28 November 1865.
[85] 31 January 1866, 4, 10, 13 November 1865.
[86] A.R., II, pp. ccx–ccxii; also J. Reddie in *ibid.*, p. 281.
[87] J.A.S., II, p. xxxii; *ibid.*, pp. cclxxv–cclxxxiv; VII (1869), pp. clix–clxi.
[88] *Freed-Man*, 1 March 1866, p. 198.

employers and alienate and spoil the Negroes in the South and the West Indies alike.[89])

Among Metropolitan newspapers the *Daily News* likewise condemned the 'worn-out nonsense about negro laziness and squatting' being peddled by *The Times*. The difficulties in Jamaica were caused not by this, but by the British failure to secure justice equally to black and white.[90] The *Morning Star* took a similar line, and the *Bee Hive*, as was to be expected, was contemptuous of the conservative Press, opening its columns to men like Beesly, who argued that the Jamaican planters were a lazy, inefficient, vicious class, unwilling to pay proper wages, and suggested that no man, of whatever race, could be expected to work 'that some individual just as capable of it as himself may sit with folded hands'. It was also pointed out by the *Bee Hive* that if the character of the Jamaican Negro was as bad as some detractors claimed – which the paper took leave to doubt – then this was because they had inherited, through enforced association, 'the vices and bad habits of their former masters', and were therefore as much to be pitied as blamed.[91]

A comparable note of pity – though pity is dangerous in racial matters, as denoting too often contempt and not love – was occasionally displayed by interested individuals who left accounts of the Jamaican labour question. After defending the freedmen against the charge of idleness, William Arthur went on to add, in connection with the rebellion itself and the violence it involved: 'As to the black, in this day of his reproach shall we not stand by him! . . . by every principle, Christian, manly and true, let us face the people who say that such faults belong to his race and not others.'[92] Charles Roundell, Secretary of the Commission which investigated the Jamaica troubles, concluded that the island's stagnant economy was the result of planter mismanagement, preference for coolie labour, hostility to Negro land-ownership and unwillingness to pay decent wages, rather than the failure of free black labour.[93]

[89] *Jamaica: Its State and Prospects etc., op. cit.*, pp. 8–19.
[90] 18 November 1865.
[91] 17 February 1866, 25 November 1865, 23 February 1866.
[92] *Op. cit.*, p. 14.
[93] *England and Her Subject-Races with Special Reference to Jamaica* London, 1866), pp. 25–40.

Such sympathizers looked comparatively optimistically to the future, setting their hopes upon the extension of education (and particularly vocational training) among the freedmen. The female emancipation society of Edinburgh suggested sending out funds for education, so that the black population 'may be able to expand to the moral dignity of free citizens' – and in more practical terms understand contracts, the regulation of wages and other matters in which the whites had previously been able to impose upon them.[94] British freedmen's aid workers, and especially the Quakers involved, who stressed the importance of founding schools for the American Negroes, also turned their attentions to the intellectual needs of the Jamaican freedmen (having attempted to alleviate physical hardship by the setting up of the Jamaica Commercial Agency Company, to foster Negro surplus exporting co-operatives on the island, and boost the import of British goods in return).[95]

In the opinion of the Radical *Manchester Examiner and Times*, Britain deserved some credit for freeing the West Indian slaves, but had notably failed in not subsidizing education, since Christian preaching among ignorant peoples was apt to produce 'a narrow and selfish fanaticism' of value neither to individuals nor society. *The Times* defended the ability of the Negro to learn, and its own willingness to see compulsory education, even though British parents would resent this, on the grounds that physical coercion of blacks had been accepted cheerfully by Britons through generations of slavery.[96] We see here a liberal version of the familiar appeal for strong government of 'uncivilized races' – an appeal usually made with reference to the best interests of the governed, the latter being deemed incompetent to pass an opinion on the subject. As it happened, however, black and white opinion coincided in stressing the need for schools, in Jamaica as in America, even though application

[94] *Annual Report . . . 1867, op. cit.*, p. 4.

[95] See, for education, Minute Books of the Gloucester and Nailsworth Monthly Meeting, Society of Friends, Book 1854–67, reports of Meetings at Nailsworth, 12 July 1865, Cirencester, 14 March, 9 May 1866, Cheltenham, 11 April 1866, and *Freed-Man*. For details of the Company, *Freed-Man*, 1 December 1866, p. iv. See also on education and the need to train teachers, E. B. Underhill, *Life of James Mursell Phillippo, Missionary in Jamaica* (London, 1881), pp. 132–8, 355–68.

[96] 16 January 1866.

might be difficult to sustain in an unprogressive and divided community.[97]

It was this difficulty – along with implicit assumptions of white cultural superiority – which led the Marquis of Lorne, when writing of education as the great want of Jamaica, to argue that it must be made obligatory. In Haiti, he believed, once the black population was left without direction there was little mental progress, and none 'should be allowed to possess such an island who does not use every exertion to make the most of its wonderful capabilities'. Equally there was potential for development in Jamaica, though small prospect of any rapid intellectual improvement among the Negroes; all races were seen to benefit from education, however, and a government system of industrial schools, with competent masters and government inspectors, was advocated by Lorne. Attendance, he argued, could not be voluntary, otherwise children would be taken away to work after learning a little, which would make them 'infinitely more disagreeable member[s] of society than [they] . . . would otherwise have been. Nowhere is it more true that a little knowledge is a dangerous thing than it is here'.[98]

The Jamaica revolt was important to most Victorians as a crisis for British liberalism; historians have written of the Governor Eyre rather than the Paul Bogle or George Gordon controversy.[99] We should not, however, overlook the importance of the events of 1865 in the development of Victorian attitudes to race. The degree of race prejudice which these events revealed was in fact recognized with shame by some contemporaries, something which Dr Williams' study only perfunctorily acknow-

---

[97] See, for instance, J. Clark, W. Dendy, J. M. Phillippo, *The Voice of Jubilee; a Narrative of the Baptist Mission, Jamaica, From Its Commencement; With Notices of Its Fathers and Founders* (London, 1865), pp. 81, 88, 92, 116; D. Hall, *op. cit.*, pp. 30–1, 34, 261. There was some disagreement, however, about the desirability of purely industrial education: see G. R. Mellor, *British Imperial Trusteeship, 1783–1850* (London, 1951), pp. 144–6, 162.

[98] *Op. cit.*, pp. 32–3, 64–5, 110, 145, 148–9. See also, for a poor view of Negro intelligence, A. Lindo, Jamaican magistrate, *Dr Underhill's Testimony on the Wrongs of the Negro in Jamaica* (London, 1866), pp. 26–7.

[99] Bogle, a prominent black Baptist landowner, was, with Gordon, one of the main leaders of the revolt.

ledges. As Charles Dilke admitted, 'if it is still impossible openly to advocate slavery in England, it has, at least, become a habit persistently to write down freedom. We are no longer told that God made the blacks to be slaves, but we are bade remember that they cannot prosper under emancipation. All mention of Barbados is suppressed, but we have daily homilies on the condition of Jamaica.'[100] Dilke himself, as his biographer points out, while deploring British treatment of natives in Tasmania, India, Jamaica and elsewhere, believed implicitly in the supremacy of the English-speaking peoples and noted without too much alarm that 'the Anglo-Saxon is the only extirpating race on earth'.[101]

Among leading British journals, *The Scotsman* suggested that, in spite of the nation's tradition of sympathy towards the West Indian Negro and suspicion of the planter, and in spite of the criticisms of Governor Eyre, public sympathy was less engaged than it would have been for white 'rebels'. The reason for this was that 'devil of hatred or at least contempt of race' that lurked – usually dangerously unacknowledged – in all Britons.[102] In alarmed agreement was the *Freeman's Journal*, whose leader-writer declared, somewhat inaccurately, that the Black Hole of Calcutta and the Massacre of Amboyna were trifles compared with the prolonged horrors of Jamaica, and could only explain these horrors with reference to the colour prejudice for which Americans were censured, but which now 'breaks out as strongly in Englishmen without the same motive for the display'.[103] Though it is conceivable that the *Journal*, having on occasion indignantly rejected suggestions that Irishmen were peculiarly prejudiced against the Negro, was here still defending the honour of the Irish in a self-righteous rebuke to the English. Certainly some American abolitionists, long reproached by British writers for their ineffectiveness against slavery, took the opportunity for revenge which the Jamaica revolt provided.

Sarah Remond, writing to the *Daily News* during a visit to

[100] *Op. cit.*, I, p. 25.
[101] R. Jenkins. *Sir Charles Dilke. A Victorian Tragedy* (London, 1958), p. 34.
[102] 4 August 1866; see also *Aborigines' Friend*, II (1859–66), p. 40.
[103] 20 March 1866.

Britain in the mid-1860s, detected 'in the minds of many Englishmen' a 'share of the same feeling of hatred towards the coloured race' that disgraced the planters of the Southern states.[104] Ever since the Civil War, Miss Remond maintained, the planter interest in the South and the West Indies had combined to hold up the freedmen 'to the scorn and contempt of the civilized world'. More was now expected of the black than the white race, in terms of good behaviour, and any crimes committed by the former were made 'the occasion of the most insulting attacks upon a whole race, on account of a difference of complexion'.[105]

A change, indeed, had taken place in British opinion, as the Negro abolitionist alleged. This had first been indicated during the Civil War when – notwithstanding the excuse that the conflict was not clearly over slavery – even the anti-slavery movement had been slow to rally to the Union cause, and perturbed at the effects of immediate emancipation. As Moncure Conway had written in 1864, 'there is a very serious doubt as to *how many of the most influential men of England*, if asked to-day to unite in a protest against the existence of slavery for one moment longer, *would utter some cant or fatuity about the bad results of emancipation in the West Indies, or the unfitness of the slaves for freedom* (which is about as wise as to talk of the unfitness of an invalid for health)'.[106] Similar conclusions were reached by a correspondent of the *Pall Mall Gazette*, referring to a letter from William Rathbone Greg which had thrown doubts on Negro capabilities, but somewhat defiantly, predicting that his views would be taken to 'indicate an almost cynical courage, an almost Carlylean contempt of the popular creed'. On the contrary, it was maintained, in mid-Victorian Britain, even before the Jamaica revolt, 'Self-styled men of the world have quite a pet aversion to negro emancipation as an object of vulgar enthusiasm, and are never tired of quoting Jamaica and St Domingo'.[107]

This hostile climate of opinion clearly had an adverse effect upon the fund-raising efforts of the London Freedman's Aid

[104] 22 September 1866.
[105] 22 November 1865.
[106] *Testimonies Concerning Slavery* (London, 1864), p. 138.
[107] 25 April 1865.

Society. Local contacts in Bath and Leicester reported that sympathy for the planters was strong, and that 'such is the prejudice against the Negro, strengthened by the Jamaica outbreak', that prospects for eliciting money for the freedmen of either Jamaica or the United States looked bleak.[108] The story in London, Bristol, Birmingham and Leeds was much the same.[109]

The nervousness aroused by the Indian Mutiny and the protracted New Zealand wars, and given a theoretical justification by the scientific exponents of the 'war of races' doctrine, had strengthened a perhaps inevitable instinct of powerful minorities in a threatening environment to bolster their position and confidence with a massive display of force. Superior weapons were to demonstrate, if all else failed, the superiority of the Anglo-Saxon. This sinister development did not go unnoticed – any more than the increase in colour prejudice – but neither could be contained. The dangers were emphasized by Frederic Harrison in a series of letters to the *Daily News* during 1867, and by Charles Roundell; both men appealed for control of the 'wild beast' of militarism, the ferocity born of desperation, and Roundell shrewdly pointed out what Mannoni has since highlighted in the colonial mentality – the insatiable desire for obedience and gratitude on the part of the colonizer. The insurrection of the Negro in Jamaica was, he remarked, 'resented as a kind of personal insult'.[110] (This type of reaction is very apparent in *The Times* reports on Jamaica.)

By the 1860s, as the supporters of the Jamaica Committee complained, the upper and middle class of the English people, especially the latter, had come to believe that Negroes were innately inferior beings who consequently did not rate equal consideration with themselves. Such a principle was not yet proudly and openly expressed, however, without some sort of rationalization. But if it was possible for genuine humanitarians to argue for the abandonment of the democratic experiment in Jamaica, how much easier for the uncommitted majority, who

[108] See letters in A.P., C117/100, C118–52, 53.
[109] A.P., C119/101, C118/16, C119/62, C118/88.
[110] *Jamaica Papers, No. 5, op. cit.,* p. 41; *England and Her Subject-Races, op. cit.,* pp. 18–19; and O. Mannoni, *Prospero and Caliban. The Psychology of Colonization* (trans. P. Powesland, New York, 1964), pp. 105–8.

might also claim to be arguing against the planters and in the interests of the Negro.[111] And so, as the *Spectator* pointed out, proceedings which would have been received with shouts of execration if they had taken place in France or Austria were 'heartily admired as examples of "strong government" when they take place in the British West Indies'.[112] The racialist in the nineteenth century, as to day, disguised his prejudices; Victorians behind discussions of the forms of government best suited to keep order in the tropics, Britons 100 years later with reference to inadequate job opportunities, housing, welfare and educational facilities to cope with demands made by Commonwealth immigrants. No great step was needed before the expression of more overtly imperialistic attitudes would be acceptable – as witness, for instance, Lecky's proud justification of the British Empire in 1893 as the epitome of 'strong central government', the 'greatest and most beneficient despotism in the world'.[113] The advice of early anthropologists – that, in dealing with the colonies, 'the special moral, intellectual, and social capabilities, wants and aspirations of each particular race' should be considered – was accepted as a denial of equality and subtly altered to justify a special degree of repression and exploitation.

In Jamaica itself, and the West Indies in general, the immediate story, however, is one of neglect rather than oppression; the principle of race prejudice, which was exposed during the debates on the revolt, was instead extended to justify British activities in Africa, to which we shall now turn. In consequence, solutions for the most pressing problems of Jamaica were not found. Educational progress was slow in the face of upper-class convictions that it was both undesirable and useless for the black population. Such instruction as there was – generally unsuited to local conditions – went to those who could afford to pay, usually not the black majority, thus increasing the colour-class consciousness which was to become such a feature

[111] See, for instance, W. Arthur, *op. cit.*, p. 14, for a humanitarian's version of this argument; for a conservative justification of Crown Colony rule see M. E. Egerton, *A Short History of British Colonial Policy, 1606–1909* (London, 1897), pp. 405–6.

[112] Quoted in B. Semmel, *op. cit.*, p. 171.

[113] W. E. H. Lecky, *The Empire: its Value and its Growth* (London, 1893), pp. 25, 45.

of West Indian society, as Kenneth Little has shown it to be of our own. Poverty remained the fundamental characteristic of the islands.[114]

To this situation British policy contributed directly. There is, however, little new awareness on the part of Victorian observers; rather, one is struck by the resilience of old ways of thought (a confirmation of the view of sociologists that mental rigidity is one of the chief characteristics of prejudice).[115] Thus taking up the cudgels on behalf of the Negro we find the British Anti-Slavery Society, at its Jubilee Meeting in 1884, presenting the testimony of Lord Derby, who defended the diligence of the black population of Barbados and Jamaica, and their quiet, unaggressive character. It is significant that Derby also commented, to cheers, that 'the future of the negro race is one with which we are only indirectly concerned. What does concern us is that we should do our duty by them.' This performed – once the Negro was given freedom and 'a fair chance,' in other words – Britain's responsibility was covered. 'We are not answerable for their doing well,' concluded the speaker. 'We are answerable for putting no obstacles in their way to prevent their doing well,' and in his view they would never do as well as the inhabitants of Australia and Canada.[116] Here is clear evidence of the declining ambition of the British anti-slavery movement, and it was matched by a decline in missionary effort, as the various societies operating in Jamaica became increasingly preoccupied with African developments. (The Church Missionary Society virtually withdrew from work on the island.[117]) Speakers at meetings of the Royal Colonial Institute also came to the defence of the inhabitants of the West Indies, and the Negroes of Jamaica in particular, but had to admit that the island was generally viewed as 'a hopelessly ruined community, which was once prosperous, but has become a wreck of its former self', and

[114] See P. Sherlock, *op. cit.*, pp. 129–32; M. Ayearst, *op. cit.*, pp. 42, 55–7; Little, *Negroes in Britain* (London, 1948).

[115] See, for instance, M. Banton, *White and Coloured* (London, 1959), p. 31.

[116] *Anti-Slavery Jubilee, August 1st, 1884. Meeting of the British and Foreign Anti-Slavery Society, in the Guildhall of the City of London, Under the Presidency of His Royal Highness the Prince of Wales* (London, 1884), p. 14.

[117] C.M.I., I, x (October 1865), pp. 302–6.

whose black population was 'an idle, thriftless, vagabond people, refusing to work, and fast lapsing into heathenish savagery'.[118]

Visiting the West Indies in 1887, the historian Froude – epitomizing such conservative opinions – made out a positive case for neglect, since the Negro, he argued, when partly raised in the scale of civilization was spoilt as a black (for Froude believed that the educated Negro despised his own people) without being able to achieve white standards and status. The West Indian freedmen, alleged the historian, were the happiest and most fortunate peasantry in the world, enjoying perfect liberty, a mild climate, and with no ambition to make them restless they had 'nothing now to do save to laugh and sing and enjoy existence' – the persistent 'child of nature' theme again, echoes of Carlyle, of *The Times* and the planter view. The Asian coolies, by contrast, were seen as hard-working, dignified, attractive in appearance, operating a colour bar against the black population, and therefore thoroughly acceptable to Victorian prejudices. (We shall see more of this attitude when surveying British attitudes to India and the Indians.) The need for strong government was taken for granted by Froude, if the islands – or indeed any colony – were not to lapse into barbarism, as witness the state of affairs in Haiti; he was hopeful that in the long term the Negro might be 'improved', but concluded, with truth, that the average Englishman had little concern for the West Indies. As early as 1859 Trollope had remarked that 'Few European white men now turn thither in quest of fortune'.[119] The planter had had his day, and in terms of geography the islands seemed to belong more naturally to the United States than Britain.[120]

[118] *Proceedings of the Royal Colonial Institute*, 6 (1874–5), pp. 228–52; 11 (1879–80), pp. 226–70 (in future simply P.R.C.I.).
[119] *Op. cit.*, p. 81.
[120] *Op. cit.*, pp. 25, 43, 49, 50, 56, 73–6, 99, 107, 125, 173, 182–8.

IV

<hr>

Africa rediviva?

<hr>

> The European lands on the Coast of Africa, as a Man of
> Science, or a Man of Commerce, or a great Hunter, or a
> mighty Explorer, totally regardless of the rights of others ...
> he treats the tribes, who have had the prescriptive possession
> of the country for centuries, as if they were in the category
> of the wild beasts, mere 'ferae naturae': he cares neither for
> their souls, nor their bodies.
>
> R. N. CUST, 1891.[1]

M ORE detailed monographs have recently been produced on
British attitudes to Africa and the Africans than on any other
aspect of Victorian racial thought in the second half of the nineteenth century. This is scarcely surprising, for by then the conquest of India had already been accomplished, while the great
phase of expansion in Africa was just beginning, though in fact
the contemporary Press continued to pay more attention to
Indian affairs until about the 1880s, and North America, for
instance, continued to prove far more appealing to prospective
settlers than 'the dark continent'. This essay will be concerned
primarily with the anthropologists, explorers, casual travellers,
missionaries, anti-slavery advocates and journalists who have
left a copious record of their activities and impressions during
the years before formal empire in Africa. The developments of
the 1890s, well known already, will be treated only briefly.

It soon becomes clear that the writings of all the groups named

[1] *Africa Rediviva. Or the Occupation of Africa by Christian Missionaries
of Europe and North Africa* (London, 1891), p. 7.

above are so lacking in objectivity as to be almost useless as the base for an accurate assessment of African societies in the nineteenth century. They go far to explain the sort of defensive counter-propaganda which resulted, in Victorian times, in books like H. D. Adams' *God's Image in Ebony*, and in recent times prompted Joel Rogers' *One Hundred Amazing Facts About the Negro* and *Real Facts About Ethiopia*, and Gabriel Osei's *The Forgotten Great Africans*.[2] The motives of the pioneers who went to Africa seeking freedom, or adventure, improved status and the possibility of leadership, or converts, geographical knowledge, or (too often) the confirmation of anthropological theories already held, colour profoundly their reactions to real situations often far different from those optimistically anticipated in Britain. Few, notwithstanding the undoubted hazards to health and even life which they encountered, were prepared to admit failure: on the contrary, a conviction of success was necessary to quench self-doubt, to bolster the notion of white superiority which a hostile environment and enforced contact with despised natives often seemed to undermine. However, we can learn much, not just about Victorian attitudes to race, but about nineteenth-century modes of thought in general. Thus, for instance, the moralizing language which even the most complaisant explorers of Africa frequently used is significant as an indication of the curiously lasting impact of the anti-slavery movement, at a time when that movement was extremely weak in terms of money, personnel, and direct influence over governmental policy.

In the course of the analysis which follows of some of the most typical British attitudes towards African customs, character and appearance, an attempt will be made to estimate their importance, and to point out the more obvious instances of bias, together with the possible explanations for this.

Of all aspects of African culture which interested Victorian writers in the period before 1890, religion was the most crucial, and here the views of British missionaries and missionary journals are particularly important. In his study of Christian

[2] Published respectively in London, 1854, New York, 1934 and 1935, and London, 1965.

missions, Stephen Neill comments that 'Christianity alone has succeeded in making itself a universal religion', with 'adherents among all the races of men, from the most sophisticated of westerners to the aborigines of the inhospitable deserts of Australia; and there is no religion of the world which has not yielded a certain number of converts to it'.[3] Success, he argues, was largely assured during the nineteenth century, thanks to missionary activity undertaken primarily by English-speaking peoples. During that century dramatic progress was made by British societies representing the Baptists, the Congregationalists (the L.M.S., ostensibly independent), the Methodists, the Anglicans (the C.M.S.), the Presbyterians, and to a lesser extent the Catholics (the Society for Foreign Missions). World Missionary Conferences met in Liverpool (in 1860), in London (1885), in New York (1900); missionary periodicals acquired a large, popular readership, and the work of evangelization – in spite of the difficulties and doubts we shall notice – proceeded as never before. These facts alone would help to explain the intellectual arrogance for which the missionaries have been so much criticized.[4] Instead of simply taking the Christian religion to foreign lands as their numbers increased in an imperialist century, some British missionaries came to believe that they were the advance-guard of a supreme spiritual and material culture. And thus although, as has been pointed out by Neill, the progress of the Gospel was not 'tied to the political or economic fortunes of any one part of the human race', these Victorian evangelists argued that the British role was uniquely important.[5] As the *Church Missionary Intelligencer* put it, England's 'high position amidst the nations of the earth is a providential dispensation. Her vast colonies, her extended influence, her universal commerce, afford astonishing facilities for the wider dissemination of Gospel truth.'[6] The sense of spiritual superiority, which a missionary must often possess, was in Africa (and to a much lesser extent in India) easily transformed into a feeling of racial superiority, because of the enormous barriers existing between

[3] S. Neill, *A History of Christian Missions* (London, 1964), pp. 14–15, 256–7.

[4] See *ibid.*, pp. 250, 259–60; and for more vigorous condemnation see H. A. C. Cairns, *op. cit.*, pp. 238–40; P. Curtin, *op. cit.*, pp. 267–8, 324–8.

[5] *Op. cit.*, p. 245.   [6] I (London, 1850), p. 3.

Europeans and Africans in terms of colour, habitat, industrial achievement and social organization, as well as religion.

It should be said at the outset, however, that the British missionary faced a basic challenge to the validity of such assumptions, not only from the many setbacks and hardships encountered and from cynical opponents of his work, but from the apparently superior progress made in Africa by Islam, along with Christianity and Buddhism one of the three great proselytizing religions of the world. This issue is worth examining in some detail because of the light missionary attitudes shed on Victorian ethnocentrism, which we shall notice again in other contexts.

The main lines of the controversy between those who believed that the results of the Moslem faith were beneficial and those who did not were drawn, as we have seen, by the 1860s. In the second category we find primarily the Christians, clergymen at home and missionaries abroad, whose condemnation of other rivals was often equally severe. Thus it was suggested by the C.M.I. that Catholicism made no headway in Africa because that religion was too tyrannical in its practices, and because the natives had an even greater command of 'miracle-working' and superstition.[7] Furthermore, it was alleged, the Catholic missions had made no attempt to stem the slave trade, and mission personnel had always treated their prospective converts with excessive severity.[8]

By the 1880s it was reluctantly admitted that Moslem successes among the Negroes had been steadily increasing, and it was more vital than ever to point out that Mohammedanism bore the greatest share of blame for oppressing and enslaving the African; that it was a religion which pandered to man's sensuality and passions, a course not open to Christianity, which aimed to act as 'the regenerator of society'; and that its acceptance of polygamy was an insult to womanhood which no Briton could be expected to stomach.[9] The standard defence of Islam – namely, that it suited the African's temperament and accommo-

[7] IX (July 1873), pp. 236–8, and I (July 1865), p. 195.
[8] XII (November 1887), pp. 655–6.
[9] C.M.I., I (July 1865), pp. 196–7; XII (1887), pp. 649–54; T.E.S.L., V (1867), pp. 85–6; D. J. East, *Western Africa* (London, 1844), p. 272; Rev. R. M. Macbriar, *Africans at Home* (London, 1861), p. 394.

dated his vices – was, in other words, no defence at all, but a clear admission of the need for the moral regeneration which Christianity alone could effect.[10]

Friction between Arabs and missionaries in central and east Africa increased in the 1870s and 1880s as the Moslem drive for converts mounted, while devout Victorians, without apparent embarrassment, raised the cry of 'Africa for the Africans' and pressed for a new crusade against 'the fury of the Mohammedan oppressor' (and incidentally 'the covetousness of the grasping Hindu trader').[11] Livingstone had reported in his journals that the Moslems in fact neglected educational and missionary work among the heathen, and naturally most Europeans involved in such work wanted to believe him, but this was difficult.[12] The Scotsman's explanation of this state of affairs was that, though the Arabs 'it is well known, are great in commerce, [they are] not much elevated thereby above the African in principle'.[13]

There were, of course, others – and not all professional missionaries – who believed with Livingstone that the Arab influence in Africa should be destroyed. Professor Henry Drummond described the Arab-dominated slave trade as the heart-disease of the continent, and, though ideally he would have liked to see Africa belong to the Africans, reluctantly urged that the traders' influence should be undermined, not just by missionary effort, but through intervention instigated 'by the people of England', whose motives could scarcely be misunderstood or opposed. Zanzibar, the centre of the traffic, he described as Arabian in its morals, a 'cesspool of wickedness'.[14] A sympathetic account of mission work in East Africa was also given by the Rev. Charles New, a Methodist who had spent much of his own missionary career at Ribe, a station to the north-west of Mombasa.[15]

[10] J.A.S., III (1865), pp. ccxviii–xi.

[11] C.M.I., X (October 1874), p. 321; F. D. Lugard, *The Rise of Our East African Empire* (London, 1893, 2 vols.), II, p. 288.

[12] *The Last Journals of David Livingstone in Central Africa, from 1865 to his Death* (London, 1874, 2 vols.), I, pp. 278–80; II, p. 210.

[13] *Proceedings of the Royal Geographical Society* (in future P.R.G.S.), XXVII (1857), p. 357.

[14] *Tropical Africa* (London, 1888), pp. 5, 69, 85, 205–6.

[15] *Life, Wanderings, and Labours in Eastern Africa* (London, 1874), pp. 3, 29–30, 33–6, 41, 50, 57, 103, 166–7, 489–508; see also T.E.S.L., V (1867), pp. 85–6, views of T. Valentine Robins on the Niger Expedition.

Predictably, New dwelt upon the horrors of the Arab slave trade, which he regarded as the chief barrier to progress in the region. Conversion to Islam rendered the Somali tribes more vicious than if they had remained heathens, he believed, and all possible steps should be taken to counteract the influence of the Arabs, who were 'a detestable race, with scarcely a redeeming quality'. It was 'a thousand pities that they should ever have put their foul hands upon, and brought their paralysing religion to, Eastern Africa', where it fostered black magic and every form of vice. The country was, wrote New, 'doomed to the dust as long as Arab and Muhammadan influences predominate'.

The argument for British occupation was supported by Bartle Frere and F. D. Lugard. The latter saw this as the speediest way of ending the slave trade, warning the British public, however, that 'the Arab slave-raider is not the only curse of Africa but is rivalled . . . by the awful and intolerable tyranny of the dominant tribe'. (It was further noted that British travellers, traders and even missionaries in Africa had all used slave labourers, particularly as porters, and could therefore scarcely adopt too superior an attitude.[16]) In fact, Britons of every type who became familiar with African conditions were publicly united in claiming that the suppression of the Arab slave trade, and hence the institution itself, was a top priority.[17]

By keeping the link between Islam and slavery constantly before the British public, the missionaries were partly able to combat the charge that it was a religion more suited to the Africans than Christianity. To accept this view was tantamount to accepting the argument that Africans were suited to be slaves, and although abolitionist enthusiasm had long since faded in Britain, such an attitude was still not respectable or practical, given the ending of the Atlantic slave trade by 1865, and the death-blow dealt to slavery in Cuba and Brazil by the

[16] Op. cit., pp. 87, 196–210, 480–7, 576.

[17] See, for instance, quoted in P.R.G.S., Samuel Baker during his expedition to central Africa for the Khedive of Egypt, XVIII (1874), pp. 52–4; Lieutenant V. L. Cameron during his search for Livingstone, XX (1876), pp. 304–25; Rev. Chauncy Maples of Universities (East Africa) Mission, II (1880), pp. 341, 349; R. W. Felkin on journey to Victoria Nyanza in ibid., p. 362; E. A. Maund on new British possessions in Central South Africa, XII (1890), p. 655; R. Burton, The Lake Regions of Central Africa (London, 1860, 2 vols.), II, pp. 340, 366–78.

simultaneous emancipation of the American Negroes. Hence it seemed quite reasonable to maintain that although Christian missions could only claim limited success in the Moslem-dominated parts of Africa, this was because of the superior spiritual doctrines which they were attempting to disseminate, and which could not be basically adapted to suit local needs without courting disaster. The conflict with Islam raised most dramatically all the queries which sceptics brought up about the value of missionary work anywhere, and in the last resort the defence could only be that the Christian message had a universal application, and that the missionary was fulfilling a mandate placed on all those who embraced its truth to 'Go . . . into all the world and preach the Gospel to every creature'.[18]

But in spite of the high moral ground taken up by the missionaries the conflict was a depressing one. Moslem lands had been traditionally neglected by Christian missions as unproductive fields of endeavour, but now a direct confrontation was unavoidable, not just in Africa, but in India also, where a prominent civil servant, Sir William Muir, had produced one of the first authentic studies of Mohammed in English.[19] A growing number of writers and scholars came to the defence of Arab culture.[20] Even supporters of the missionary effort complained about the misguided propaganda in which the 'Mahometan Africans are described for the benefit of the untravelled home-public, as sunk in every kind of debauchery, disgusting sin, and degradation'.[21]

The most famous apologist for Islam was the explorer Richard Burton, who maintained flatly that 'the Arab and the negro . . . combine better than the European and the black. El Islam, by forbidding impure meats and spirituous liquors, by enjoining ablutions and decent dress, and by discouraging polygamy and polyandry, has improved the African's *physique*, and through it, by inevitable sequence, his *morale*.'[22] The emphasis on the practical advantages of the Moslem faith was important, and Burton returned to it frequently. Since he held that the natives

[18] J.A.S., III (1865), p. ccxxvii; *London Missionary Society Chronicle* (1863), p. 193, (1965), p. 180; and Mark xvi. 15–18.

[19] Neill, *op. cit.*, p. 366.

[20] See, for instance, Pope Hennessy in *Journal of the Society of Arts*, XXI (London 1873), No. 1,067.

[21] *Africa Rediviva, etc., op. cit.*, p. 14.

[22] *A Mission to Galele, op. cit.*, II, p. 192.

of every part of Africa were without conscience, without thought for the future, and insensible to the force of reason, Christianity – with its refined spirituality – was seen as doomed to failure. The Arabs, however, had first concentrated on secular education, and then persuaded their converts to modify practices like cannibalism, ordeals, incest, murder of albinos, twins and other unacceptable offspring, witch-torture, and the like. Intermarriage between the two races was not frowned on, and was of great value to the black population. Whereas the Christianized African, confused by contact with an alien culture, became either 'sheepish and servile, or forward and impudent', Burton found the Moslem inhabitants 'kind, obliging, and manly in demeanour'. Furthermore, the latter had the very important advantage of approximating in appearance to European standards of beauty. He predicted a Moslem conquest of the African continent.[23]

The practical superiority of Islam over Christianity was repeatedly taken up by Victorians. Joseph Thomson, a geologist familiar with Africa and a popular speaker at anthropological and geographical society meetings, noted that in the Sudan the population had been improved in every way through Moslem influence, which had been used, for instance, against the corrupting liquor traffic, whereas the methods of Christian missionaries – who asked too much of prospective converts – made failure inevitable.[24] Similar praise came from the Rev. Alexander Mackay, himself a missionary in Uganda, who recognized that the Arabs had succeeded in Africa by their intrepidity, perseverance and determination, while Europeans had withdrawn at the first hint of danger, for all their preoccupation with the evils of the slave trade.[25] Of like mind was Anglican clergyman Canon Isaac Taylor, whose arguments about the futility of Christian missions (revolving round the assumption that Islam was better suited to the needs of the barbarous) were hotly rejected by the

[23] See Burton's *The Lake Regions of Central Africa, op. cit.*, II, pp. 325–6, 335; *Notes on the Dahoman* (London, 1865), pp. 124, 126; *Wanderings in West Africa* (London, 1863, 2 vols.), I, pp. 177, 180–1, 188, 210, 255; *Two Trips to Gorilla Land and the Cataracts of the Congo* (London, 1876, 2 vols.), II, p. 308.

[24] J.A.I., XVI (1887), p. 185; *Contemporary Review*, December 1886, pp. 876–83.

[25] C.M.I. XV (1890), p. 42; see also XIV (1889), p. 22.

C.M.S.[26] They may also be found in the writings of Winwood Reade, who maintained that Christianity was too abstract a religion to appeal to Africans, and approved – in terms identical to those of Burton – the improvements in their customs brought about by Islam; of F. L. James, who praised the Christian Mission at Sanheit in the Sudan for its efforts, but pointed out that its converts were unemployable – outcasts from their own people and shunned by the Moslems; and of schoolmaster Bosworth Smith; while explorer Harry Johnston made the point that Europeans and Moslems had equally enslaved and partially civilized the docile African.[27]

These works combined afford a depressing indication of the degree of prejudice entertained even by philanthropic Victorians towards the African. Christian missionary activity was opposed not, as missionaries sometimes alleged, because later nineteenth-century explorers and anthropologists were all atheists, still less because they were Moslems in the making, even though the Arab physique might be admired, as well as Arab culture and skill in commerce. Although doubts were raised by the admission of Islam successes – for surely a truly superior religion, such as Christianity claimed to be, would find ways of proselytizing effectively, even in Africa – the main implication was that an inferior religion, cunningly adapted, was best suited to inferior peoples.

The difference between the missionaries and their detractors was, in fact, frequently one of emphasis only, in spite of their mutual animosity and misunderstandings. The former believed that natives could be Christianized and radically improved; the latter that they could be improved, but not under the auspices of Christian missions which also insisted on transplanting unsuitable Western institutions and modes of behaviour to the forbidding African soil. Both agreed that there was ample room

26 *Times*, 8 October 1887.

27 W. Reade, *Savage Africa* (London, 1863), pp. 576–85, and *The African Sketch Book* (London, 1873, 2 vols.), I, p. 315; W. L. James, *The Wild Tribes of the Soudan* (London, 1884), p. 212; B. Smith, *Mohammed and Mohammedanism* (London, 1889), pp. 238–9, 258–9, 209–11; Sir H. Johnston, *British Central Africa* (London, 1897), p. 155, and *The Uganda Protectorate* (London, 1902, 2 vols.), II, p. 487; see also *Transactions of the Aborigines Protection Society, 1890–6* (February 1893), p. 331 (in future T.A.P.S.).

for improvement, and occasionally came together. Thus one finds among laymen a willingness to praise the work of missionaries if only these men will be practical and firm. Lugard, for instance, argued that the evangelist should steer clear of politics, avoid sectarian squabbles, and concentrate on providing industrial schools to train and discipline the young, writing off the older Africans as hopeless.[28] One sees here the very familiar prejudice – frequently advanced about the effects of missionary work in the West Indies – that Christianity might produce dangerous notions of democracy, of human equality, among those who should rightly be kept in a position of inferiority; this might be avoided, without embarrassment to the conscience, and with the blessing of modern science, through the implementation of separate labour codes and legal and educational facilities for colonized peoples. Here disguised is the white passion for strong government over 'savages'. Early missionary work in South Africa had been largely unsuccessful, wrote James Bryce in 1897, and he welcomed the new tendency to emphasize secular education and training shown, for example, by the Free Church of Scotland's mission at Lovedale, Eastern Province.[29] Some years earlier James Chapman had argued that missionaries in this part of Africa, though over-inclined to take the part of the natives, and demanding unreasonably quickly the abandonment of such practices as polygamy, could prove of value in persuading the black population to wear clothes, attend school and pursue agriculture more diligently.[30] Johnston, Reade and Speke all approved of the practical side of mission work while finding little enthusiasm for its spiritual aims.[31]

Part of the contempt for the African revealed in this context was the result of erroneous beliefs that throughout the continent, if Islam were excluded, he had produced no recognizable religion. (This view, of course, was shared by the missionaries themselves, who made it one justification for their activities.) It is important to emphasize that Victorian attitudes to primitive

[28] *Op. cit.*, I, pp. 69–74, 189–90, 223–4, II, pp. 453, 457–8, 483, 557–8.

[29] *Impressions of South Africa* (London, 1897), pp. 466–92.

[30] *Travels in the Interior of South Africa* (London, 1888, 2 vols.), I, pp. 129, 220–2, 290.

[31] Speke, *What Led to the Discovery of the Source of the Nile* (London, 1864), p. 366; Johnston, *The Story of My Life, op. cit.*, p. 162; and Reade, *The African Sketch Book, op. cit.*, II, pp. 123–4.

religions give us a far better insight into the religious atmosphere of Britain than of Africa, particularly in the apparent preference of anthropologists like Tylor for presenting savage beliefs as a product of irrational individual thoughts and fears rather than with reference to the tribe and its arrangements.[32] The use of the concept of 'survivals' by Tylor, McLellan, Spencer, Frazer and others to explain otherwise anachronistic elements of social life as simply relics of past states of society, has also been criticized for inhibiting 'the study of social facts as living items of culture'; for encouraging 'an antiquarian rather than a socio-logical attitude to contemporary society'.[33] And all too often a lack of sympathy with primitive religions denotes a crisis of belief or a contempt for organized ritualistic religion in the Victorian observer which made a detached understanding of the phenomena observed virtually impossible.

The late nineteenth-century anthropologists were not nearly so crude in their indictments of primitive religion as were often – for propaganda purposes – the missionaries, or the frequently ill-informed travellers and traders. Thus while Tylor noted that idol and spirit worship was necessarily contemptible to English-men, and that as 'a rule, the faiths of the higher nations have more and better moral influence than the faiths of the ruder tribes', he was also prepared to admit that the curiosity which seeks to explain the mysteries of existence was equally strong among men of every stage of development, and that 'even among savages the practical effect of religion on men's lives begins to show itself'.[34]

Rejecting the argument of Max Müller and other linguists that mythology was simply a 'disease of language' and hence fell within the domain of philology, Tylor, Huxley and Andrew Lang threw open the subject of religion to anthropological treatment. But the connections which they found between savage and modern belief (for instance, in spiritualism) constituted a clear attack upon the latter and an assumption of inferiority in the former. Both barbarous and civilized religions were a mass of curious notions and contradictions, remarked Edward Clodd; superstition, however, was to be expected of Africans,

[32] J. W. Burrow, op. cit., p. 239.
[33] Ibid., pp. 240–1.
[34] E. Tylor, op. cit., pp. 366–88.

but not of Victorians.[35] Sir John Lubbock expressed the more optimistic, Christian, version of this attitude when he wrote that 'while savages show us a melancholy spectacle of gross superstitions and ferocious forms of worship', taking in fetishism, nature worship or totemism, shamanism, idolatry or anthropomorphism, yet 'the religious mind cannot but feel a peculiar satisfaction in tracing up the gradual evolution of more correct ideas and nobler creeds'.[36] It was the anthropologist's critical attitude to religions both ancient and modern which provoked a series of three articles in the *Contemporary Review* by the Rev. W. W. Peyton, who argued that the modern scientist (he criticized particularly Spencer and Huxley) was usually too literal-minded and unsympathetic, even atheistical, to appreciate spiritual symbolism. For this the poetic faculty was required, and anthropology would only come into its own when it had 'brought some poetry into its task of explication, and . . . cast aside the theories that the human mind is the victim of a big hoax, and that the religions of the world are a cancerous growth or an overlaid germ which has been saved from death by the healing virtue of the unknowable in the latter half of the nineteenth century'. Anthropologists had dwelt too long upon the savage customs of ancient times, Peyton maintained, and had transformed words like 'polytheism', 'idolatry' and 'superstition' into terms of emotion and abuse, even though the theory of 'survivals' was meant to exclude both.[37]

The conservatism of primitive peoples in religious matters was noted by Haddon, and this was an important theme elaborated by other writers, with the devout among them taking the view that Christianity was the only religion of true progress, breaking down the integration of religion and society characteristic of tribalism.[38] (Islam, of course, was not deemed progressive,

[35] See J. W. Burrow, *op. cit.*, pp. 237, 256; A. Lang in *Custom and Myth* (London, 1884), *Myth, Ritual and Religion* (London, 1887), and *Anthropological Essays, op. cit.*, pp. 2, 7–8; A. Haddon, *History of Anthropology, op. cit.*, p. 140; A. Clodd, *op. cit.*, pp. 119, 122; and T. Huxley, 'The Evolution of Theology; an Anthropological Study', *Nineteenth Century*, XIX (1886), pp. 346–65, 485–506.

[36] *Op. cit.*, pp. 114, 116, 119.

[37] 80 (1901), pp. 213, 229–30, Article I; Article II, pp. 438, 445; Article III, p. 835.

[38] *The Study of Man, op. cit.*, pp. xx–xxi; and Cairns, *op. cit.*, p. 201.

demanding only a minimal alteration of social habits among its African converts.)

Victorians who passed judgement on primitive religions without the benefit of any scientific training or any prolonged acquaintance with African conditions were predictably less restrained in their comments. The standard attitude was contained in the *Encyclopaedia Britannica*'s entry on the Negro for 1884, which declared that the race had no religion beyond mere fetishism and ancestor-worship.[39] This was in fact supported by the more prejudiced contributors to the anthropological journals. John Crawfurd, for instance, believed that the spiritual beliefs of the Negro added up simply to witchcraft: he had produced no doctrines, no rituals, no temples, no prophets.[40] Elaborating such statements in his usual unpleasant manner, the explorer Samuel Baker was of the opinion that the races of the Nile Basin, whom he visited, lacked any belief in a supreme being, nor were their minds 'enlightened by even a ray of superstition. The mind is as stagnant as the morass which forms its puny world.' The inhabitants of the entire region, with the exception of Abyssinia, which had felt the beneficial effects of Christianity (though the writer was no friend of the missionary), were in fact little better than brutes, according to Baker, who doubted their common creation with the white races.[41] Burton, though he believed that African religions were so vague as not to be worth studying, spent some time condemning the evils of witchcraft and fetishism (polygamy he could condone),[42] while Harry Johnston, with reference to the Congo region, and Bryce, to the tribes of South Africa, argued that there was no evidence of belief in a deity, no moral significance in native religion, but only the worship of spirits and ghosts. Winwood Reade and the traveller T. V. Hutchinson maintained that it was useless to

[39] XVII (Edinburgh), p. 317.

[40] T.E.S.L., III (1865), p. 216.

[41] Quoted in T.E.S.L., V (1867), pp. 231, 236–8; *The Albert Nyanza, Great Basin of the Nile, and Explorations of the Nile Sources* (London, 1866, 2 vols.), I, pp. 241–2, II, pp. 316–17; *The Nile Tributaries of Abyssinia and the Sword Hunters of the Hamram Arabs* (London, 1867), pp. 504–7.

[42] Burton, *Lake Regions of Central Africa, op. cit.*, I, pp. 341–61, and *Two Trips to Gorilla Land, op. cit.*, I, pp. 89–105; Johnston, *The River Congo, etc.* (London, 1895), pp. 289–90; Bryce, *Impressions of South Africa, op. cit.*, p. 109.

appeal in the name of religion to peoples who were not yet humanized, who, as the former put it, lived 'a life without a future or a past, without hope or regret', and died 'the death of a coward and a dog, for whom the grave brings darkness, and nothing more'.[43]

On this subject the attitude of the missionary was unconsciously ambivalent; clearly the superiority of Christianity had to be proclaimed, but if the details of savage practices disclosed to the Victorian public were too highly coloured, then support funds might not be forthcoming. In addition, it was necessary not to frighten away prospective missionaries and their families. (These difficulties were quickly pointed out by cynics like James Hunt, who accordingly dismissed the evidence of missionaries as valueless for this reason.[44]) All too often, in fact, the missionary accounts are indistinguishable in their generalizations and sense of moral superiority from the verdicts of British travellers. Thus the C.M.I., though complaining of the 'ethnological folly' which destroyed 'all sympathy between Christ and the inferior races', when writing of the material attractions of Africa still gloomily concluded: 'In bold relief against the brightness of this land stands the blackness of her moral degradation. She lies, as of old, in the outer darkness.'[45] None the less, partially contradicting this statement, the journal went on to argue that the inhabitants of Africa were capable of receiving 'Christian education', had been unfairly singled out for 'the outpourings of prejudice and detraction', rejected the theory of polygenesis, and suggested that if the Negro was degraded morally it was simply 'owing to a prolonged condition of isolation and ignorance', which conditions might produce a similar state of affairs even among Europeans.[46]

The notion of the non-existence of African religion was often accepted; hence one finds Calcutta missionary Macleod Wylie laying it down that evangelical work in India was far more difficult than it was in Africa, because the 'poor Negro' looked

[43] Hutchinson, reported in T.E.S.L., I (1863), pp. 340; Reade, *Savage Africa, op. cit.*, pp. 257–8, 261.

[44] *Introductory Address . . . Before the Anthropological Society of London . . . 1863, op. cit.*, p. 12.

[45] I, No. 9 (1865), p. 264, and V, No. 1 (1869), p. 53.

[46] *Ibid.*, pp. 53–4, 57.

upon the missionary as his deliverer, and his mind was 'pre-occupied by no antecedent belief of any power or influence', whereas in India there were peoples 'whose religion presses on them . . . like the atmosphere'.[47] This view was supported by Charles New, but strongly challenged by the Rev. J. E. Carlyle, who maintained that the tribes of south and west Africa enter-tained a complex of religious beliefs, but he then went on to itemize 'its grovelling superstitions, its spiritual pretensions, its charlatanism, ventriloquism, and scarcely disguised fraud and legerdemain, [which] hold under . . . cruel control countless millions of the African race'.[48] Similarly, the Rev. S. W. Koelle, at pains to show the value of Christianity to Africans, presented a very uncomplimentary picture of the latter when he wrote that the Gospel was 'the true means of elevating the lowest, civilizing the most barbarous, and converting the most perverted, of our race'.[49] Difficulties and setbacks, however, revealing another aspect of missionary propaganda, were often blamed upon 'the evil influence of ungodly settlers';[50] and to counteract tales of the savagery of Ashanti and Dahomey, of the superstition, dishonesty and self-indulgence encountered by those stationed at the C.M.S.'s Nyanza, Yoruba and Niger Missions, these same missionaries – conscious that they might be spreading gloom at home – testified to the intelligence, perseverance, enterprise, respect for law, and general affability of the tribes they en-countered.[51]

Slavery and the slave trade provided further embarrassment for the missionary, who had to meet the assertions of laymen that these institutions were in fact devised by Africans before the coming of the Arab, proof positive of the barbarism of the black races. And at a time when the results of emancipation in America and Jamaica were being regarded dubiously by Victorians, it comes as no surprise to find a man like Baker, who

[47] *Ibid.*, VII, No. 6 (1856), p. 282.
[48] New, *op. cit.*, pp. 105–6; C.M.I., VI (1881), pp. 453–5, 463–5.
[49] C.M.I., VI, No. 3, pp. 59–60.
[50] *Ibid.*, VIII, No. 1, p. 19; reference to Yoruba mission.
[51] *Ibid.*, II (1877), p. 201, *ibid.*, p. 409; III (1878), p. 228, and VII (1882), pp. 100, 551, for unfavourable accounts; for favourable accounts, C.M.I., VIII, No. 9, pp. 194; X (1874), pp. 97–9; III (1878), p. 483; VII (1882), pp. 97, 541; XIV (1889), p. 66; and P.R.G.S. for Uganda Mission, XI (1880), p. 356.

put forward this argument, extending it to show that the African was useful everywhere as a slave, but when freed became 'a useless burden to the community, . . . a plotter and intriguer, imbued with a deadly hatred to the white man who had generously declared him free'.[52] Generally Christians left the delicate question of origins alone. It was enough to point out that Europeans had profited from and greatly extended the slave trade, and that 'Christianity is the grand agency for [its] . . . subversion. It brings the mercy and goodness of God into immediate contrast with the cruelty and iniquity of man. . . . Conferring spiritual freedom, it is repugnant to all slave-holding and slave-trading; and, in the influence it exercises over individuals and nations, must be hostile to, and eventually destructive of, all such tendencies.'[53]

Interesting for the light which it sheds upon missionary attitudes to race is the belief, strongly upheld by some groups, that the connection between Christian teaching and the setting up of expensive, white-controlled Churches in Africa should be played down, and priority given instead to the creation of an African clergy and the raising up of an indigenous Church. To some extent, all missionaries aimed to achieve the latter, of course, but the emphasis of the Anglican Universities Mission to Central Africa and the various C.M.S. ventures was unusually marked. Did this emphasis indicate that some evangelists, at least, entertained a genuine respect for African culture? This question is very difficult to answer. H. A. Cairns points out that, as far as the U.M.C.A. was concerned, determining factors were an admiration for the art of the possible, dislike of Africans apeing Europeans, and the superior educational attainments and tolerance of the missionary personnel, whose class background made them indifferent to the merits of industrial training for their converts.[54] The attitude of C.M.S. agents was rather more confused.

Great importance was attached among them to the study and recording of native languages.[55] Wide publicity was given to the

---

[52] *The Albert Nyanza, op. cit.*, I, pp. 293–4.
[53] Report on the Abbeokuta Mission, C.M.I., I, No. 9 (1850), pp. 196, 198.
[54] *Op. cit.*, pp. 219–21.
[55] C.M.I., I, No. 11 (1865), p. 324; IX, No. 12 (1884), p. 724.

views of Bishop Samuel Crowther, who, under the Society's auspices, in 1864 had become the first African bishop of the Anglican Communion, in charge of a purely African mission in eastern Nigeria. According to Crowther, it was necessary, in order to know his people, 'to mingle with them, study their mode of doing things, and yield to them according to their own idea for the time being'. Only then could one hope successfully to implant the teachings of Christianity.[56] Furthermore, native Churches would be comparatively cheap both to establish and run, their pastorates would face no language or social problems, and the European missionary would be able to spread his influence over a wider area. Climate alone, according to one report, made it inevitable that Africa must be evangelized 'by her own sable sons'.[57] The Society's Secretary, Henry Venn, was a particularly ardent spokesman for these ideas, arguing that if individuals of the superior race were always in charge, local initiative and interest would be stifled – again the Victorian fixation with self-help.[58] (In actually implementing his policy of short-lived European missions followed by self-governing and self-supporting native Churches, particularly in Sierra Leone, Venn was less than successful.[59]) As to motive, while pride might be at the back of European control, lack of manpower, an equally unedifying fact, partly explains the C.M.S. attitude: the latter, unlike the U.M.C.A., could not claim that its British recruits were particularly aristocratic. The importance of industrial education was, however, also played down – by Crowther, for example, and the Rev. Alexander Mackay, writing about conditions in Uganda, who emphasized that missionary education should be conducted '*on the basis of African peculiarities*', by properly trained teachers and without any thought of racial superiority.[60]

The vision of a Church in which African and foreigner could work together on a basis of real equality was missing; most

[56] C.M.I., I (1865), pp. 60, 162, 323–4; XXVI (1901), p. 304; and R. N. Cust in *The Times*, 31 January 1901.

[57] *Ibid.*, II (1866), p. 58, III (1871), p. 50.

[58] *Ibid.*, III (1867), p. 123.

[59] S. C. Neill, *op. cit.*, p. 260.

[60] C.M.I., III (March 1867), p. 74, XV (1890), p. 46; one of the Society's New Zealand missionaries – V, No. 12 (1854), p. 268 – remarked that the natives tolerated religious education so as to get the practical variety.

evangelists, in spite of concessions to African culture, seem to have accepted without question the inferiority of their converts. As Bishop A. R. Tucker of the C.M.S. Uganda Mission confessed, though he himself was guided by such a vision, it was not easy for the European missionary, 'with all his abounding energy and vitality, to sit quietly by and train the Native to do that work which in his inmost heart and soul he believes he can do so much better himself'.[61]

A brief consideration of missionary motives confirms this impression of race prejudice and pride. As we have seen, the primary justification for foreign missions in Africa, in the face of domestic critics and Arab opponents alike, was that they were – for Christians – an inescapable religious responsibility. But there were other defences. The missionary saw himself as beloved and admired throughout Africa. 'Goodwill, gratitude, and confidence in the minds of the native races towards England are the precious argosies which have been brought home to England by her missionaries,' wrote the Rev. John Mackenzie. Even the cynical Joseph Thomson, while critical of the methods of Christian missionaries, was prepared to admit that they had made the name of Englishmen revered and admired throughout the length and breadth of East Central Africa.[62] It was also argued that the missionary was carrying freedom – literally as well as from superstition – to Africa's inhabitants, performing 'for their dark-hued neighbours an office like that which in the later Roman Empire was entrusted to the *Defensor Civitatis*', and if powerless to prevent wrong at least able to ensure 'that the national conscience shall be stung to agony by the knowledge of its commission'.[63] As one-time missionary and British agent in Bulawayo J. S. Moffat put it, the evangelist was all too often occupied in applying plasters to sores irresponsibly made on the body of Africa by the white settlers.[64]

But, quite apart from their effects upon Africa, foreign missions had a lure for the Victorian seeking fame or adventure, or merely escape from a routine Church appointment in Britain.

[61] *Ibid.*, XXVI (1901), pp. 838–9.
[62] *Contemporary Review*, X (1874), p. 754, and LV (1889), p. 44.
[63] C.M.I., I (1850), p. 7, VIII (December 1872), p. 362; Thomas Hodgkin in the *Contemporary Review*, LXXIII (January–June 1898), p. 69.
[64] *Contemporary Review*, LXXX (July–December 1901), p. 323.

The C.M.S. was sensitive on the point that its training schools in Britain recruited mainly from the lower ranks of society, and that its missionaries might therefore be accused of ignorance or social climbing; but in default of better agents no other course was open to the society, and it felt that, anyway, simplicity of character and wants might be a positive advantage.[65] Particularly unattractive to the layman was the clear desire for martyrdom evident in some missionary writing: service to the 'benighted African' was just a means to this self-glorifying end, which the former thought might have been avoided with a little common sense, to the benefit of the evangelists' protégés. The frequency of missionary deaths certainly seemed to confirm the savagery of the African, as well as the African continent (much the more common cause of fatalities), in the minds of the Victorian public. Commenting on a spate of deaths and disasters in its foreign missions, however, the C.M.S., apparently undeterred, declared that 'the martyr's death is the Church's seed, and as the Saviour's word can never fail, there must be a bountiful harvest from this seed sown'.[66] The soldiers of Christ, it was predicted, would march on to victory over the graves of those who had fallen before them.[67] When appealing for recruits, English clergymen made frequent reference to the missionaries' 'sainted lives', 'true heroism and devotion', and 'conspicuous nobility'.[68] Anna Hinderer explained her reasons for undertaking religious work among the Yoruba thus: 'I longed to be a martyr, to be one of that "noble army"'.[69] The degree of risk was confirmed by outsiders (often impatiently); as Lord Northbrook, President of the Royal Geographical Society, stated – in his case, admiringly – missionaries in foreign countries must be prepared to carry their lives in their hands, and were bound to lose them rather than offer physical force in their own defence.[70]

There were other attractions, other temptations. With the exception of those few who attempted to show serious respect for African institutions, missionaries were often in danger of

[65] C.M.I., III, No. 9 (1867), pp. 258, 261–3.
[66] Ibid., XVII (1892), p. 357.
[67] Ibid., II, No. 5 (1866), p. 155.
[68] Ibid., XV (1890), pp. 440, 659.
[69] R. B. Hone (ed.), Seventeen Years in the Yoruba Country. Memorials of Anna Hinderer (London, 1872), pp. 4–5, 13.
[70] P.R.G.S., XI (1880), p. 414.

surrendering to the imperialist impulse, consequently becoming inseparably associated with the progress of British colonialism. It was difficult to follow the maxim that converts could be Christians, yet still 'remain Africans, on their own platform of human civilization', in face of a conflicting desire to implant British civilization in Africa, though Winwood Reade once sarcastically remarked that even if it were 'to be proved that Christian missions retarded civilization in savage countries, they would not cease to be popular. Devotion and enterprise are the two cardinal passions of mankind. In missions these are united, and are therefore irresistible.'[71] It should be said at once, however, that the relationship of missionaries to imperialism is a complicated one which, in this brief space, it is difficult to treat adequately.[72] But if – and this is not to be wondered at – British evangelists sometimes shared the cultural arrogance and expansionist attitudes of their lay contemporaries, it is necessary always to recall that Europe's contact with Africa at this time saw the latter uniquely disturbed and disorientated, and the former unusually confident and prosperous. In addition, a study of missionary literature conveys not merely an impression of pride and prejudice, but also a genuine humanitarianism, instances of heroism which was not wasted, and of genuine friendship between the races.[73]

On the question of the wider purpose of missionary enterprise, the *Spectator* commented in 1865 that the evangelists were taking not just Christianity to the natives, which would be difficult enough to grasp, but 'their own form of Christian civilization'.[74] The term 'civilization' apparently required no elucidation on this occasion, but the journal did attempt a definition some time later when reproving Matthew Arnold for his views on Victorians' repellent, *bourgeois* values. The British, avowed the *Spectator*, were brusque and unfriendly, but British colonies and Britain itself attracted immigrants on an unparalleled scale, all seeking 'the specialities of English civilization – order,

[71] *Africa Rediviva*, op. cit., p. 78, and Reade, *Savage Africa*, op. cit., p. 567.

[72] See below, pp. 153, 155–6, 213–14.

[73] See, for example, J. F. Ajayi, *Christian Missions in Nigeria, 1841–91* (London, 1965), and E. Ayandele, *The Missionary Impact on Modern Nigeria, 1842–1914* (London, 1966).

[74] 22 September 1866, p. 1,058.

justice, fair wages, utter tolerance'. The strangest fact in the history of the world was 'the attractiveness of the British civilization, in which millions of every race and degree of development have been and will be voluntarily submerged'.[75]

Although the missionary regarded immortal souls as the richest possession of Africa, wrote one, and was thus free from the profit motive which consumed the explorers, travellers and traders, it was necessary to guide the natives in a practical fashion, because – like children – they learnt quicker through their eyes than through their ears.[76] Given missionary difficulties with African languages, this statement is unimpeachable. But civilization as viewed by the evangelist often seemed to consist of industrial training, commerce, and 'decent' habits. Charles New, in the light of his experiences in East Africa, typified the missionary emphasis on education, improving the lot of women, developing natural resources and inculcating a love of work (and clothes) among the natives.[77] Although Livingstone advised against the missionary fulfilling the dual function of preacher and trader, he did urge that Britain ought to 'encourage the Africans to cultivate for our markets, as the most effectual means, next to the Gospel, of their elevation'. (The notion that diligence was next to godliness, central to the freedmen's aid movement, seemed equally applicable, in the minds of Victorian humanitarians, to the non-white populations of America, the West Indies, Africa – and indeed India.) Livingstone's belief that commerce was a most important aid to civilization – 'for it soon breaks up the sullen isolation of heathenism, and makes men feel their mutual dependence' – was warmly supported by his friend and correspondent, Sir Roderick Murchison, President of the Royal Geographical Society, who maintained that it was an object 'dear to all philanthropists'.[78]

In putting the case for missionary work to a public which it admitted was often hostile, the C.M.S. argued that the nations evangelized by Britain would prove to be her best allies and

[75] *Spectator*, 4 June 1881, pp. 730–1.

[76] Rev. E. W. Bickley, *The Central African Mission at Urambo and Lake Tanganyika* (London, 1894), pp. 3, 8–9.

[77] *Op. cit.*, pp. 90–1, 119, 129, 506.

[78] *Missionary Travels and Researches in South Africa, etc.* (London, 1857), p. 33, and *Last Journals, op. cit.*, I, p. 675; and Murchison in P.R.G.S., XXVII (1857), pp. cixvi, clxxi, 357.

commercial partners; missionaries, it believed, were 'the best heralds of civilization: they acquire and retain a footing where no other men can', thereafter making savages aware of new wants which the civilized nations could at once supply.[79] In order to advance the interests of humanity, civilization, and commerce, the C.M.S. was even prepared to support political intervention on the part of Britain in barbarous regions and unwilling to limit its activities to areas where British rule was established. The 'spiritual imperialism' of missionaries and the 'Anglo-Saxon imperialism' which could not tolerate breaking faith with treaties or abandoning African tribes to internecine strife and massacre were seen as 'absolutely at one'. Christ for the world and the world for Christ became a feasible proposition to some, and the views of men like Bishop Tucker of Uganda gained steadily in popularity. Tucker believed that 'nothing but an Imperial policy deliberately adopted and unswervingly pursued by our Church in her missionary enterprise can ever meet the necessities of the great heathen world in general, and of the dark continent of Africa in particular'. Such expansionist tendencies found best expression in the maxim adopted by the Student Volunteer Missionary Union of Great Britain in 1896 – 'The Evangelization of the World in the Present Generation'.[80]

It is possible to see anticipated here almost all the assumptions about the advantages of western civilization and Christianity, and the sense of moral responsibility as well as superiority implicit in British imperialism, which coloured the writing of non-philanthropic Victorians on the subject of race, and to which the rest of this chapter is devoted.

The pattern of prejudice which emerges is by now fairly familiar to the modern reader, and very much what our survey of British reactions to other primitive peoples would lead us to expect.

[79] C.M.I., X, No. 10, pp. 220–2.
[80] C.M.I., V (1880), p. 724, XIX (1894), pp. 8–9, 12; XXV (1901), pp. 840–1, XXI (1896), pp. 253, 260 – the C.M.I. was in fact sceptical about the Student Volunteers' slogan, in view of current contributions to missionary work, though the maxim was not meant to be taken absolutely literally.

The Victorian who actually visited Africa was struck first by what he saw: by the exotic natural geography of the continent and the strange aspect of its inhabitants. And almost always he was attracted to the former, repelled by the latter. The most offensive comments I have encountered (in an area where outspokenness is the rule) have been descriptive of the appearance of Africans in general, and Negroes in particular, and unfortunately now blind prejudice was given a veneer of respectability through the writings of the phrenologists and anthropologists. The Rev. Horace Waller, for instance, describing the Yaos of East Africa with obvious distaste, noted from the head shape that although 'they had just room for some brains, . . . certainly a phrenologist would say there was no depth of feeling, or kindness, or nobility in them'.[81]

It is impossible to explain the savagery of these comments simply with reference to national or European standards of beauty, though these were clearly important. The Western preference for a light skin was nothing new. An article in *Nineteenth Century* on varying ideals of human beauty noted, after a survey of Greek, Assyrian, Egyptian, Italian and English art: 'It is odd how persistently the supreme ideal of female beauty is fair.'[82] This observation, with only a few exceptions, applied equally for men. In English literature, Othello and Oroonoko notwithstanding, the most famous black beauty is not a human, but a horse. The colour of imported Africans, which made them easily identifiable as fugitives, had been one reason why they were preferred to white indentured servants in the American colonies from the seventeenth century, and by the eighteenth the terms 'white' and 'black' were being used to indicate free and slave (as well, incidentally, as Christian and pagan, civilized and barbarous, European and African).[83] Colour symbolism in the English language has been closely investigated, and it is a commonplace that by the Victorian period the word 'black' had come to evoke evil, sin and treachery, ugliness, filth and degradation, night and funeral mourning, while 'white', on the other hand, was associated with qualities like cleanliness, purity, beauty, virginity and peace (though it might occasionally have

[81] II (1880), p. 350.
[82] XLIX (January–June 1901), p. 127.
[83] W. Jordan, *op. cit.*, pp. 94–7, 108.

less reputable associations – as in whitewash, whited sepulchre, white-livered and white feather).[84] Although, following Fuller, the abolitionist set up the Negro as 'God's image cut in ebony', and Sierra Leone, the colony founded by ex-slaves, was described as a 'humble gem, "black but comely"', to the missionary Africa – in the standard terminology of the day – was still this 'darkest of dark lands', which only the light of Christianity could illuminate.[85]

It has been noted that from earliest times some English observers displayed a certain sophistication about the Negro's colour, developing a preference for jet blackness over the lighter tawny hues.[86] There is little evidence of this preference by the nineteenth century: in fact, the position had been exactly reversed, with the blackest peoples of Africa seen as the grossest. The C.M.I., while taking a very sensible attitude about the question of European conventions of beauty, and noting that long arms, short necks and other Negro characteristics were to be met with among whites, when they were equally condemned, was forced to admit that 'it is the hue of the negro's skin which, in the eyes of modern anthropologists, forms an inseparable obstacle to his admission within the pale of our species'. Only very occasionally was this view disputed.[87] This is perhaps surprising, in view of the debate about the inferiority and infertility of hybrids and half-castes, but the contradictory notion that only mulattoes had ever attained positions of eminence – whether in Africa, America or the West Indies – was still widely held.[88] H. A. Bryden, in his *Tales of South Africa*, recounted a romantic fable about the female head of a tribe in Umfanziland who, 'for a woman of native blood, was astonishingly fair'. The explanation of Mapana's beauty, it soon transpired, was that

[84] See H. Isaacs, 'Blackness and Whiteness', *Encounter*, XXI (1963), pp. 8–21; P. J. Heather, 'Colour Symbolism', *Folk Lore*, XLIX (1948), pp. 170–82.

[85] C.M.I., VIII (1872), p. 362; VI (1881), p. 150.

[86] W. Jordan, *op. cit.*, pp. 9–10.

[87] C.M.I., V, No. 1 (1869), pp. 54–5; for the view that colour was unimportant see A. F. Sim, *Life and Letters of Arthur Fraser Sim* (London, 1896), pp. 138, 156, and P. A. Bruce in *Contemporary Review*, LXXVII (January–June 1900), p. 284.

[88] See Burton, *A Mission to Galele*, *op. cit.*, II, p. 197, for a typical account of the infertility of mixed breeds.

'white blood ran strong within her'.[89] The normally critical
Burton commented favourably upon the fierce Fans of the
Gaboon because, with their fine features and pale complexion,
they were almost of European appearance.[90] For similar
reasons, Charles New was able to admire the Waknari tribe of
eastern Africa, Lugard to praise the Masai and the Wahuma,
R. J. Mann the 'Kaffirs' of Natal, Chapman certain South
African tribes, Thomson the M'henge and Waheke of East
Africa, and Baker and Johnston to admire the Gallas, described
by the latter as 'surely one of the world's handsome races'.[91]
A similar attitude was adopted by a great many of those whose
views were publicized in the British anthropological journals.[92]

Observers with some pretensions to knowledge deplored the
confusing of the Arab, Moorish, Abyssinian, Egyptian, Nubian
and Berber peoples of the north, those most frequently in contact with European influences, and 'the ignoble pure negro'.[93]
By unanimous consent, said the *Encyclopaedia Britannica*, the
African Negro occupied the lowest position in the evolutionary
scale, his abnormal length of arm, prognathism and lightweight
brain supposedly affording the best material for 'the comparative study of the highest anthropoids and the human species'.[94]
The Victorian fixation with the notion of a 'missing link' becomes
apparent here. The search for such a link, encouraged by the
skeleton findings in Java in 1891, became the theme of several
novels, including J. C. Rickett's *The Quickening of Caliban* and
J. P. Webster's *The Oracle of Baal*; each author, significantly,

[89] (London, 1890), pp. 162, 173.
[90] *Selected Papers on Anthropology, Travel and Exploration* (ed. N. M.
Penzer, London, 1924), p. 94.
[91] New, *op. cit.*, p. 356; Mann, T.E.S.L., V, p. 287; Lugard, *op. cit.*, I,
p. 340, II, p. 158; Baker, *The Nile Tributaries of Abyssinia, op. cit.*, p. 516;
Johnston, *The Story of My Life, op. cit.*, p. 138; Chapman, *op. cit.*, I, pp.
64, 74; Thomson in P.R.G.S., II (1880), pp. 117, 121; see also H. E.
O'Neill, consul at Mozambique, in *ibid.*, VI (1884), p. 724.
[92] J.A.I., XXI (1891–2), p. 359, Mrs French Sheldon on East African
tribes; XXVI (1896–7), p. 133, R. M. Connolly on Fans; XXVIII (1898–9),
p. 42, Captain G. Burrows on natives of Upper Welle District of the
Belgian Congo; T.E.S.L., V (1867), pp. 91–2, Colonel C. P. Rigby on the
Somali.
[93] Burton, *A Mission to Galele, op. cit.*, II, p. 191; Reade, *Savage Africa,
op. cit.*, pp. 511–16.
[94] XVII, p. 316.

made his 'missing link' essentially Negroid in type.[95] Accordingly, Burton depicted the Negro facial angle in terms of 'quasi-gorillahood', and believed that Negroes would not eat ape on account of its likeness to themselves.[96] (The simian characteristics of the race were also stressed by Harry Johnston.)[97]

Burton's description of the typical Negro itself highlights what the average Victorian disliked:[98] 'In his lowest organization he is prognathous, and dolicho-kephalic, with retreating forehead, more scalp than face; calfless, cucumber skinned, lark-heeled, with large broad and flat feet; his smell is rank, his hair crisp and curly.' Only the familiar criticism of the African mouth and nose are omitted from this offensive passage.[99] Those who wished to present an attractive picture of Africa to the Victorian public maintained, like Livingstone, that the Negroid features popularly believed to be universal were fortunately rare, except on the west coast; elsewhere there were, in fact, many light-coloured Africans with 'finely-shaped heads, straight or aquiline noses and thin lips, magnificent forms, with small feet and hands, graceful limbs; and barn-door mouths, prognathous jaws and lark-heels are never seen'.[100] Sir Harry Johnston and Richard Burton also made the comforting point (which has been much used by modern racists, and to which we shall return when considering India) that the Negroes themselves admired those of their number who possessed the lightest skins, though it has never been determined how far this was due to a simple adoption, through prolonged contact, of European standards.[101]

Nineteenth-century sensibilities were also, of course, assaulted by African nudity, which was generally associated with a

[95] Published, London, 1893 and 1896.

[96] Burton, *Wanderings in West Africa, op. cit.*, II, p. 86; *Two Trips to Gorilla Land, op. cit.*, I, p. 164.

[97] *The Uganda Protectorate, op. cit.*, I, pp. 471, 473.

[98] Burton, *Wanderings in West Africa, op. cit.*, I, p. 178.

[99] For condemnation of these features see, for instance, Reade, *Savage Africa, op. cit.*, p. 516, and for other condemnations of the Negro appearance F. L. James, *op. cit.*, p. 79, J. Chapman, *op. cit.*, I, p. 63, C. New, *op. cit.*, pp. 275, 331, J. Thomson, P.R.G.S., II, pp. 728–9.

[100] *Missionary Travels, op. cit.*, pp. 291, 379; *Last Journals, op. cit.*, I, p. 230; and P.R.G.S., XVIII, pp. 260–1.

[101] Johnston, *British Central Africa, op. cit.*, p. 394; Burton, *A Mission to Galele, op. cit.*, II, p. 189.

deliberate shamelessness and immodesty, clothes, conversely, being synonymous with decency and civilization.[102] Occasionally it seems clear that there was little enjoyment for a convention-bound Victorian male in contemplating naked 'savages'. Reade's curt comment – that 'nothing is so moral and so repulsive as nakedness. Dress must have been the invention of some clever woman to ensnare the passions of the men' – rings true.[103] The pendant breasts of the older woman particularly offended, as a reminder perhaps of frequent child-bearing, itself presumed to be the product of unrestrained sexual licence. It was in line with British disapproval of the precocity of African children that the beauty of the young females should be emphasized; all too soon retribution – in the form of ugliness and obesity – overtook these hot-house flowers.[104]

Very possibly Victorians were writing with a view to what would please the women they left behind. Certainly reticence was always expected of the missionary. Latin was resorted to when the subject-matter was indelicate, and the response to over-enthusiastic accounts of native charms was frigid – as witness the condemnation of the details given by Speke of his convivial encounters with tribal chiefs.[105] But sometimes even those who took exception to nudity were forced to admit that the African was not improved by the assumption of a motley array of cast-off – usually unwashed – European garments, and that lack of clothes might be the result of a dearth of suitable materials or a sensible response to the hot, wet climate.[106] And from time to time one comes across passages of lyrical description in the 'noble savage' tradition. Thomas Baines, who as an artist (working in Australia, the Cape, and various other parts of Africa) had perhaps unusual licence, reported that the figures

---

[102] Burton, *The Lake Regions of Central Africa*, *op. cit.*, II, p. 337; *Wanderings in West Africa*, *op. cit.*, II, p. 18; Livingstone, *Missionary Travels*, *op. cit.*, p. 276; New, *op. cit.*, pp. 356–7, 391, 467; Lugard, *op. cit.*, I, pp. 366, 488; Johnston, *British Central Africa*, *op. cit.*, p. 419.

[103] *Savage Africa*, *op. cit.*, p. 546.

[104] *Ibid.*, pp. 244, 447; New, *op. cit.*, p. 95.

[105] J. McQueen, *The Nile Basin* (London, 1864), pp. 98–9.

[106] Burton, *Wanderings in West Africa*, *op. cit.*, II, p. 16; Chapman, *op. cit.*, II, p. 202; E. Clodd, *op. cit.*, p. 74; P.R.G.S., V (1895), p. 43, testimony of W. A. Eckersley (railroad surveyor) on east Mashonaland Negroes; J.A.I., II (1881–2), pp. 340–1, Bartle Frere.

of the Matabele women 'were in many instances sufficiently perfect to serve [a sculptor] . . . as models of beauty'.[107] Thomson, not a man disposed to flowery tributes, condemned the customs of the Masai but admitted: 'They are the most magnificently modelled savages I have seen or even read of. Beautifully proportioned, they are characterized by the smooth and rounded outline of the Apollo type.'[108] Writing of the inhabitants of the upper Congo, Harry Johnston compared them to 'antique statues cast in bronze', a compliment which could scarcely have been paid to most of the British travellers and traders in Africa, who very often returned home with gaunt features, yellow skin and falling hair.[109] The pathetic – often no doubt ludicrous – appearance of the Victorian abroad was generally ignored, however, though Lugard did have the grace to admit, in the course of a flattering description of the aristocratic-looking north and east African tribes, that 'To me there was a sense of incongruity in the obeisance of these courtly old savages [Yoruba], in their robes of snowy whiteness or of brilliant colours, before a dirty, tattered, and unimportant-looking individual like myself'.[110]

Lack of modesty on the part of Africans was equated, in the mind of the European, with lack of sexual restraint: publicly deplored, often privately envied. This supposition was, in turn, linked up with a number of basic assumptions about the character of 'savages', and especially the Negro. Excessive sexuality was related specifically to a tropical climate, nudity, superior physical equipment and 'a remarkable absence of personal self-respect' in the African.[111] Professor A. H. Keane, after identifying four main racial groups in the world – Negritic (black), Mongolic (yellow), Amerind (red or brown) and Caucasian (white) – noted that the most characteristic qualities of the first-named were sensuality, sloth, passion, affection and lack of self-respect.[112] Other anthropologists confirmed this view.

[107] *The Northern Goldfield Diaries of Thomas Baines* (London, 1946, 3 vols.), ed. J. P. R. Wallis, I, p. 76.

[108] P.R.G.S., VI (1884), p. 696.

[109] *The River Congo, op. cit.,* p. 289, and H. A. Cairns, *op. cit.,* pp. 3–4.

[110] P.R.G.S., VI (1895), p. 222.

[111] *Encyclopaedia Britannica*, XVII, p. 319.

[112] *The World's Peoples. A Popular Account of Their Bodily and Mental Characters, etc.* (London, 1908), pp. 13, 16.

Groom Napier, for instance, who followed the standard British three-fold classification of man, defined his Ethiopian group as basically passionate (his other group divisions were moral or intellectual), while in the scheme of Robert Dunn the Negro was characterized by a love of enjoyment and an abnormal susceptibility to excitement.[113]

In this context allegations of the childishness of African peoples were brought into play (an alternative comparison was between Africans and young animals); hence to some extent their behaviour might be comprehended, if not condoned. The character of the African also justified the treatment he met with from Europeans. Thus Lionel Phillips, who described the South African 'Kaffirs' as a 'complex mixture of treachery and cunning, fierceness and brutality, childlike simplicity and quick-wittedness', concluded that such people 'require a master, and respect justice and firmness: generosity is a quality they do not understand'.[114] Burton, writing of the typical tribesman of the eastern part of the continent, concluded: 'He seems to belong to one of those childish races which, never rising to man's estate, fall like worn-out links from the great chain of animated nature.' The minds of such creatures could not 'escape from the circle of sense'; they were the slaves of impulse, infantile passion and instinct – wilful, lazy, and improvident, selfish, irreverent, impatient, and without conscience; 'Retaliation and vengeance are . . . their great agents of moral control'. Singing, dancing, eating, fighting and love-making were their occupations; honest labour was despised, cultivated pursuits unknown, and the women were, if anything, less restrained in their lusts than the men.[115] Burton explained this partly in terms of the hot, humid climate, something to which Baker also gave emphasis, and which he saw as conducive to immorality and hampering both missionary work and European colonization. Even more than Burton (and like Johnston and Lugard), he believed that the needs and behaviour of Africans were akin to those of

[113] Groom Napier, J.A.S., V (1867), p. clxi; Dunn, T.E.S.L., III (1865), p. 20.
[114] *Contemporary Review*, LXXVIII (July–December 1900), p. 768.
[115] *The Lake Regions of Central Africa, op. cit.*, II, pp. 280, 324–31, 335, 337–8, 376; *Zanzibar: City, Island and Coast* (London, 1872, 2 vols.), I, p. 379.

animals.[116] According to Speke, their most characteristic qualities were susceptibility to mirth, garrulity, self-indulgence, impulsiveness and inconstancy – the African was 'a grown child, in short'.[117]

Other travellers bore witness to the 'greediness, caprice, superstitiousness and dishonesty of the African character', to the prevalence of sexual promiscuity and the degradation of women.[118] In view of the Victorian reverence for a virtuous wife, it is not surprising to find men like Winwood Reade condemning the 'children of nature' who instructed their female offspring in vice from the earliest age and sold them for marriage as soon as they reached puberty; who made their wives mothers when they were scarcely girls, treated them as slaves when they were women, and killed them when they were old. However, Reade proceeded to point out that, in his experience, Africans were affectionate rather than lascivious, and that while they could not control their passions, neither did they show any refinements of vice. This was also the view of Harry Johnston, who agreed that while mental advance was halted in the Negro at puberty, because he was unfortunately endowed 'with more than the usual genetic faculty', Europeans were more prone to viciousness and obscenity.[119] It was widely believed that the institution of marriage in the European sense – apparently the only sense acceptable – was unknown: F. R. Statham contemptuously remarked (completely oblivious of the full significance of lobola)

[116] *The Albert Nyanza, op. cit.*, I, pp. xxiii–v, 48, 241–2, 287–8, II, pp. 310, 315; Lugard, *op. cit.*, I, pp. 74, 285–6, 309–10; Johnston, *British Central Africa, op. cit.*, p. 472 (also 441).

[117] *Journal of the Discovery of the Source of the Nile* (London, 1863), pp. xxviii–xxx.

[118] Richard Thornton on East Africa in P.R.G.S., XXXV (1865), pp. 20–1; Burton, *Lake Regions of Central Africa, op. cit.*, I, pp. 334, 337, and *Two Trips to Gorilla Land, op. cit.*, I, pp. 100–7; Johnston, *The River Congo, op. cit.*, pp. 274–5, 289; Reade, *Savage Africa, op. cit.*, pp. 255, 257–8, 542, 549–50, 555, and in A.R., II, p. 337; *The African Sketch Book, op. cit.*, II, p. 359; Livingstone, *Missionary Travels, op. cit.*, p. 226; and *Last Journals, op. cit.*, I, p. 300; Bryce, *op. cit.*, p. 116, 452–3; Drummond, *op. cit.*, pp. 57, 59, 65; Dr H. Blanc on 'Natives of Abyssinia', J.E.S., VII (1869), p. 298; T.E.S.L., III (1865), pp. 88–90, V (1867), p. 82, T. V. Robins on inhabitants of Niger Region.

[119] Reade, *op. cit.*, pp. 46, 51, 244, 261, 545, 547–8; Johnston, *British Central Africa, op. cit.*, pp. 408–9.

that the Zulu's existence revolved round cows and marriage, but that the latter's importance derived solely from the fact that it was a means to obtaining the former.[120] Early marriage and polygamy were seen as an insult and a burden to African women, even though they did not seem to be aware of their shame, and supposedly sailed through repeated childbirth without pain. The second institution might serve a useful purpose, it was sometimes acknowledged, among savages whose only friends were their blood relations, when favouritism was not shown, where women faded quickly and sterility and high child mortality rates were a problem, and when the number of wives was limited by economic circumstance.[121] Precipitate missionary efforts to destroy polygamy were even, on occasion, deplored.[122] Another objection to African family practices was prompted by a belief that native children were sometimes neglected, sometimes rendered precocious beyond their years, and sometimes murdered because they had the misfortune to be born with a deformity.[123] However, it was at times admitted that those youngsters who were allowed to grow up were carelessly but affectionately treated, by European standards.[124]

The question of miscegenation was approached with greater difficulty in regard to Africa than, say, America or the West Indies. Although unofficial liaisons were made between the races in the latter, intermarriage was made difficult by the barrier of slavery, both before and after its abolition. In Africa, especially before the settlement of large numbers of white women, the possibilities and temptations for the pioneer – excluding the evangelist – were very much greater. The missionary could not

[120] F. R. Statham, *Blacks, Boers and British. A Three-cornered Problem* (London, 1881), p. 152. See also G. Burrows in J.A.I., XXVIII (1898), pp. 39–40, and R. M. Connolly in J.A.I., XXVI (1896), pp. 143–4.

[121] Burton, *Two Trips to Gorilla Land, op. cit.*, I, pp. 79–80, and *Wanderings in West Africa, op. cit.*, II, p. 28; Reade, *Savage Africa, op. cit.*, p. 576; Chapman, *op. cit.*, pp. 220–2; New, *op. cit.*, pp. 66–7, Mrs French Sheldon in J.A.I., XXI (1892), p. 360; H. Johnston, *British Central Africa, op. cit.*, p. 441; Sir J. Lubbock, *op. cit.*, pp. 99–100.

[122] Bishop Colenso, reported in J.A.S., III (1865), p. cclxxiv.

[123] Sir J. Lubbock, *op. cit.*, p. 99; Reade, *Savage Africa, op. cit.*, pp. 244, 555; J. Crawfurd in T.E.S.L., IV (1866), p. 218.

[124] Johnston, *British Central Africa, op. cit.*, p. 417; Mrs French Sheldon, J.A.I., XXI (1882), pp. 361, 372; Rev. J. MacDonald on South African tribes, J.A.I., XX (1890–1), p. 139.

take advantage of the opportunities which presented themselves for acquiring an African wife or mistress, had racial or religious scruples been no barrier. He was closely watched by those financing him at home, so that secret relationships were out of the question or would bring recall, and it was widely felt that during the early years of missionary work in Africa women were out of place, because of the financial strain and potential for distraction which a family involved. (The attitude of the C.M.S. with regard to India was somewhat different, as we shall see.) Even when missions were well established, the aim of founding a native Church with Europeans acting as itinerant preachers and supervisors made marriage difficult, while the high rate of missionary deaths threatened, in the case of the married evangelist, to saddle the home society with the cost of supporting widows and orphans.[125] The missionary who contemplated taking an African wife would also have to contemplate bringing her back to England, since the climate made permanent residence unattractive to all but the most hardy until towards the end of the century.

The obvious way out – taken, in fact, by many missionaries, despite criticism – was to marry a white woman before leaving England. Missionary wives were virtually the only important female element in the British contact with Africa in the period before the 1890s. Those who made out a case for the married missionary emphasized that the degraded position of the native women – a problem difficult for men to tackle – might be improved through female influence and the example of monogamous marriage; the wife might also relieve her husband of much menial work about the mission. Unfortunately, however, the presence of such women also served to strengthen the racial pride of the missionaries, who often became more concerned about imaginary threats to their wives and daughters from African males than for improving the lot of African women.[126]

For the traveller, the trader and adventurer in particular, the situation was far different. 'Going native', which Lugard so deplored in the missionary, might for the layman be an advantage, not a crime;[127] and although it is doubtful whether notions of white superiority were ever surrendered, miscegenation

[125] C.M.I., III, No. 9 (1867), p. 258.
[126] H. A. Cairns, *op. cit.*, pp. 59–62.   [127] *Op. cit.*, I, p. 74.

undoubtedly took place, with evidence of willingness on both sides in, for instance, central Africa.[128] Veiled acknowledgement of this state of affairs is to be found in the admission by Britons that those tribes who had most contact with the coast and with the whites were frequently the most degenerate,[129] such contact bringing not only overtures from men interested in casual sex, which could be bartered like any other commodity, but an introduction to gin and other European liquor, a trade which sparked off a vigorous campaign by the Aborigines Protection Society in 1895, following the disclosures of Joseph Thomson and other travellers and administrators, and the publication by the Society of its 'Poisoning of Africa Papers'.[130]

The justification of liaisons between black and white, if such were thought necessary, might be – and this was Burton's argument – that the association of a coloured woman with a European was regarded by her tribe as an honour.[131] However, H. H. Johnston, although aware of the popular travellers' view that the white man was regarded not as a mere mortal, but as a spirit by the African,[132] denied emphatically that in consequence the latter wished to encourage adulterous relations between their wives and white men, or intercourse between unmarried native women and whites.[133] John Crawfurd, for the anthropologists, confirmed that the Negro, like the lower animals, was opposed to the mixture of different races and groups.[134] (A degree of interbreeding, particularly for the Negro, was regarded as beneficial, if unlikely.[135]) Separation of the races was already strictly maintained in South Africa by the end of the century. Writing in 1897, Bryce noted with astonishment the strong feeling of dislike and contempt, almost hostility, shown by the bulk of the whites to their black neighbours, which he believed was the legacy of slavery, native wars, and the bigotry of poor whites. Physical aversion was also important, and Bryce predicted that the races were unlikely to marry or mingle, even

[128] Cairns, *op. cit.*, pp. 55–7.
[129] Mrs French Sheldon in J.A.I., XXI (1892), p. 361.
[130] T.A.P.S., 1890–6, 1895, pp. 493–503, 535 f.
[131] *Wanderings in West Africa, op. cit.*, II, p. 24.
[132] See, for instance, H. Drummond, *op. cit.*, p. 97; Chapman, *op. cit.*, pp. 268, 285.
[133] *British Central Africa, op. cit.*, p. 412.
[134] T.E.S.L., III (1865), pp. 102–3.   [135] P.R.G.S., VI (1884), p. 724.

though intermarriage was legal in other British colonies, and such mixing would improve the African stock, because the 'stronger [race] despises and dislikes the weaker'.[136]

The predisposition to generalize about the African character was as strong as the inclination to generalize about savage religions. As the *Anthropological Review* put it, with regard to both the landscape and inhabitants of the continent, 'a sad monotony prevails'. All savages were alleged to resemble one another physically, and were also believed to possess 'no more individuality than other creatures which live in herds: examine a thousand minds, and you will always find the same cunning, curiosity, sloth, and . . . good-natured dishonesty'. The article concluded, interestingly: 'We have tasted the ennui of civilization . . . and the ennui of savage life. We must own that we prefer the former.'[137] Those who believed this to be true would necessarily develop a certain scepticism about the excitement and value of African exploration (though it must be remembered that the London Anthropological Society was right at the centre, in 1866, of the famous debate begun by Hunt over the Negro's place in Nature, which was encouraging the view that one Negro, at any rate, was just like any other.)[138] Thus Winwood Reade warned that the traveller could only hope to find minor variations among the numerous tribes, according to climate and local circumstances, and Harry Johnston maintained that Negroes all looked much alike.[139] However, Reade himself also made the point that generalization – for instance, about African treachery – often stemmed from the fact that 'all Africans are supposed to be negroes, and that which is criminal is ever associated with that which is hideous', and Livingstone in the same vein complained of 'bogiephobia', in which the patient believes everything horrible, if only 'it is imputed to the possessor of a black skin'.[140]

[136] *Op. cit.*, pp. 444, 458, 460.   [137] A.R., IV (1866), p. 144.
[138] See J.A.S., II (1864), pp. xv–liii; A.R., I (1863), pp. 388–91; *Memoirs Read Before the Anthropological Society of London*, 1863–4, I (1865), pp. 3–49.
[139] Reade, *Savage Africa*, op. cit., p. 241; Johnston, *British Central Africa*, op. cit., p. 393.
[140] Reade, *op. cit.*, p. 551; Livingstone in P.R.G.S., XVIII (1873–4), p. 259.

The more discriminating traveller, such as Thomson, deplored the tendency to represent all Africans as blood-thirsty savages and cannibals, and suggested such a description was ludicrous when applied to a gifted people like the Yoruba.[141] None the less, the tendency – and particularly that of thinking of every African as a Negro – remained, even if it did not manage to diminish the prestige of the traveller (although contributing to an often-cynical note in the Press: 'Africa', said the *Daily Telegraph*, 'is a bore').[142] The response, for instance, to Livingstone's crossing of Africa, or to the anti-slavery activities of Baker and Gordon in the Sudan, is evidence of this. So, too, are the self-congratulatory meetings of the Royal Geographical Society, where respected explorers bore witness, in the words of Thomson, to the 'boundless sense of liberty' and adventure engendered by their profession, and African travel was depicted as calling into constant exercise the endurance of a Stoic, the self-command of a Red Indian, the meekness of a saint, and the constitution of a camel.[143] Britons were believed to possess these attributes in abundance, together with 'that stout English quality which we call pluck – a quality which rises higher the more difficulties increase'. Bartle Frere joined in the chorus of applause, adding two more characteristics – keen powers of observation and a determination not to be beaten; all the above virtues, he believed, were more common among Englishmen of every age than in most other races, but he did add that this very abundance of natural gifts was 'apt to give us a dangerous contempt for artificial culture'.[144]

This was a crucial admission, for by the late nineteenth century race as a biological concept had been confused with a variety of cultural characteristics, such as religion, and, since Victorians held the African cultures, whose functioning they did not properly understand, to be inferior, the linking of race and culture led to a wholesale condemnation of African tribes as racially inferior. As Livingstone expressed it:[145] 'I think that

---

[141] P.R.G.S., VI (July–December 1895), p. 223.

[142] 17 August 1866.

[143] P.R.G.S., XIV (1869–70), President's Address, pp. 689–90, and Thomson in *ibid.*, II (1880), pp. 306, 727.

[144] *Ibid.*, XVIII (1873–4), p. 579.

[145] *Ibid.* (1873–4), p. 262.

we . . . travellers have of late years got too much into the novel-writer's habit of turning up the whites of our eyes, and holding up our paws, as pious people are all thought to do, whenever we meet with any trait not exactly "Europe fashion".' At a conference on the native races of the British Empire held at the anthropological institute in 1886, Sir James Marshall, speaking of the West Coast of Africa, deplored the contempt shown by Europeans for native culture, and argued that from his own experience the best chance of success lay with white administrators who treated Africans 'with consideration for their native laws, habits and customs, instead of ordering all these to be suppressed as nonsense, and insisting upon the wondering negro at once submitting to the British constitution, and adopting our ideas of life and civilization'.[146] Bartle Frere, when discussing the relations between civilized and savage peoples, was not content simply to notice the decline of the latter, according to the laws of Nature, but was at pains to point out that much depended on the policies adopted by the superior power. Britain had little to boast of to date in her dealings with South African natives (though Frere was confident of the long-term value of British civilization), having persecuted the Bushmen and deprived them of game, introduced the Hottentots to measles, smallpox, venereal disease and liquor, and undermined the power of the chief, so producing anarchy among the Bechuanas.[147] Similarly, journalist Edward Dicey complained that the Baker–Gordon campaign in the Sudan had destroyed slavery, but also the old social order; nothing new was set in its place, thus paving the way for the success of the Mahdi.[148]

In spite of a dangerous tendency to generalization and chauvinism, there remained, in fact, some Victorians who were conscious of their own intellectual shortcomings, and unwilling to present the inhabitants of Africa as the victims of an undifferentiated savagery. There were aspects of African life – and even, occasionally, of African character – which evoked respect. As one would expect from those who prided themselves on their pluck, Britons admired (perhaps unconsciously feared) the warlike individual or tribe. The eighteenth-century concept of the

[146] J.A.I., XVI (1887), p. 180.
[147] Ibid., II (1881–2), pp. 325, 327, 331.
[148] Nineteenth Century, XV (January–June 1884), p. 376.

noble savage was dead, as witness the comment of the *Saturday Review* that the qualities of the savage life were 'a combination of the seamy side of the gamekeeper's profession and of the gypsy's business, with a considerable dash of the discomforts of a pauper lunatic asylum without keepers'[149]. But traces of the mythology remained. When South African difficulties were debated, frequent reference was made to the fact that although black military strategy might not be worth much, the natives were 'otherwise fine people' and 'formidable antagonists'.[150] In an article on the fighting power of Negroes, the *Spectator* paid the Zulus, the Masai, and the Matabele the supreme compliment of suggesting that they might, with advantage, be drafted into the British Army, while, according to a South African correspondent of the *Contemporary Review*, many of the natives would 'compare favourably with ourselves'.[151] A poem published by the Aborigines Protection Society in 1879 on the capture of Cetewayo contained the following defence:[152]

> Savage, brutal, if you will;
> He fought for home, a hero still.

Bishop Colenso's tribute to Cetewayo's nobility of character and influence over his people was supported by the A.P.S., and the society was prepared to argue for his restoration to power, as was the *Spectator*, dismissing as nonsense the allegations that he was merely 'a black brute'. (Such support the *Saturday Review* condemned as imbecile.)[153]

British travellers were no less attracted than the Press to Africans with a reputation for valour. The Masai were admired by Thomson, not just as a good-looking tribe, but as a conquering race, while Colonel J. R. L. MacDonald, journeying to northern Uganda, was impressed by the Karamojo – frank,

[149] 20 April 1878, pp. 490–1, and see Tylor on this, *op. cit.*, p. 408.

[150] *Saturday Review*, 2 March 1878, p. 270; *Fortnightly Review* (Frederic Mackarness), XXXVI (July–December 1884), p. 400.

[151] *Spectator*, 12 November 1898, p. 680; *Contemporary Review*, LXXIX (January–June 1901), p. 324; but see also *Spectator*, 29 October 1898, p. 592, for view that Africans will offer no military threat until able to organize a European-style army.

[152] T.A.P.S. (1878–82), pp. 182, 266.

[153] *Ibid.*, p. 481; *Spectator*, 24 June 1882; *Saturday Review*, 24 May 1884, p. 666.

outspoken, excellent raiders and fighters – and by the Swahili and Sudanese troops accompanying him.[154] To Bartle Frere the 'Kaffirs' were admirable because they could not be enslaved – the apparent inability of the Negro to resist oppression, including slavery, was one of the most potent reasons in the nineteenth century why he should be despised.[155] Those tribes who enslaved or raided their neighbours, though criticized by Britons as a bar to their own influence, were infinitely preferable to those who allowed themselves to be victims. Since the English believed that 'there are races which must lead, and races for which it is good . . . to follow', and were themselves unable to avoid 'the intoxication of the military spirit', in South Africa and elsewhere, it was no doubt soothing to the conscience to find evidence of such an 'imperial' quality among those they enslaved.[156] There are clear signs, with regard to Africa, of the uneasiness about militarism which the Jamaica revolt so strongly aroused. The explorer Stanley, in particular, was criticized for unnecessarily resorting to force in his encounters with hostile tribes during the famous search for Livingstone.[157] Missionaries themselves sometimes seemed to expect military aid when faced with native opposition, even in regions outside British control, and they were censured for this.[158] The publicity given to African ferocity helped to quell such arguments. Hence one commentator on V. L. Cameron's journey across Africa admitted that he had initially thought Cameron too mild to deal with the 'roughs and savages' he was likely to meet there, and Samuel Baker defended Stanley's methods as necessary in a country where the only law respected was that of force.[159] Even missionaries displayed a sneaking admiration for the bold

---

[154] P.R.G.S., VI (1895), pp. 215–16; *The Geographical Journal*, XIV (1899), pp. 136–7, 148.

[155] *Proceedings of the Royal Colonial Institute*, XII (1880–1), p. 142 (in future P.R.C.I.); for condemnation of the Negro as easily enslaved see, for instance, J. Crawfurd in T.E.S.L., III (1865), p. 103.

[156] *Spectator*, 7 February 1880, p. 168. See also Bryce, *op. cit.*, p. 118, for defence of European actions in South Africa on the grounds of the warlike activities of the Matabele.

[157] P.R.G.S., XXI (1876–7), pp. 59, 62–3.

[158] See, for instance, *Contemporary Review*, LXXVIII (July–December 1900), p. 870. Louise Brown on 'Missionaries and Governments'.

[159] P.R.G.S., XX (1875–6), pp. 327, 48.

and successful, as can be seen, for instance, in Livingstone's description of the warlike Chief Sebituane of the Makololo.[160]

African cruelty and indifference to suffering, however, were deplored; the ordeal, mutilation, summary executions, these were not to be equated with the martial spirit, but were blamed upon tribalism, or slavery, or – as General Gordon saw it – African susceptibility to groundless fears. 'All craven creatures are cruel,' he declared, 'and when terror has overwhelmed masses of men, they are indistinguishingly furious and bloodthirsty.'[161] Even African folklore glorified force and cunning rather than milder qualities, a book of Zulu nursery tales reviewed by the *Spectator* revealing 'a graphic and almost cruel imagination', and none of the 'innocent wonder . . . the golden visions' of Western stories in the same idiom.[162]

In addition to admiration for the valour of certain African tribes, some evidence of African industrial, political and artistic skills was admitted by Victorians, who did exempt the groups concerned from the usual complaints about Negro ignorance and sloth. The potential of the African as a free labourer was not quite so hotly debated as that of the American or West Indian Negro, as no commercial group yet exerted the political influence of the planters of these two areas; but since, as Captain Younghusband put it, most pioneers in Africa were motivated by a belief that they could 'make money more rapidly there than elsewhere', this was not an unimportant consideration.[163] For this reason, E. A. Maund spoke out against the much-admired and warlike Matabele. Killing and slavery were to be replaced by civilizing influences: just what these were was soon clear. 'We English,' he said, 'colonise native territories to make them pay.' Khama's people were, in fact, rapidly becoming civilized – in other words, peaceful, and prepared to take British goods.[164] Where commerce was not the spearhead of civilization, it was 'the handmaid of progress', an equally potent force and one to which, it was believed, savage races were indifferent.[165]

[160] *Missionary Travels, op. cit.*, pp. 86, 90.
[161] Quoted in C.M.I., XII (1887), p. 71.
[162] 8 September 1866, p. 1,003.
[163] *South Africa of To-day* (London, 1898), pp. 113, 123–4, 146.
[164] P.R.G.S., XII (1890), pp. 650–1, 655.
[165] Lord Aberdare in *ibid.*, VI (1884), p. 196.

To S. W. Baker Christianity followed civilization, commerce introduced it, and Britain as 'the great chief of the commercial world', obviously had 'the force to civilize. She is the natural colonizer of the world.' Cotton, coffee and sugar might be grown to advantage, and exchanged, with ivory (not to mention gold, palm oil, ground-nuts, pepper, ginger and gum), for European products, once the African could be induced to labour steadily.[166] In Sierra Leone, believed Burton, if only laws of labour – however offensive in England – had been adopted, the world would have been spared the sight of decaying villages, and a population anxious for gentility, but incapable of sustained agricultural labour, trusting simply 'to the allurements of a petty, demoralizing trade'.[167] Here is a passage clearly indicative of the preoccupation with 'steady industry' which, as the *Spectator* stated, 'in English opinion, is the single virtue, except reverence for white faces, to be demanded of black men'. And because the native did not need to work, reported Professor Drummond gloomily, Africa was a nation of the unemployed.[168]

In this context a number of tribes were, however, singled out for praise. Winwood Reade, generally a most hostile observer, actually noted that all Africans have 'a grand commercial faculty', and predicted that a society for the diffusion of practical knowledge would have a great success among them, though it would doubtless not appeal to Christian missionaries. He also observed that even the cannibalistic, half-naked Fans were skilful blacksmiths and boasted a metallic currency.[169] The Wanyamwesi, wrote Speke, were an industrious people, cultivating extensively, keeping herds, trading, manufacturing cloth and iron.[170] Chapman bore witness to the excellent metal production of the Makololo, and the Bechuana women in general (though the strenuous manual work which African

[166] *The Albert Nyanza, op. cit.*, I, pp. xi–xiv; II, pp. 309–10, 314. See also *Ismailia, A Narrative of the Expedition to Central Africa for the Suppression of the Slave Trade, Organized by Ismail, Khedive of Egypt* (London, 1874, 2 vols.), II, pp. 505, 509.

[167] *Wanderings in West Africa, op. cit.*, I, pp. 222, 265.

[168] *Spectator*, 24 June 1882, p. 824, and Drummond, *op. cit.*, p. 56.

[169] *Savage Africa, op. cit.*, pp. 551, 576; *The Story of the Ashanti Campaign* (London, 1874), pp. 5–6; see also *The African Sketch Book, op. cit.*, p. 426.

[170] *Journal, op. cit.*, pp. 84–5.

females were expected to perform did not as a rule call forth favourable comment), and even Bryce, whose account of the native races of South Africa was disparaging, admitted that the European mine-owners might complain of the indolence of their black employees, but added that in their natural state the 'Kaffirs' had not been savages 'of a low type', for they tilled the soil efficiently and could work in metals.[171] While deploring the lack of cultivation and morals among the Wanika, Charles New admitted that in all that concerned the affairs of everyday life they were as keen and sharp-witted as Europeans, and Lugard was impressed by the honesty and intelligence of the Kikuyu, by their extensive agriculture and well-contrived system of irrigation, suggesting that Carlyle's famous denunciation of Negro laziness was much exaggerated, even though the African might require considerable supervision.[172] As Sir H. Johnston paid tribute to the considerable gifts of the Ibos as farmers, smiths and producers of fabric, so the Baganda were praised for their fine houses and roads, attractive metal goods and thriving trade.[173]

The study of African languages did not develop sufficiently or in such a way as to change the low opinion of native culture entertained by most Victorians. Attempts to classify man according to language have already been noted, together with their effects on the debate over polygenesis and monogenesis, and on the Aryan controversy. We have also seen that the structure of African languages led British writers to condemn them as complex, but inferior, as did the absence of abstract terms, of concepts of a single, beneficent deity in the Christian idiom, and of a recorded literature, except in the Arab-dominated parts of the continent. The Negro was regarded as particularly backward in these respects.[174] Thus H. B. Evans, a surgeon

---

[171] Chapman, *op. cit.*, I, pp. 172, 206, 268–9; Bryce, *op. cit.*, pp. 105, 108.

[172] New, *op. cit.*, pp. 94–5; Lugard, *op. cit.*, I, pp. 327–8, 472–3.

[173] Johnston, *The Story of My Life, op. cit.*, p. 204; A. M. Mackay – *Pioneer Missionary of the Church Missionary Society to Uganda* (by his sister, London, 1898), pp. 106 f.; see also J. MacDonald on 'East African Tribes' in J.A.I., XXII (1892–3), pp. 118–19, and Mrs French Sheldon on same, XXI (1891–2), p. 388; R. M. Connolly on 'Fans', XXVI (1896), pp. 148–9; and G. Burrows on the Congo Region (the Mangbetton) in XXVIII (1898), p. 44.

[174] See above, pp. 11–15.

who had spent much of his life in the West Indies, exclaimed: 'How forcibly does language illustrate the characteristics of a people? We cannot for an instant compare the jabbering jargon of the Negro to the bold, forcible cosmopolitan tongue of the Anglo-Saxon. An Englishman can imitate the nigger dialect, but the Negro cannot speak English.'[175]

British missionaries have, in fact, recorded their own intellectual shortcomings and frequently inhibiting inability to master the dialects of their prospective converts. (This was one of the reasons for encouraging the activities of native evangelists of perhaps otherwise unimpressive educational attainments.) It is also clear that their studies brought to some members of this group an unusual awareness of the beauty and subtlety of African languages, and were in themselves an important contribution to nineteenth-century philology.[176] Nevertheless, when Robert Cust, a prolific writer on African and missionary subjects, produced his *Modern Languages of Africa* in 1884, he introduced it with the words: 'Here is something in the place of nothing. The book may be thrown into the abyss and form a platform on which a better edifice may be raised.' His work was accordingly well received by the *Saturday Review* as fulfilling a real need, even though Cust was thought to be a compiler rather than a philologist in his own right, and was criticized for over-emphasizing the linguistic achievements of British missionaries.[177] Important work continued to be produced, both by missionaries and laymen, but at the turn of the century Cust, while welcoming the foundation of an institute at King's College, London, to study South African vernaculars, still emphasized the inadequate state of European knowledge.[178]

Notwithstanding slow progress in this area, and despite a willingness to generalize about the Negro's barbarism and inability to learn (on the lines that he had produced no literature, no written language, no architecture, art, music or religion of merit), some Victorians found aspects of African culture which

[175] *Op. cit.*, p. 26.

[176] See Curtin, *op. cit.*, pp. 392–7; Cairns, *op. cit.*, p. 33; Ajayi, *op. cit.*; S. W. Koelle, *Polyglotta Africana, etc.* (London, 1854); R. N. Cust, *A Sketch of the Modern Languages of Africa* (London, 1883, 2 vols.), I, pp. 2–3, 22, 24, 26, 30, 33, 34–5, 38, 65, 67–8, 70, II, pp. 457–8.

[177] *Saturday Review*, 14 June 1884, p. 785.

[178] C.M.I., XXVI (1901), p. 304.

they could admire.[179] Unusually enthusiastic was the verdict of Pope Hennessy, one-time Governor of Sierra Leone, that the Africans of the interior, 'possess natural ability, a love of knowledge, a capacity for culture, a taste for music and poetry, a generous and hospitable disposition, patience and even cheerfulness under long-suffering, gratitude, honesty in their dealings, and a strong domestic love'. Hennessy did, however, confirm Burton's complaint that the young men in Sierra Leone were disinclined to go into agriculture and manufacturing if clerkly or other high-status occupations were available.[180] His impression of the educational progress being made in the colony was confirmed by an inhabitant of eighteen years' standing, Robert Clarke, and R. J. Mann, a superintendent of education in Natal, dismissed the familiar charge that black children could not learn or mature beyond the age of puberty.[181] (Speaking at an anthropological society meeting in 1863, Professor Wilson rightly pointed out that this theory would never be proved as long as so few opportunities existed for Africans to pursue education after that age.[182])

Although he believed that in general level of intellect the Bantu were below the Red Indian, the Maori or the Hawaiian, Bryce did admit that the 'Kaffirs' spoke a highly developed language and had a sort of customary law, and that since the process of systematic native education was not long under way, the situation was always changing. He also pointed out – and this is most unusual – the talents of exceptional individuals like 'the Zulu Tsaka, the Basuto Moshesh, and the Bechuana Khama' and 'the eloquent missionary Tiyo Soga'.[183] Livingstone's admiration of Sebituane has already been noted, and the exploits of Cetewayo, of Susi and Chuma, and the achievements of Mtesa, King of Buganda from 1857–84, Chief Lobengula of the Matabele, or Mirambo, the Wanyamwesi chief, could scarcely

[179] For typical condemnations of African intellectual abilities see T.E.S.L., IV (1866), p. 215 (Crawfurd); Burton, *The Lake Regions of Central Africa, op. cit.*, II, p. 337, and *Wanderings in West Africa, op. cit.*, I, p. 175; Johnston, *British Central Africa, op. cit.*, p. 472.

[180] C.M.I., IX (1873), pp. 241, 243, 246. See also C.M.I., V (1869), p. 53, on the African's ability to learn.

[181] T.E.S.L., V (1867), p. 295, II (1863), pp. 331, 335.

[182] A.R., I (1863), p. 390.

[183] *Op. cit.*, pp. 80, 440–1.

be ignored, though as a rule Victorians concentrated on tribes rather than individuals.[184] Equally concerned with the potential of the South Africa natives, Bartle Frere was impressed by the intellectual power of the 'Kaffirs', which he believed exceeded that of most Indian races, and even acknowledged the extraordinary aptitude for both music and drawing among the Bushmen and the Hottentots.[185]

In short, while Victorians might deplore the slave trade and the aggressive policies of tribes like the Matabele and the Masai (though admiring the tribes themselves), it was impossible to deny that kingdoms like that of Buganda and tribes such as the Wanyamwesi had real claims to civilization by their own definition (which was the only one in question). The discoveries of anthropologists alone, claimed Tylor, had refuted the popular notion that savage life observed no rules by providing detailed studies of marriage and kinship laws; had shown that public opinion was a force even among savages, who also widely frowned upon manslaughter and theft within the tribe.[186] The Rev. Henry Johnson, a native preacher attached to the C.M.S.'s Upper Niger Mission, could thus in 1882 write in the Society's magazine without fear of occasioning surprise that the Yoruba showed a respect for lawfully constituted authority which could not be surpassed by the most civilized nations.[187] Similarly, Harry Johnston had to modify his general view of the African's intellectual potential with a tribute to the sensibility to beauty, graceful dancing and skill in music of the inhabitants of the Upper Congo, and Winwood Reade softened his criticisms with an admission that the Mpongwe of the Gaboon were refined, perceptive and clever, and that Dahomey's elaborate system of government was a monument to human ingenuity as well as cruelty.[188] Tylor himself, according to his disciple, Lang, by

[184] H. A. Cairns, op. cit., pp. 116–18; though frequently the despotism, of African chiefs was deplored: see, for instance, C.M.I., XII (1887), p. 70, on Mwanga of Uganda, and X (1885), p. 713.

[185] P.R.C.I., XII (1880–1), pp. 140–1.

[186] Op. cit., pp. 402, 405, 408, 412–13.

[187] C.M.I., VII (1882), p. 541; and see similar comments about elaborate systems of law among tribes of East Africa in P.R.G.S., V (1884), p. 635 (H. E. O'Neill's testimony).

[188] Johnston, The River Congo, op. cit., p. 289; Reade, Savage Africa, op. cit., p. 74, and The African Sketch Book, op. cit., II, pp. 221–5.

his comparisons between savage and civilized societies had gone
a long way towards demonstrating 'that man, in Byron's words,
is "always and everywhere the same unhappy fellow", whatever
the colour of his hair or skin, and the shape of his skull'.[189]

But if the polygenesists and racists no longer dominated anthropology by the end of the nineteenth century, and there are signs
that some Victorians could distinguish one African tribe from
another, and admire some aspects of African culture, the
generalizations and the extremism had not been without effect.
Even the arguments of evangelists and opponents of slavery and
the slave trade posed enormous dangers for the future of
tribalism and traditional ways in Africa. It may be argued that,
in fact, the missionaries who tried to preserve these ways were
just as wrongheaded as those who could not comprehend, and
contemptuously destroyed them. (Certainly in time their efforts
brought conflict between missionary and settler, which strengthened the persistent undercurrent of hostility towards the
former in the British Press.) However, well before the period of
direct European control over Africa, which began in the 1890s,
some missionaries clearly shared the imperialist outlook which
was never absent during Victoria's reign, though occasionally
muted. Thus although the C.M.I. was to express doubt in 1887
that any beneficial impression was 'being made upon Africa by
the multitudes of adventurers now swarming into it' – a 'dele-
terious commerce rather than substantial benefit for the Negro
bids fair to be the result' – appeals for funds in the journal from
the 1850s, as we have seen, had stressed the benefits which would
accrue to British trade from an extended evangelical effort.[190]
According to the Rev. W. W. Peyton, missionary work was 'the
most successful experiment and experience of evolutionary
principles going on before our face', and it was an easy step
from seeing Christianity as ordained to vanquish inferior
religions to believing Christian peoples were meant to overcome
savages.[191] (The admiration which missionaries as well as laymen
expressed for the strong, conquering tribes of Africa is a further
indication of their acceptance of social Darwinianism.)

[189] *Anthropological Essays, op. cit.*, p. 6.
[190] C.M.I., XII (1887), p. 665.
[191] *Contemporary Review*, LXXX (July–December 1901), p. 839.

Victorians of every shade of opinion also managed to convince themselves that the destruction of the slave trade would clear the way for the development of a legitimate commerce, and that as long as Britain operated only unofficial 'spheres of influence' in Africa, these desirable changes could not be effected. We see again the British admiration for strong government, which led Speke as early as 1863 to advocate for Africans a government 'like ours in India', to rescue them from the perpetual warfare produced by polygamy and slavery.[192] Burton's almost simultaneous condemnation of the slave trade likewise depended on the assumption that this was the chief cause of tribal warfare, a barrier to population increase and trade, and both men deplored the corrupting influence of 'semi-civilized' European arms and liquor merchants.[193] Burton, however, was dubious about the effectiveness of the British occupation of West Africa, but partly, one feels, because it was only half-hearted – for years, he commented in 1876, travellers had been advising English statesmen not to despise the cunning of barbarians and not 'to attempt finessing with Asiatic or African'.[194] Writing about the same time, Winwood Reade declared that the Ashanti War of 1874 had been caused by the weakness of the British Administration, which had inhibited trade and given the natives 'encouragement, hope, and provocation'. He looked now to see a strong government in the new protectorate.[195] Among missionaries, even before the 1880s, there are similar pleas for an extension of the British Empire, as witness Charles New's proposals for the establishment of a colony in East Africa, modelled on Sierra Leone, and intended as a haven for those Africans freed by Britain from slavery.[196]

The actual economic prospects for 'good' commerce driving out 'bad' do not seem to have concerned Victorians as much as the immorality – commonly accepted even outside Exeter Hall –

[192] *Journal, op. cit.*, pp. xviii, xxii. See also R. A. Freeman, *Travels and Life in Ashanti and Jaman* (London, 1898) for admiration of strong governments in Africa.

[193] *The Lake Regions of Central Africa, op. cit.*, II, pp. 340, 366–78, and *Selected Papers on Anthropology, op. cit.*, p. 105; Speke, *op. cit.*, p. xx.

[194] *Two Trips to Gorilla Land, op. cit.*, I, pp. viii, x–xi.

[195] *The Story of the Ashanti Campaign, op. cit.*, pp. 409, 417; see also *Savage Africa, op. cit.*, pp. 293–300.

[196] New, *op. cit.*, p. 506.

of slavery, and the slave and liquor trade. The prestige attached to owning domestic slaves as servants or concubines, for instance, was seldom considered as a factor making for the continuation of the institution. This emphasis can clearly be seen in the Archbishop of Canterbury's condemnation of the sale of gin to Africans because 'Uncivilized people are weaker to resist, and are unable to control, temptations of this kind', and the complaint of *The Times* that the traffic led to 'the demoralization and degradation of the races concerned'. (Furthermore, this evil trade was able to threaten with extinction all beneficial forms of commerce.[197])

There were dangers here for humanitarians, and especially the missionary. If, indeed, the slave trade was curtailed through British action and occupation of Africa, would the process of occupation or the effects of 'legitimate' commerce be entirely beneficial? And if the morals of the early traders and trading companies were sometimes questionable,[198] could it be taken absolutely for granted that these would improve with a change of government, or that Christian values would be upheld? It was alarmingly true, as Burton had predicted, that above all 'the world still wants the black hand'. Enormous tropical regions still awaited the clearing and draining operations which were necessary to make them fit habitations for civilized men, and which only the 'lower races' were physically suited to perform.[199] The dilemma produced by the extension of British power during the 1880s and 1890s may be demonstrated by the debate over the treatment of the native peoples of South Africa. Although Englishmen frequently congratulated themselves that their actions never indicated the degree of race prejudice that was to be found among the Boers,[200] a bitter debate developed between those (mainly the settlers) who believed that philanthropists at home were sentimental meddlers out of touch with the realities of native conditions, and those – epitomized by the Aborigines Protection Society – who felt that the Europeans had usurped native land, confined civil and political rights to whites, had

[197] T.A.P.S., 'Poisoning of Africa Papers', IV (1890–6), pp. 1–2, VII, p. 4.
[198] *Ibid.*, p. 336 (1893).
[199] *Two Trips to Gorilla Land, op. cit.*, II, p. 311.
[200] Chapman, *op. cit.*, I, pp. 123–4; Bryce, *op. cit.*, p. 443; *Spectator*, 12 January 1901, p. 41.

savagely repressed native rebellions, exacted forced labour, and were infused with 'a profound contempt for all coloured men, and an inordinate self-esteem'.[201] The settler counter-attack concentrated on the improved physique of the natives who worked voluntarily in the European mines (for they were denied liquor and received regular food); on the benefits received in the way of education and security from intertribal warfare; and stressed the necessity of breaking up tribal lands in the interests of 'civilized progress'.[202] The debate was essentially insoluble, and there grew up among some Englishmen a fear, well founded as events were to prove, that the new imperialism might produce a realization of Dryden's bitter verse:

> Thieves, pandars, pallards, rogues of every sort,
> These are the manufactures we export.
> And these the missioners our zeal has made,
> For, be it with my country's pardon said,
> Religion is the least of all our trade.

[201] For settler defence see *Saturday Review*, 2 March 1878, p. 270; Bartle Frere, T.A.P.S. 1878–82, pp. 182–3 (1879), p. 341 (1881); and for criticism of settler treatment of natives see *ibid.*, 1878–82, pp. 239–40, 252–3, 268; *Spectator*, 6 November 1880, p. 1,409; *Contemporary Review*, LVI (July–December 1889), 'South Africa and the Aborigines Protection Society', pp. 347–56; J. McDonnell, 'The Question of the Native Races in South Africa', *Nineteenth Century*, XLIX (January–June 1901), pp. 901–2.

[202] See J. S. Moffat in *Contemporary Review*, LXXIX (January–June 1901), pp. 320–1, 324; Statham, *op. cit.*, pp. 133, 138–9, 143–4 (see also his *South Africa as It Is* (London, 1897)); Bryce, *op. cit.*, pp. 439–40.

V

The Indian Empire

> The natives respect us, they acknowledge that we make them rich and prosperous, that we are very just and very well meaning; but they cannot bear us. There is no mistake about this.
>
> *Saturday Review*, 1868.[1]

A SENSE of failure and a sense of achievement are combined in much of the British writing about India after the revolt of 1857, which, according to one London journal, ended the romantic age in Anglo-Indian relations and began a new era of realism and caution.[2] The Mutiny created a sense of outrage in Victorian Britain (in the same way that the Jamaica rebellion was resented) because it seemed to indicate a gross ingratitude on the part of the Indian people. Moral and political reforms begun in the 1830s and designed to create an efficient administration had instead alienated princes and landowners, alarmed traditionalists, and offended the religious – and particularly caste – sensibilities of the native troops, provoking two major revolts before 1857. A motley coalition of the discontented during that year took advantage of the mutiny in the Bengal Army (triggered off by the introduction of a new cartridge said to be greased with cow or pig fat, the first offensive to the Hindus, the second to the Moslems), but were united by little except opposition to the consolidation of British power. Accordingly the revolt was suppressed without serious difficulty, but with great bloodshed and bitterness.

[1] *Saturday Review*, 28 March 1868, p. 403.
[2] *Ibid.*, 14 July 1877, p. 41.

The immediate result of the Mutiny was a further spate of administrative reform: Company rule was ended and power assumed by the Crown. The government of India was conducted from the British end partly through a Council in London, established in 1858, but mainly by the Secretary of State. The Central Legislative Council in Calcutta was enlarged in 1861, and Indian representatives were included among its non-official members; however, the Council continued to have no control over the Viceroy and his Executive Council. Legislative councils were established in the provinces, and by the 1890s there was a limited admission of the principle of election. After 1860 the system worked fairly well and the country was peaceful, although the North-West Frontier continued to cause apprehension and induce heavy expenditure, as did the Second Afghan War in 1879 and the annexation of Burma in 1885.

In the long term the Mutiny served to confirm the mutual distrust which had been growing up between rulers and ruled for over twenty years. The ensuing study will be concerned with Victorian attitudes to Indian religious beliefs and civilization generally, to the country and its people, and the principal sources used are books and articles by missionaries, travellers, administrators and soldiers, and the British Press. The contrasting viewpoints revealed in the Anglo-Indian and purely English material brings out, even more clearly than did the African survey, the potential for conflict between the stay-at-home philanthropist or philosopher and the settler groups. Equally, the contrast between secular and missionary activities is even more apparent.

The Mutiny of 1857, a monstrous shock to the complaisant British community in India, was hailed by missionaries both there and in Britain as a sign of Divine displeasure. In an article entitled 'National Sins the Sources of National Calamities', the *Church Missionary Intelligencer* explained the revolt as the result of temporizing with false religions and neglecting Christianity, out of a mistaken belief that this was the easiest way to ensure loyalty in the native.[3] Those who maintained

[3] C.M.I., VIII, No. 11 (1857), pp. 243–53. For a similar view see Rev. Dr J. Cumming, *The Great Tribulation; or, The Things Coming on Earth* (London, 1859), p. 348.

that disaster could have been averted had the religious scruples of Moslem and Hindu been respected – specifically, over the question of the cartridges – were entirely mistaken, the journal argued, proceeding to deny any revolutionary implications to Christianity, even if the natives had falsely believed that it was to be pressed upon them, had been, as Argyll put it, in 'a genuine religious panic'.[4] On the contrary, 'Christianity strengthens lawful authority, concurs with it in action, makes the man more loyal, more submissive to his superiors, more attentive to their commands'.[5] Supposing the road to success had lain in recognizing the caste system and other traditional Indian practices, the Christian could never hope to prosper by allying himself with 'irrational despotism' and 'gross superstition', but relied instead upon 'moral superiority': as a foreigner, uninvited, neither elected nor placed in power by the people, this was the Englishman's sole justification for being in India.[6]

Fundamentally, what all missionaries objected to was the policy adopted towards Christianity during the period of East India Company rule (the Company being hostile to their entry from fear that the disturbance caused by the preaching of the Gospel might threaten its always uncertain control of its dominions). From the end of the eighteenth century, however, the effects of the Evangelical Revival in England were making themselves felt as far afield as India.[7] The first Anglican bishop arrived at Calcutta in 1814; Bishop's College was established there to train young men for the ministry; the Baptists established an important mission and college at Serampore, not far from Calcutta, and began the herculean task of translating the Bible into the main languages of the East. In 1816 the Church Missionary Society sent a party of evangelists to Travancore, southern India, where they founded what is now the Society's college in Kottayam, and much earlier had established itself at Tinnevelly, on the other side of the Western Ghats, while the

[4] *George Douglas, Eighth Duke of Argyll . . . 1823–1900. Autobiography and Memoirs* (ed. Dowager Duchess of Argyll, London, 1906, 2 vols.), II, p. 81.

[5] C.M.I., VIII, No. 10 (1857), pp. 217, 227. See also IX, No. 4 (1858), pp. 73, 75.

[6] *Ibid.*, IX, No. 1 (1858), pp. 21–2, and XII, No. 3 (1861), p. 68.

[7] S. Neill, *op. cit.*, pp. 262–80.

London Missionary Society enjoyed some success at Mayiladi, Southern Travancore. By 1835 the Bishopric of Madras had been constituted, and valuable educational work undertaken by Britons in Madras, Nagpur, Bombay and elsewhere.

Official Company restrictions on missionary enterprise in India were lifted in 1833, and the C.M.S., the Baptists, and the Wesleyan Methodists accordingly extended their activities. But old attitudes were difficult to break down, and the task of the evangelist in the vast, disturbed states of India was daunting. By 1851, in the whole of India, there were still only 339 ordained missionaries, who, with their wives, constituted a force of about 600 in a country with a population of 151 million. Christians were reckoned at 91,092, most of whom were concentrated round the Anglican missions in Tinnevelly and the London Missionary Society area of South Travancore.

The administration had contributed to this dismal state of affairs most obviously, missionaries felt, by refusing – in the face of steady pressure – to introduce religious instruction into Government schools, although with the adoption of Sir Charles Wood's Educational Despatch of 1854, grants-in-aid were given by the Government to private institutions involved in higher education, with the hope of releasing public funds for the basic education of the largely rural masses. (Some criticism of this decision had been made by those who feared political repercussions, and their arguments were to seem most convincing after 1857.[8])

The Indian Mutiny thus paradoxically provided missionaries with an opportunity for arguing against religious neutralism, on the grounds that it had failed to enlist the gratitude of the native population, while their critics maintained that the departure from strict neutralism in 1854 had offended Indian traditionalists and led directly to the uprising three years later. Well before the Mutiny the C.M.I. had noted with pleasure the decline of the old belief that 'The Natives of India were . . . so religious and moral in their own way, as fully to exonerate us from attempting to innovate on their prejudices and habits', a belief 'endangering the loss of our empire in India'. It was recognized by 1850, in fact, that 'Christianity best consolidates

[8] M. Edwardes, *British India, 1772–1947* (London, 1967), pp. 116, 121.

a conquest'.[9] Although the inadequacy of Indian missions and the abominable character of native practices were deplored, confidence was expressed in the ultimate decline of the Hindu religion in the face of 'civilization and trade'. By 1857 this confident note was muted.

There is no evidence that the mutineers especially directed their violence against Christians or missionaries; as far as can be estimated, nearly forty missionaries, chaplains and members of their families and twenty Indian Christians died in the course of the outbreak, which was virtually limited to the Ganges Valley. This was pointed out in India by representatives of the C.M.S., who argued that had missionaries been permitted access to the native regiments there would have been 'Christians in the ranks; and had there been, this vast insurrection could never have been organized'. It was hoped that the Government would see the wisdom of this argument, and also be persuaded to abandon its mistaken policy of secular education, which was simply 'training up a race of infidels'. The grants-in-aid were deemed so insignificant as to constitute no real breach in this policy. Furthermore, Catholics and Protestants had together been at work in India for some 350 years without provoking an uprising comparable to that of 1857.[10] If the missionary was guilty of interference with the native population, then so, too, was the Government, the latter having departed from its avowed neutralism in religious matters by legislation curbing polygamy, *suttee*, and infanticide, although the view of Sir John Lawrence, who rose from service in the Punjab to be Viceroy in the 1860s, was in fact heartily supported – namely, that 'Christian things done in a Christian way . . . will never alienate the heathen'.[11]

In India the missionary's position was even more awkward than it was in Africa. After many years of labour, little apparent progress had been made. The grasp of Hinduism, Islam and Buddhism, religions more fully developed, in the eyes of Victorians, than the 'mere fetishism' of African tribes, had if anything been strengthened by internal reform movements;

[9] C.M.I., I, No. 11 (1850), p. 243.
[10] C.M.I., VIII, No. 9 (1857), p. 214, and Appendix, pp. 4, 7, 8.
[11] *Ibid.*, IX, No. 4 (1858), p. 75, No. 5, p. 99. Lawrence quoted in Neill, *op. cit.*, p. 356.

while there were many – and this was emphatically not the case with Africa, where no aspect of religious practice was applauded – who admired at least the Sanskrit and Arabic literature which the great native religions had produced, as well as the temples and other artefacts they inspired. (As W. W. Hunter observed, 'Religion and philosophy have been the great contributions of India to the world'.[12]) After 1857 the situation, as one would expect, did not immediately change for the better. Queen Victoria's 1858 proclamation, designed to restore the confidence of Moslems and Hindus, promised that '*Firmly relying ourselves on the truth of Christianity, and acknowledging with gratitude the solace of religion*, We disclaim alike the right and the desire to impose Our convictions on any of Our subjects. We declare it to be Our royal will and pleasure that none be in anywise favoured, none molested or disquieted by reason of their religious faith or observance, but that all alike shall enjoy the equal and impartial protection of the law.' It is possible to see here, in addition, a guarantee that in future missionaries were to be free from the discrimination of which they had been the objects under the Company's régime. The proclamation was, however, an undeniable confirmation by the new Government of the old principle of religious neutralism. The London Missionary Society was quick to point out the anomalies in this policy, since the collection and disbursement of temple dues was still undertaken in a few areas, a clear breach of neutrality, and it made out a strong case for introducing Christian instruction in Government schools and colleges based on the evidence of Anglo-Indians, who were convinced that secular education produced national self-consciousness, hatred of Britain, 'pernicious errors', and 'the most demoralizing and revolutionary principles'.[13] The C.M.I. also urged that if a ban on proselytism was implied, then the royal Proclamation would be a serious imposition on Christians, who believed this to be an essential duty. Lord Ellenborough's protest against State aid to mission

[12] *The Indian Empire: Its People, History, and Products* (London, 1886), p. 163.

[13] *The Indian Crisis. Memorial to the Queen from the London Missionary Society, on the Religious Policy of the Government of India. With an Explanatory Statement on the Policy of the Indian Government in Respect to Religion, and the Education of the Natives* (London, 1858), pp. 4–5, 12, 20–3, 26–9.

schools was strongly criticized, and an Indian correspondent of *The Times* quoted to the effect that Europeans there would bear anything except an 'anti-Christian policy'.[14] But despite these complaints and misgivings the *Intelligencer* felt able to rejoice that British supremacy had been 'wondrously preserved'; 'God's hand was outstretched for our defence', and this should be taken as a sign of grace, of the beginning of a new epoch.

This was to be the case. After 1858 the activities of Christian missionaries gradually increased, with the covert approval of the Government and the advantage of a period of unusual peace and progress.[15] In response to this renewed effort, the indigenous religions, more than ever aware that Christian penetration constituted a threat not only to their own members, but to the entire way of life and the ancient traditions of India, rallied for a counter-offensive. Social reform was initiated by such Hindu reformers as Keshub Chunder Sen and Debendraneth Tagore; such teachers as Ramakrishna Paramahamsa and Swāmi Vivekānanda urged the mutual recognition of the spiritual teachings of East and West and an end to proselytism; the Ārya Samāj was founded by Swami Dayānand Sarasvati, aimed at purifying Hinduism and combating Christian and Western influences; while among the Moslems important doctrinal reforms were effected by Syed Ahmed and Syed Amir Ali. This religious ferment rendered the task of the growing numbers of Christian missionaries more difficult and attracted the notice of the foreign observer.

Whereas on contact with the African, Victorians emphasized alien appearance, brutal savagery, and a generally primitive way of life, what first impressed the visitor to India, or the Anglo-Indian, was the knowledge that the only subject which had power to raise the population from its 'normal condition of mental torpor . . . is religion'.[16] According to Monier Williams, Professor of Sanskrit at Oxford and author of numerous books on Indian life, 'The voracious appetite of a Hindū in any matter connected with religious superstition far outdoes that of any other nation on earth', and in fact 'almost every religious idea that the world has ever known has in India been stimulated

---

[14] C.M.I., X, No. 1 (1859), pp. 5, 6, 8–9.
[15] Edwardes, *op. cit.*, pp. 263–5.
[16] *Saturday Review*, 12 April 1884, p. 489, quoting Monier Williams.

to excessive growth, and every religious usage to preposterous extremes'.[17] The missionaries themselves were very conscious of the fact that in India 'for centuries subtle and profound faiths of remote antiquity have affected and determined the life of the people'.[18]

Indeed, this uneasy consciousness served to increase the missionary propensity to fluctuate between extreme optimism and despondency which we have already noticed.[19] Thus in sanguine mood 'a growing distaste to Hinduism' and its reactionary influence might be recorded among the Indian people – the sort of unfounded assertion which led critics to attack 'the sensational, pharisaical, self-laudatory, and narrow-minded style' of missionary reports.[20] In this style was the tribute of a layman, Lord Napier, Governor of Madras, who praised the progress of Christianity, and depicted missionaries as 'walking between the Government and the people with devotion to both, the friends of right, the adversaries of wrong, impartial spectators of good and evil'; or the tribute of General Sir Arthur Cotton, who after sixty years' experience in India confidently reported that 'this favoured land is now the head-quarters of God's truth'.[21] Although such statements bear witness to the sense of superiority which sustained Victorians in spiritual matters, it is, however, possible to match them with admissions of the slow progress being made by Christianity – even if this was generally set down to the indolence, conservatism and vice of the natives – for, as the *Calcutta Review* put it, 'The Anglo-Saxon in India moves upon the surface; darkness is upon the face of the deep beneath him'.[22]

Gratifying to British sensibilities on this point, therefore, was the conviction that the rites involved in the Hindu and Moslem

[17] *Modern India and the Indians: Being a Series of Impressions, Notes, and Essays* (London, 1878), p. 77; see also Bartle Frere, *Indian Missions* (London, 1873), p. 75.

[18] C.M.I., XXIV (1899), p. 176.

[19] See above, pp. 112–13, 122–3, 127–30.

[20] C.M.I., V, No. 9 (1869), pp. 257–60, and VI (November 1870), p. 345; *Africa Rediviva, op. cit.*, p. 75.

[21] C.M.I., VIII (February 1872), p. 45, VI (April 1881), pp. 241–3.

[22] *C.M.S. Godda District Report. Santal Mission* (Pokhuria, Manbhoom, 1898), p. 3; C.M.I., I, No. 9 (1850), p. 211, and VIII (September 1872), p. 264; *Review*, No. 31 (1855), p. 82.

religions, and the caste system supported by the former, were the major barriers to missionary work and evidence of the most advanced moral degradation: again the argument to explain failure which our study of attitudes to Africa revealed – namely, that Christianity was a superior religion which only succeeded among superior peoples. Sir John Lubbock once remarked that the main difference between the deities of savage and civilized man was that those of savages were evil and not good, requiring sacrifices, demanding an approach through dances and ceremony, not prayer, approving what in highly developed societies was regarded as vice.[23] These remarks, in the minds of most Victorians, were applicable not only to the rude beliefs of African tribes, but also to Hinduism and Islam, in India as in Africa regarded as a challenge to Christianity by its accommodation of the human weaknesses which that faith condemned. The intensity of dislike for Indian religions displayed by evangelists and laymen alike after 1858 was a new departure from the easy tolerance of Company rule, and one which helped to widen the gulf between the British and those they ruled.

A pamphlet put out by the Anti-slavery Society dwelt gloomily upon the 'idolatrous and sensual services of the Hindoo temples', while W. W. Hunter, historian and Director-General of Statistics at Calcutta, condemned Siva worship when practised by the lower classes in India as 'simply a religion of pleasure', with a deplorable emphasis on sacrifice and phallic symbolism.[24] According to R. N. Cust, Commissioner of Amritsar and a Secretary of the Royal Asiatic Society, although there was much that was admirable in the Hindu, Britons should cease to talk with him of his worship 'except in the same manner as we should, gently and reprovingly, in pity and disgust, talk of drunkenness, folly, and libertinism'.[25] Predictably, there was little sympathy for Indian religious rituals among British anthropologists, though some interest in recording these: thus Dr J. Shortt of Madras noted with pleasure that civilization was at last undermining the religious beliefs of the

[23] *Op. cit.*, p. 115.
[24] *A Brief View of Slavery in British India* (London, 1841), p. 1; Hunter, *op. cit.*, p. 223.
[25] *Pictures of Indian Life Sketched With the Pen From 1852 to 1881* (London, 1881), p. 99.

hill tribes of The Nilgiris, exposing the 'utter folly and inutility of all [their] . . . self-imposed and austere practices'.[26]

Equally critical was Monier Williams, who, although he was described by the *Saturday Review* as adopting towards the Indian people the attitude of 'a genuine philanthropist', condemned the bloodthirsty nature of the more primitive forms of Hinduism, and dismissed the religion of the masses as a mere matter of selfish superstition – maintaining none the less that there were more points of contact between Christian and Hindu, despite the latter's 'hideous idolatry', than between Christianity and Islam or Buddhism.[27] Williams was particularly concerned to point out that various objectionable social usages, such as early marriage, endogamy, and the prohibition of widow marriage, formed no part of the original Hindu religion, but the destruction of these was necessary before Christians could hope for genuine success in India. While they prevailed, 'a feeble condition of brain' among the Hindus would prevent their conversion, 'For Christianity is a religion which, before it can dominate over the human heart, requires a clear apprehension of certain great facts, and a manly assent of the reason to the doctrines and practice they involve'. In the meantime, however, missionaries should not underestimate Hinduism's 'comprehensiveness, its super-subtlety, its recuperative hydra-like vitality'. Indeed, an intense pall of ignorance, prejudice and superstition lay over the land, in some places 'a veritable Egyptian darkness thick enough to be felt'.[28]

Among British journals, the *Saturday Review* marvelled at the contradictions in the Eastern temperament which allowed the Hindu to worship licentious gods and yet set great store by a life of asceticism and contemplation, while the usually restrained *Spectator* spoke of that 'strange pit full of jewels, rags, and filth, of gleaming thoughts, and morbid fears, and horrid instincts – the Hindoo mind'.[29] Christianity would make no headway in India, according to the latter, until it attacked not

---

[26] J.E.S., VII (1869), pp. 249–50.

[27] *Saturday Review*, 12 April 1884, p. 488; Williams, *op. cit.*, pp. 40–1, 96, 100, 191.

[28] *Ibid.*, pp. 135–9, 232; *Religious Thought and Life in India, Part I, Vedism, Brahmanism and Hinduism* (London, 1883), pp. 18, 520.

[29] 4 March 1871, p. 263, and 14 July 1866, p. 771, respectively.

only the ridiculous ritual of Hinduism, along with the more extreme practices it still tolerated, such as *suttee*, but also its basic philosophy which induced such absolute stoicism and tranquil confidence among adherents.[30]

The most severe indictments of the Hindu religion, however, came from the missionaries themselves, even though – as Professor Neill has pointed out – the native reform movements and a better appreciation of Indian languages and scholarship were producing by the end of the century a novel degree of uncertainty about the unique and surpassing attributes of Christianity.[31] An article written by the Rev. J. S. Robertson of the Church Missionary Society's Bombay and West India station was typical in its condemnations of the 'abominable festival' called the Kôli, the 'yearly carnival of the polluted Hindoos, during which they practise abominations such as may be supposed to be acceptable to the demon of lust'.[32] The deities of Hinduism were described as 'stained with every vice', and the 'foulest crimes' were said to be perpetuated in the name of religion.[33] This created problems for the missionary, since, naturally, Hindu literature about the gods was likewise gross and immoral, and such organizations as the Madras School Book and Vernacular Society concerned themselves to provide literature for the masses which they would find equally attractive, but which was also 'pervaded by a healthy, moral tone'.[34] Monier Williams' studies were praised by the Church Missionary Society primarily because they exposed 'The darkest feature in the whole compass of heathen life, namely, the perpetration of vice in the name of piety, and the clothing of the vilest degradation with the sanction of a sacred service to the gods'.[35]

In fact, the degree of corruption was such that the Hindu faith was believed to be without real principles. 'There is

---

[30] *Spectator*, 11 December 1880, pp. 1,582–3, and 25 June 1898, p. 902.
[31] *Op. cit.*, pp. 358–9.
[32] C.M.I., I, No. 1 (1850), p. 8.
[33] *Ibid.*, VI, No. 4 (1855), p. 78.
[34] C.M.I., III (1878), pp. 138–40. See also for condemnation Hindu toleration of vice, *ibid.*, XVII (1892), p. 26, and R. Burton, *Sindh, and the Races that Inhabit the Valley of the Indus; With Notices of the Topography and History of the Province* (London, 1851), p. 231.
[35] C.M.I., XVII (1892), p. 328.

nothing left but an elaborate formalism', declared the C.M.I., refuting the *Spectator's* argument still further with an assertion that Christianity achieved successes by a direct appeal to the intelligence and the affections, concerning itself only marginally with such evils as caste.[36] This assertion was not even true in the case of the C.M.I. The very same volume contained an impassioned attack upon the institution.[37] Furthermore, the journal held the view, unlike some other periodicals – the *Pall Mall Gazette*, for instance – that religion was not independent of, but directly influenced, social manners.[38]

In addition to charges of immorality, the Hindu most commonly faced criticism on the grounds that his religion tolerated idol-worship, cruel habits, such as widow-burning, *thuggee*, infanticide, hook-swinging, self-mutilation and human sacrifice, and certain reactionary customs, such as polygamy, prohibitions on widow remarriage and female education.[39] By 1858 legislation against the practices involving physical menace had been successfully effected by the Government.[40] The memory of them continued to influence British attitudes to the Indian people, however, as Williams' work makes clear, and legislation concerning such matters as female education simply could not be enforced. Not unexpectedly, a greater degree of barbarism was detected in the black races of southern India, whose kin were to be found in Africa, the Malay Peninsula and elsewhere, and who were regarded as the most inferior of the Indian peoples. According to Charles Johnston, writing in the *Contemporary Review*, it was 'To this black race, passion-

[36] *Ibid.*, VIII, No. 10 (1857), pp. 231–2.
[37] *Ibid.*, No. 11, pp. 251–3.   [38] VIII (October 1872), pp. 292–3.
[39] *The Hill Tribes of India. An Account of the Church Missionary Society's Work Among the Santals, Paharis, Gonds, Kors, Bheels, and Hill Arrians* (London, 1891), p. 22; W. W. Hunter, *England's Work in India* (London, 1881), p. 44; J. Cumming, *The Destiny of Nations* (London 1864,), p. 166; C.M.I., XLIII (1892), p. 25, quoting J. Moore; and T.E.S.L., VI (1868), pp. 264–81, for indictments of Hindu savagery; see C.M.I., VII, No. 12 (1856), pp. 280–1, for condemnation of other Hindu customs; and T.E.S.L., V (1867), pp. 127–43, for indignant rejection by Professor Dadabhai Naoroji of wholesale attacks on Indian practices; and C.M.I., X (1874), pp. 42–3, for allegations and denials of idol-worship (denials by F. Max Müller).
[40] See *Contemporary Review*, II (May–August 1866), p. 231, on abandonment of *meriah*.

ate, magnetic, of wild imaginings, we must trace every lurid and demoniac element in the beliefs of India. This is their contribution to the common sum: a contribution fitting in the kin of the African Voodoo, the Australian cannibal, the Papuan head-hunter.'[41] Although it was sometimes asserted that the 'respectable' classes in India would not tolerate poly-gamy, the position of women aroused great indignation among Victorians, who complained not – as in Africa – of the hard physical work they undertook, but of their seclusion, ignorance and consequent bigotry.[42] (Such complaints, in turn, helped to increase the apprehension in India about the effects of Western ideas, which was a contributory factor to the Mutiny of 1857 and later manifestations of native protest.)

Missionaries, even during the days of Company rule, had refused to tolerate the Hindu prejudice against female education, and the London Missionary Society, the Church Missionary Society, and the British and Foreign Schools Society made a little headway in this field. After 1858 the Government con-tinued to move very cautiously in deference to Indian suscepti-bilities, but the missionary societies pressed ahead, sustained by the conviction that, as things remained, Indian women were, quite innocently, degraded – in a 'miserable state of secluded ignorance'.[43] Special appeals were made to British women to contribute financially to their elevation.[44] Through the female population of India their sons, over whom they exercised great influence, might be reached, and the C.M.S. was far more anxious to see women missionaries or missionary wives em-ployed than it was in Africa, actively co-operating with three agencies, the Society for the Propagation of Female Education in the East, the Indian Female Normal School and Instruction Society, and the Church of England Zenāna Missionary Society.[45] A doctor in Amritsar who asked a friendly Hindu

[41] LXXX (July–December 1901), p. 409.

[42] See R. N. Cust, *op. cit.*, p. 339, for comment on polygamy; also G. Campbell, *Modern India: a Sketch of the System of Civil Government. To Which is Prefixed, Some Account of the Natives and Native Institutions* (London, 1852), pp. 65–6.

[43] *Papers Referring to the Educational Operations of the Church Missionary Society in North India* (London, 1864), p. 7.

[44] C.M.I., III (1867), pp. 200–3.

[45] *Ibid.*, X (1885), pp. 697, 707, 709, XXIV (1899), pp. 627–8.

what were the evangelist's most effective weapons was told that, above all, '"we dread your women, and we dread your doctors; for your doctors are winning our hearts and your women are winning our homes, and when our hearts and our homes are won, what is there left of us?"'[46]

This approach received the support of laymen familiar with Indian conditions. In the opinion of Cust, the well-being of the continent depended on the moral and religious education of its female population, at present in a pitiable condition; Hunter delighted in the fact that 'European ideas are knocking at the door of the zenāna, and we hear confused cries from within which seem to show that the death-like monotony of women's existence in India is broken'; while, according to Williams, the children of mere children would probably remain so all their lives – in-breeding, he believed, produced deterioration of the brain tissue, and weakly offspring were 'brought up by ignorant, superstitious, narrow-minded mothers in a vitiated atmos- phere', and he concluded that the adoption of Western ideals of womanhood was necessary for progress. W. A. Rogers, an Indian civil servant, made the additional point that as long as the seclusion of the female population continued, Anglo- Indians and natives could never mix socially in a manner acceptable to the former.[47] However, as the *Spectator* rightly pointed out, the attempt to educate Indian women in this way constituted an attack upon their entire way of life and an attempt to substitute the values of the English society, which was based upon 'a brutal individualism, such as even the civilized Celt abhors'.[48] And there were some admissions that Indian society had its advantages as well as drawbacks. Richard Burton, for instance, who visited Sind in the 1850s and 1870s, remarked that family feeling was infinitely stronger than among Europeans, and that the behaviour of children was generally admirable, and Sir George Campbell, Lieutenant-Governor of Bengal, testified that the position of Hindu women was good, in that the

[46] J. C. Thomson, *Our Medical Workers and Their Work* (London, 1894), p. 13.

[47] Cust, *op. cit.*, pp. 97, 334–43; Hunter, *England's Work in India, op. cit.*, p. 50; Williams, *Modern India, op. cit.*, pp. 136–7; and W. A. Rogers in P.R.C.I., I (1869), pp. 123–4.

[48] 14 July 1866, p. 771.

marriage bond was sacred and their influence great, while Indian society looked after its poor better probably than did Britain.[49] Other writers bore witness to the fact that the population as a whole were 'obedient to parents, reverential to old age, . . . compassionate towards the helpless', strong and affectionate in their family commitments.[50]

If women constituted one major barrier to the progress of Christianity – and, in fact, to all change – the caste system constituted the other. Christian missionaries, regarding caste as an essential part of Hinduism (for a Hindu believes that reincarnation continues until the highest caste is reached, after the soul has returned many times and suffered much) and recognizing the extent to which the Hindu religion permeated the social order, just as Christianity aimed to do, attacked caste laws as cruel and stultifying.[51] Thus a correspondent of the C.M.I. in Calcutta complained bitterly of British lay support for a system 'which only differs from slavery because it is more offensive, more absurd, and more unscriptural'.[52] And again the layman (where not directly involved in fashioning Government policy) often agreed. Burton, for example, dismissed the Hindu with his seven castes as 'ever essentially . . . unprogressive; society was fossilized as soon as formed, and in point of civilization, "thus far and no further" became its law'.[53] He emphasized here an aspect of caste with which Victorians were particularly impatient. In reviewing at the time of the Mutiny, the improvements in the administration of India over the years, Mill had commented that reform was difficult because of the 'passive and slavish character' of the people, and these characteristics were seen to be the direct result of a static, rigidly stratified society.[54]

[49] Burton, *Sind Revisited: With Notices of the Anglo-Indian Army; Railroads; Past, Present, and Future, etc.* (London, 1877, 2 vols.), I, pp. 293–4, II, pp. 137–8; Campbell, *Modern India, op. cit.,* pp. 65–7.

[50] See article by J. Seymour Keay, long resident in Hyderabad, in *Nineteenth Century,* XIV (July–December 1883), p. 12; article in *Aborigines Friend,* I, No. viii (November 1857–January 1858), pp. 346–7.

[51] Edwardes, *op. cit.,* pp. 2–3, 150.

[52] C.M.I., IX, No. 1 (1858), p. 22; see also V, No. 9 (1869), p. 259.

[53] *Sind Revisited, op. cit.,* II, pp. 305–6.

[54] J. S. Mill, *Memorandum of the Improvements in the Administration of India During the Last Thirty Years* (London, 1858), p. 40.

Monier Williams, though he condemned European ignorance of caste rules, which gave rise to unnecessary offence, and noted that even the lower castes found satisfaction in their position, was obliged to confess that by British standards the system tended to arrest progress, paralyse energy, crush 'manly independence', stifle public opinion, and to make nationality, patriotism, and true liberty almost impossible.[55] Caste, it seemed, having the ancient sanction of religion, was an even greater barrier to Westernization and technological progress, to the ideal of the self-made man, than African tribalism, and in spite of the predictions of optimists like Dr J. Cumming, who believed that with the increase of missionary work in India caste had received a massive, if not final, blow, it seemed infinitely resilient.[56] Hence the best prospects for Christian missionaries were frequently seen to be among the tribes of southern India, whose primitive state was believed to rule out a well-developed caste system.[57] A survey of Indian affairs presented to the British Association by Major T. B. Jervis (for the East India Company) was prefaced by a verse which well summed up British feelings on this subject:[58]

> In links of steel, here superstition binds,
> The unenlighten'd native to his CASTE;
> Tethers him; blights his genius; condemns to ply,
> Unceasingly, the trade his sires have plied,
> Like Sysiphus – for ever: – debarred
> All hope of change, all prospect to o'erleap
> Or burst her barriers to the skies uprear'd,
> Immur'd, as in the chambers of the grave.

Such defence of caste as could be made, from the Victorian point of view, was, significantly, on racial lines. To R. N. Cust,

[55] *Modern India, op. cit.*, pp. 233–5; *Religious Thought and Life in India, op. cit.*, p. 473.

[56] Cumming, *The Destiny of Nations, op. cit.*, p. 166.

[57] J. Shortt in T.E.S.L., III (1865), p. 389; Sir Walter Elliott, J.E.S., I (1868 –9), p. 128; *The Hill Tribes of India, op. cit.*, p. 26; C.M.I., II (1877), p. 265.

[58] *Address Delivered at the Geographical Section of the British Association, Newcastle On Tyne, Descriptive of the State, Progress, and Prospects of the Various Surveys, and Other Scientific Enquiries, Instituted by the East India Company Throughout Asia; With a Prefatory Sketch of the Principles and Geography* (Torquay, n.d.); see also C.M.I., VII, No. 12 (1856), p. 280, M. Wylie of Calcutta on material progress which followed weakening of caste.

the important point to grasp was that caste followed ethnic divisions and was the result, not primarily of religious doctrine, but of that same feeling of repulsion which separated a European from an Eskimo or a Negro. Missionaries, he believed, were foolish in interfering with such a basic instinct, for naturally the superior Indian Aryan looked with horror upon the peculiar practices of the inferior inhabitant of Southern India. (Cust, however, deplored the existence of such sentiments, whether on the part of Indian or Anglo-Saxon, and believed that they were very strong only among a comparatively few Brahmins.)[59] Britons who were themselves motivated by racial pride and colour prejudice were not a little amazed and annoyed, as Williams pointed out, to find that the people of India were motivated by an 'intense pride in their own supposed moral, religious, and even intellectual superiority';[60] viewed with dismay any rejection by the Indian élite of British assumptions of superiority, and still more resented the fact that the Hindu regarded social intercourse with the European as a potential source of defilement.[61] However, just as the Victorian admiration of force and success led to a defence of the more vigorous African tribes and disparagement of their weaker neighbours, so the pride exhibited by the highest castes and the hero-worship demonstrated by the lower drew forth a certain admiration and acknowledgement of shared Aryan qualities, as we shall see.

In general terms, however, setting aside the art and literature which it had inspired, there seemed little to recommend the Hindu religion, described by the Church Missionary Society as a 'deep and dark grave, in which every thing like moral principle, social and domestic happiness, public worth and national energy, lies buried'.[62] We find, also, as with Africa, a contempt for Islam and its effects, primarily upon the people of northern India and Bengal, and among laymen some of the same impatience with the unsuccessful efforts of Christian missionaries to combat its influence, which – unlike that of

---

[59] *Pictures of Indian Life, op. cit.*, pp. 273, 281–2, 287, 293, 305.
[60] *Modern India, op. cit.*, pp. 182, 188–9.
[61] See G. Campbell, *The British Empire* (London, 1887), pp. 44–5; C.M.I., IX, No. 1 (1858), pp. 21–2, Calcutta correspondent.
[62] C.M.I., I, No. 2 (1850), pp. 243–4.

Buddhism and Hinduism – was believed to be growing.[63] Though necessarily in India the last-named, as the religion of four-fifths of the population, was the chief object of missionary attack, the evangelist likewise criticized, as a worker in Oude put it, the 'fanaticism, bigotry, licentiousness and cruelty' of Islam.[64] A plea for an extension of mission work in Mohammedan lands published in 1891 referred to the characteristics of Islam in almost identical terms, noting also as typical side-effects formalism and an unpardonable opposition to progress. The seclusion of the female population was seen as a direct outcome of its successes in India, attention was drawn to the unedifying life of Mohammed, and Islam was presented as a principal cause of the Indian Mutiny. (The condemnations of Buddhism – then arousing considerable interest in Europe – were only a little less sweeping.[65])

A more judicious view was sometimes taken by laymen who recognized that the Mohammedans were sharing in the religious reformation of the second half of the nineteenth century, believed them to be superior in purity and intellectual attainments to the Hindus, and admitted that far from being a menacing force they were a repressed minority, once conquerors, but now deprived of power by the British. Although such a view admitted the impossibility of destroying Islam and welcomed the prospect of co-operation between Moslem and Christian, feelings of superiority are also apparent here. There was pity for the Mohammedans' loss of their ancient monopoly of Army and Revenue posts, for their educational disabilities, but a strong awareness that Britain was now in the role of conqueror and could therefore afford to be magnanimous.[66] When

63 Williams, *Modern India, op. cit.*, pp. 218–19.

64 C.M.I., XIV, No. 12, p. 282.

65 W. St Clair Tisdall, *Diex Li Vuelt! It is The Will of God! A Plea For a Great Extension of Mission Work in Muhammadan Lands* (London, 1891), p. 9; see also C.M.I., VIII, No. 11 (1857), p. 243, IX, No. 5 (1858), p. 110; *Papers Referring to the Educational Operations of the Church Missionary Society in North India, op. cit.*, p. 7; and J. Johnston, ed., *Report of the Centenary Conference on the Protestant Missions of the World* (London, 1889, 2 vols.), I, pp. 17–40, 50.

66 W. Scawen Blunt, 'The Mohammedan Question in India', *Contemporary Review*, XXXVI (July–December 1884), pp. 626, 631–2, 636–7; G. Campbell, *Modern India, op. cit.*, p. 209; W. W. Hunter, *The Indian*

W. W. Hunter referred to the beneficial effects of Buddhism, inculcating gentleness and charity to all men, virtues which rendered a poor law unnecessary in India and gave 'a high significance to the half-satirical epithet of the "mild" Hindu', he did so after dwelling upon the virtues of the conquering Aryan.[67] This is quite common – a version of the praise for the industrious but frequent preference for the warlike tribes of Africa which we have noticed. A good example of this kind of conflict is to be found in the *Spectator*, which in an article on 'The Arabs of the Desert', published in 1881, had pondered whether those races 'which halt and wait, as calmly indifferent to the strife outside as if their habitats were planets, may conserve energy more than the races which advance, and in advancing must expend force of some kind?', but none the less concluded on another occasion that the claims in north Africa of a people who had 'built nothing, founded nothing, achieved nothing' were scarcely worth considering.[68]

In spite of the widespread assumptions, however, about the inferiority of the Hindu religion, with its vice and cruelty, and of Islam, with its additional liabilities – namely, the hankering after past glories and reputation as the religion which still condoned slavery – British missionaries in India, even though the Protestant community multiplied tenfold between 1851 and 1901, were continually fighting a battle against self-doubt and criticism from back home. An article in the *Contemporary Review* in 1866 noted the indifference to religion in Britain, and felt that this resulted in a lowering of standards among candidates for the mission field; indicated the failure of any native Christian to rise to pre-eminence in India; and concluded that if the Hindu was influenced towards Christianity by the strength of the white Churches in India, then few converts were likely.[69] The *Spectator*'s Editor, Meredith Townsend, writing in the same journal, approached the question from a different angle,

[67] *The Indian Empire, op. cit.*, pp. 79, 162.
[68] 21 May 1881, pp. 667–8, 2 July 1881, p. 856.
[69] I (January–April 1866), pp. 123–5, 127, 133.

Musalmans: Are They Bound in Conscience to Rebel Against the Queen? (London, 1871), pp. 156–7, 176, 180–1, 192, 210–11.

stressing not the intellectual inferiority of the white missionaries, but their colour-consciousness, love of comfort, respectability and English education (when the Hindu expected asceticism in his religious leaders). To Townsend the best hope lay with the development of a native Church and missionaries, but he was not optimistic about the future.[70] His views were promptly criticized by the principal of a mission college, William Millar, who – though he admitted that there was some truth in the cynical observation that missionaries went abroad 'because they could not get a comfortable settlement at home', to satisfy the Anglo-Saxon passion to rule, if not in Britain then elsewhere[71] – argued that alone in the community the Anglo-Indian Christian evangelist took a personal interest in the native population, and defended the achievements of mission schools.[72] Other writers testified to the love which the Indians felt for the missionaries (and British rule generally), the way in which the latter provided a 'safeguard against oppression and wrong-doing in all stages of our connexion with hostile, half-civilized peoples or barbarous tribes', and the hindrance to their good work presented by ignorance and hostility at home and by Indian officials whose own lives scarcely conformed with Christian teaching.[73]

There was, however, some support for Townsend's dream of a native Church. The London Missionary Society, not un-expectedly, given its African record, emphasized that the distinctive feature of its operations was the handing over of responsibility, as soon as possible, to native converts.[74] Acknow-ledging that Englishmen were perforce 'strangers and sojourners, each for a brief season' in India, and admitting the language difficulties encountered by European missionaries – who, even where they had mastered the local vernacular, could not be

[70] *Contemporary Review*, LVI (July–December 1889), pp. 1, 3, 5, 8.

[71] See Millar in *ibid.*, p. 490; also Rev. J. Rooker, *A Missionary Criticized by an Outsider* (London, 1891), pp. 4, 8.

[72] Millar, *Contemporary Review*, LVI, pp. 489–502.

[73] C.M.I., I, No. 1 (1850), p. 9, V, No. 8 (1869), pp. 225–40, native pamphlets; IV (June 1879), p. 350, Lieut.-General R. G. Taylor of Punjab; XXIV (June 1899), pp. 456–61, article by Punjab resident.

[74] *Our Medical Workers and Their Work*, *op. cit.*, p. 18; the Baptists, Wesleyan Methodists and Scottish Free Church were also in favour, see C.M.I., VI, No. 3 (1870), pp. 314–16.

sure of appreciating native modes of thoughts or detecting insincerity – the Church Missionary Society, also predictably, set great store by the training of native preachers and the production of books in the vernacular.[75] As Robert Cust expressed it in 1885, 'The epoch for the simple, God-fearing Scripture-loving, but otherwise uninstructed, Missionary, whether man or woman, is past. Arms of precision are required to fight the Lord's battles.'[76] However, this need not imply an acceptance of racial and religious equality on the part of these societies (and Townsend himself favoured overall control of native institutions by whites). A report from the C.M.S.'s Santal Mission complained of the inefficiency and small educational attainments of most native preachers, and their lack of real enthusiasm – presumably of the 'robust and athletic piety', which missionary work was felt to require.[77] It was not felt that all local vernaculars were worthwhile or that the teaching of English should be entirely neglected, and there was widespread support (the Young Men's Christian Association excepted) for the opinion of a native speaker, during a C.M.S. meeting at Amritsar, that the most serious and important aspects of evangelization could only be undertaken by Europeans.[78] And, of course, the basic assumption that missionary activity was not simply a duty for the Christian, but that the people of India – and Africa – were eagerly awaiting and gratefully receiving the benefits of Christianity, remained unshaken. These confident sentiments were epitomized in these

[75] *The Hill Tribes of India, op. cit.*, pp. 13, 40; *A Native Church For the Natives of India; Giving an Account of the Formation of a Native Church Council, for the Punjab Missions of the Church Missionary Society, and of the Proceedings at Their First Meeting, at Umritsur, 31st March, to 2nd April 1877* (Lahore, 1877), p. 45; C.M.I., XXIV (January 1899), pp. 16–19, XXI (April 1896), p. 244, VI (1881), p. 152; III (June 1878), pp. 346, 349–56, II, No. 5, pp. 155–6.

[76] C.M.I., X (1885), p. 710.

[77] *Op. cit.*, p. 3; and *A Tribute of Affectionate Respect to the Memory and Founders of the London Missionary Society. A Sermon Delivered in Surrey Chapel, Wednesday Morning, May the 9th, 1849. By J. A. James* (London, 1849), p. 24.

[78] C.M.I., X, No. 1 (1885), p. 39; *Papers Referring to the Educational Operations of the Church Missionary Society in North India, op. cit.*, p. 19; *A Native Church For the Natives of India, op. cit.*, p. 50; S. Neill, *op. cit.*, pp. 365–6.

lines by Derry and Raphoe, published by the C.M.I. in 1899:[79]

> But oh, the exceeding bitter cry
> Of countless souls in agony!
> These, from dim shrines of dreadful creeds,
> Foul rituals and accursed deeds,
> Some whisper of the Lord have heard;
> Some pulse of hope their heart hath stirred:
> Not in a dream these myriads cry,
> Help us, ye Christians, or we die.

Although missionary attitudes towards their work in Africa and India were very similar, the average Victorian held a widely differing set of assumptions about the character, educability, diligence, appearance and broad civilization of the Indian and the African. Undoubtedly towards the end of the century race prejudice was reinforcing the British weakness for generalizing about coloured peoples. Shortly after the Mutiny, in fact, it was common to find 'Indian "niggers"' spoken of with a 'coarse contempt and vulgar hatred'.[80] But the growing nationalism and economic difficulties of the 1870s bore in upon Anglo-Indians and Britons alike the necessity of securing the co-operation of some sectors, at least, of Indian society, while as far as Africa was concerned, only relatively powerless agencies like the Aborigines Protection Society felt this was possible or desirable.

There were two conflicting notions of the Indian temperament popularly entertained by Victorians: one was the traditional stereotype of the tractable, mild Hindu, the other (directly influenced by the events of 1857) depicted the cruel, scheming Oriental, who needed and only respected strong government. Sometimes both caricatures were drawn by the same writer. H. B. Evans, writing in 1855, presented such a typical exposition of the former view (with some comparison of the Indian and the Negro) that it is worth quoting in full:[81]

> The Indian [he declared] is docile, harmless, and industrious; and, when he has the opportunity, saving . . . under the guidance and

[79] C.M.I., XXIV (March 1899), p. 168; see also similar verses in *ibid.*, XIX (April 1894), p. 270.
[80] *Saturday Review*, 20 March 1869, p. 374.
[81] *Op. cit.*, p. 34.

protection of a European, whom he reveres, he will do almost anything; and even in the lowest castes, there is a degree of refinement about them which is surprising. They are gregarious in their habits, and, unlike the Negro, do not evince that love for a savage state of life which the latter is so fond of indulging, when not under restraint. They are quick, apt, and intelligent workmen, and make capital servants: the great secret in the management of them is kindness and fair dealing, with a tolerance of their harmless prejudices.

An additional touch was added to the portrait by Burton, who bore witness to the 'soft and exquisitely polished manners of the Indians', while Sir George Campbell agreed that the Hindu possessed a high degree of industrial energy and intelligence, with none of the laziness or apathy of the Celt or Negro, 'and the more they get the more they want'. He believed that, generally speaking, the Indians were not a cruel or bloody-minded people, and though, in the north at least, less mild and effeminate than the British believed, they lacked the 'persevering, indomitable courage in *all* matters of the European'.[82] Such beliefs continued to be widespread even after the Mutiny, but with a new awareness of the difficulties involved in understanding the Indian mind – an awareness which, however, is usually a product of post-rebellion unease rather than a serious questioning of British qualities and methods. There is, in fact, a marked decline in the enthusiastic Orientalism of the early Anglo-Indians, men such as Jonathan Duncan and Horace Hayman Wilson, who, under the 'charm of a remote philosophy and a fantastic history . . . were . . . Brahminized, and would not hear of admitting into their Oriental enclosure either Christianity or any of the learning of the West', though judicious observers like W. W. Hunter did acknowledge that the greatest wrong that the English could do to their Asiatic subjects was not to understand them.[83]

In such a mood the *Saturday Review* complained that the

---

[82] Burton, *Sindh, op. cit.*, pp. 163, 296; Campbell, *Modern India, op. cit.*, pp. 59, 63.

[83] J. R. Seeley, *The Expansion of England* (London, 1926 ed.), p. 291; W. W. Hunter, *The Indian Musalmans, op. cit.*, Dedication; Burton, *Sind Revisited, op. cit.*, II, pp. 26–7; M. Roberts, *Son of Empire* (London, 1899), p. 11.

Hindu character was one of the hardest on earth to comprehend, and particularly for Englishmen who persisted in governing a 'childish, impulsive, and pre-eminently vain Eastern race, fond of display, amusements, decorations, and pomp of all kinds, precisely as we might govern a nation of hard-headed, calculating, canny Scotchmen'.[84] This was just the course which British anthropologists so much deplored. However, the *Review* went on to suggest that Englishmen were ever more convinced that India must be governed with reference to English rather than Indian ideas and officials. The justice and profitability of British rule more than compensated for its lack of popularity: this could not be expected, any more than a good schoolmaster taking over a bad school could expect gratitude from his pupils. The Tory journal also argued that only Liberals entertained the mistaken view that all men were alike, entitled to identical rights and fit to be governed identically, and that such beliefs, if applied to India, would lose it for Britain. There was no apparent awareness of the paradox involved in upholding the universal justice of British principles and denying the existence of a universal set of natural rights.[85] The reference here to Liberal attitudes incidentally concerns the Party's crusade during the 1870s against the Government's India policy, a campaign involving support for the native Press, an increase in the number of Indians in the Civil Service, opposition to the Bill creating Queen Victoria Empress of India, and support for Gladstone's basic proposition that the British title to be in India depended on its being profitable to the Indian people, in their own eyes.[86]

The *Spectator*, representing the Liberal outlook and just as proud of the ability of a small number of Britons to rule millions of Indians, likewise pointed out the inability of the former (especially the Anglo-Indians) to produce anything which revealed 'the inner character, or wishes, or motives' of the deliberately secretive Indian people. Even the Chinese were not

[84] 8 September 1866, pp. 296–7; see also C. T. Buckland, *Sketches of Social Life in India* (London, 1884), p. 139.

[85] 17 August 1867, p. 201, 28 March 1868, p. 404, 27 June 1868, p. 834, 4 March 1871, p. 263.

[86] See Gladstone in *Hansard*, CLXIII (6 June 1861), p. 641; *Spectator*, 15 June 1861, pp. 637–8, condemning British despotism in India.

so hidden from the understanding of the British, so that the Indian Empire provided 'the most marvellous example the world has ever seen of governing human beings through abstract principles, when those principles include impartial justice, perfect tolerance, and the most absolute respect, not only for personal freedom but for personal idiosyncrasy'.[87]

In spite of certain misgivings, however, most Victorians were sincerely persuaded that the British operated in accordance with these principles, believed that justice and tolerance were standard British qualities,[88] and continued to regard with a forbearance often verging on contempt the harmless foibles and attributes of the Indian peasantry. (The educated *élite*, of course, was more dangerous and hence deserved greater respect.) The average Hindu, it was stated, was a born gentleman, albeit manufactured from ages of etiquette; his chief characteristics were still said to be reserve and docility, gentleness, pity, and procrastination (while simultaneously lauded were the British virtues of determination, fearlessness and veracity).[89] These findings were supported by Monier Williams, who also stressed Indian intelligence, patience and faithfulness, but noted that physical strength and solidity of physical or mental backbone – essentially British qualities – were generally lacking[90]. But then, as the *Saturday Review* put it, falling instinctively into the imperialist frame of mind, 'if they had too much backbone, we should hardly be there to govern them'.[91] In this vein, John Crawfurd compared the Indians unfavourably with the Chinese, believing the latter to have been 'but twice conquered by strangers, and in both cases the strangers have adopted the laws and manners of China', whereas for the past 800 years the Hindus had 'been subdued by every strange people that had the power to invade their country, and they have been compelled to adopt the laws of the conquerors'.[92]

[87] 22 October 1881, p. 1,336.

[88] See, for instance, St Leger Herbert in *Fortnightly Review*, XXXV (January–June 1884), p. 249; Lord Bryce, *Studies in History and Jurisprudence* (Oxford, 1901, 2 vols.), I, p. 79.

[89] C.M.I., XLIII (1892), p. 201, and Cust, *Pictures of Indian Life, op. cit.*, VIII, pp. 80–1, 109, 139, 255–6, 258.

[90] *Modern India, op. cit.*, pp. 88, 127, 236.

[91] 16 June 1877, p. 722.

[92] T.E.S.L., I (1861), p. 160.

In apparent contradiction, after 1858, to such versions of the Indian character was the belief that at least some of the Indian races – and particularly the hill tribes – were anything but mild. The head-hunting Nagas, for instance, who yielded a few converts to Protestant missions in the late nineteenth century, were the subject of much invective, and, according to Captain John Butler, a political agent in Assam, who was reported in the *Journal of the Anthropological Institute*, their relations with Britain had been 'one long sickening story of open insults and defiance, bold outrages and cold-blooded murders on the one side, and long-suffering forbearance, forgiveness, concession, and unlooked-for favours on the other'.[93] Referring to the mountain peoples of the North-West Frontier, an Indian Army veteran paid tribute to their courage and vigour (not to mention steadfastness, hospitality, dignity and intelligence), while many travellers and civil servants detected among the non-Aryan tribes (the Marawars, Kallars, Bedars and Ramusis of the south, and the Kolis and Gujars of the north) such traits as bravery, athleticism, love of war and of hunting.[94] The *Morning Post* and numerous other journals at the time of the Mutiny rose up in venomous denunciation of the Mohammedan and Hindu rebels, united 'in crime and cruelty'.[95] Though philanthropists indignantly countered that the latter were only sensual where priestcraft inculcated it as a duty, fawning and false from the oppression of successive tyrants, pilferers from the betters who had stripped them of their property, treacherous because themselves so systematically cheated and betrayed, and cruel and callous to the cries of misery because their native rulers knew no mercy and superstition made them mad. While the absolute quintessence of the post-Mutiny re-evaluation of the Indian character, against which this protest was directed, is contained in a passage from Dr Cumming's *The Great Tribulation* (1859):

> It used to be said of the Hindoos [he wrote] that they were such a mild, amiable, and gentle race. . . . But what is the disclosure? That greater liars do not exist in the world than the Hindoos; that

[93] J.A.I., XI (1882), p. 57.

[94] Major Fosberry, V.C., reported in J.E.S., I (1868–9), pp. 182–93, Sir Walter Elliot in *ibid.*, pp. 112–13.

[95] *Morning Post*, 2 September 1857.

you cannot always trust them out of sight; that they are deceptive; and we have seen by recent events such outbursts of fanaticism, cruelty, bloodshed, and crime, that we wonder how any that knew them thirty years ago could give them such and so splendid a character.[96]

In this context it is interesting to notice Victorians arguing that the Indian people themselves, and especially their native princes, inclined to and respected conquest and violence, as witness the history of the Aryan invaders of India.[97] Morley Roberts' hero, Captain Blundell, for instance, in the novel *Son of Empire*, who spent his early years as an African explorer – 'a real traveller, a man who just walked through Africa as if it belonged to him' – made his reputation finally in exploits on India's North-West Frontier, where he paid tribute to the valour of his native troops, who responded magnificently and gratefully to his leadership. The savagery of their opponents was also stressed, and complaint made of the Nonconformist Press, in whose eyes[98] 'The noble savage could do no wrong, while the British soldier was a howling, outraging, looting scoundrel, to whom any Ghazi, drunk with fanaticism, was a quiet and gentlemanly Wesleyan'. The Hindu, declared the *Spectator*, saw a 'necessary unity of right and force' and therefore obeyed even a foreign power.[99] This afforded a very convenient and common defence of British rule, though otherwise sympathetic foreigners might complain of that mixture of 'selfishness and energy which, in the Anglo-Saxon race, degenerates too often into ferocity'[100]. Accordingly, Burton described the Indian as a dangerous, dark and deep-seeing plotter (though usually not actively courageous – he maintained that 'the belief that Sepoys will fight, without English-

[96] *Aborigines' Friend*, I, No. 1 (1858), p. 346, report from meeting held at Friends' House on Indian reform and native rights, and Cumming, *op. cit.*, p. 284.

[97] Bartle Frere in J.A.I., XI (1881–2), p. 314; C.M.I., XIV (May 1889), p. 284; *Spectator*, 14 July 1866, p. 771.

[98] *Op. cit.*, pp. 95, 130–1, 178, 180, 367.

[99] 29 January 1870, p. 135; see also R. N. Cust, *Pictures of Indian Life*, *op. cit.*, p. 98, article on 'The Indian Raja'; and testimony in Mill's *Memorandum*, *op. cit.*, p. 90, on cruel native treatment of hill tribes.

[100] *A Debate on India in the English Parliament. By M. Le Comte De Montalembert* (London, 1858), p. 13.

men to lead them is a snare, a sham, and a delusion'), and argued that all Asiatics were to be (and expected to be) controlled by strange and terrible punishments; clemency was absolutely unwise. Furthermore, it was essential for Britain to keep a firm hold of India, not only for the good of its people, but because – quoting Bismark – a nation which voluntarily surrendered territory was a nation in decay.[101]

Even the moderate Campbell stressed the savage nature of princely rule, arguing from this the necessity and superiority of British administration, which should be avowedly despotic, even though absolutism ran counter to British preferences. At this point of time – the 1850s – Campbell was prepared to encourage 'the colonization, conversion, and the introduction of European morals, manners, and arts', being more sanguine than most about 'the aptness of the people to receive these benefits'. By the 1870s, however, perhaps in response to developing Indian nationalism, while still defending British despotism, he claimed to have always favoured allowing the native population to retain its own laws regarding marriage and inheritance, religious and social rites – in fact, in all matters not absolutely inconsistent with the British system. Campbell, like many Victorians, was not prepared to see the same principle applied to African tribal administrations, believing these to be – particularly with regard to property – a barrier to settlement and progress. Africans, he wrote,

> are not the possessors of an old civilization and ancient laws, under which they have learned to manage their own affairs; they are in no degree in the position of the Hindoo and Mahomedan races in India. They are mere barbarians, with some ill-defined customs which we have reduced to law. . . . African tribes seem to be mere casual aggregations of people under the chief of the day. . . . I should judge, then, that there is little of native law or rule which we are much called on to respect when these people come under our jurisdiction.[102]

In his highly resented indictment of the British record in India, J. S. Keay was particularly scathing about this type of

[101] *Sind Revisited, op. cit.,* I, pp. 60, 81, 275–6, II, pp. 57, 60–1.
[102] *India as It May Be: an Outline of a Proposed Government and Policy* (London, 1853), pp. xii, xiv–xvi, xxiv–xxv, 9, 413; *White and Black, op. cit.,* pp. 111–12, 121–2.

rationalization, which he maintained was very strong among the Anglo-Indian population. He quoted the opinions of various civil servants who, for instance, at the time of the Ilbert Bill controversy in the 1880s, denied native officials the right to pass judgement on Europeans on the ground that a conquering people were superior to those they had conquered, even though, in Keay's view, modern political science knew nothing whatever of the claims of a conquering race.[103]

Another classic example of the Victorians' admiration of strength and courage, or, cynically put, 'the law of force and cunning', was their treatment of and attitudes towards the aborigines of New Zealand.[104] It is quite clear that outside the Aborigines Protection Society there was little support for the retention by the Maoris of large tracts of communally owned land, this being 'absolutely antagonistic to progress'.[105] It was admitted, however, that at all times the Maoris were noted for their 'fine physical characteristics, their nobility of character when at peace, and their courage when at war'.[106] (Their pride of birth and dignity, hospitality and courtesy, even though since contact with Europeans their numbers were declining, were also seen as important redeeming virtues.[107]) It was impossible, of course, to ignore the martial attributes of the Maoris during the long wars of the 1860s and 1870s, and even the *Saturday Review*, which scoffed at the land policies and the 'mawkish morality' of the A.P.S., acknowledged that of all primitive tribes they were the 'bravest in war and the most versatile in peaceful occupations'.[108] That Society itself agreed with such a verdict on the Maori character, as did the Church Missionary Society, in spite of setbacks to its work on the islands, which included the execution of a missionary at

[103] *Nineteenth Century*, XV (January–June 1884), pp. 563–4, 'The Spoliation of India', Article II. See replies from Florence Nightingale in *ibid.*, pp. 329–38; from Lionel Ashburner in *ibid.*, XVI (July–December 1884), p. 618.

[104] See Mill in *Fraser's Magazine*, XLI (1851), p. 25, on 'The Negro Question'.

[105] F. W. Pennefather in J.A.I., XVI (1887), p. 213.

[106] J. H. Kerry-Nicholls in *ibid.*, XV (1886), pp. 187–8.

[107] R. Lee in J.A.S., II (1864), pp. xcv, xcviii, and Sir G. Grey in J.E.S., I (1868–9), p. 334; Arthur Halcombe in P.R.C.I., II (1879–80), pp. 332–3.

[108] 30 September 1865, pp. 412–13.

Opotiki. As late as 1892, when the wars were over and the settlers' lust for land satisfied, missionary John Thornton testified that the Maoris' independence of character, manly bearing and frank manner made them the most attractive of all the foreign races committed to British rule.[109] The verdict of J. A. Froude in 1886, however, is significant of the change which had taken place in lay opinion, for to him the Maoris he saw at Ohinemutu, subdued, corrupted by drink and squatting about all day with nothing to do, were helpless, useless and absurd.[110]

While Victorians had conflicting opinions about the basic Indian characteristics, with perhaps the majority still inclining to view the aggregate (unlike the mass of Africans) as gentle and amenable, there was something approaching unanimity on the question of Indian diligence, and widespread agreement on the intellectual ability of the native population, although the findings of administrators, travellers and scholars resulted in the careful grading of different tribes and castes in terms of these qualities. The Indian population was not – any more than the tribes of Africa – seen always as an undifferentiated mass. Thus Monier Williams, emphasizing the racial diversity of India, spoke of the spirited Hindustani, the martial Sikh, the ambitious Marathi, the proud Rajput, the hardy Gurkha, the calculating Bengali, the busy Telugu, the active Tamil, the patient Pariah; and M. A. Sherring, in his *History of Christianity in India*, devoted considerable space to the differences between some twenty-eight racial groups then receiving instruction.[111] Generally speaking, however, Victorians were most impressed

[109] For the views of the A.P.S. see *On the British Colonization of New Zealand. By the Committee of the Aborigines' Protection Society* (London, 1846), especially pp. 46–57; *The New Zealand Government and the Maori War of 1863–4, With Especial Reference to the Confiscation of Native Lands, and the Colonial Ministry's Defence of Their War Policy* (London, 1864), pp. 2, 22–3; *Aborigines Friend*, II (1859–66), pp. 457–8, and T.A.P.S. (1883–9; December 1884), pp. 152, 155–7; for C.M.S. see C.M.I., X, No. 12 (1858), pp. 277–87, I, No. 9 (1865), pp. 265–73, 288, VIII (May 1872), pp. 158–9, XLIII (March 1892), pp. 201–6.

[110] *Op. cit.*, p. 271.

[111] Williams, *Indian Wisdom, op. cit.*, p. xxiv; Sherring, *History of Christianity in India; With Its Prospects. A Sketch* (Madras, 1895).

by the Aryan or Caucasian peoples of northern India (the word 'Aryan' is of disputed origin and meaning, but Britons chose to accept the definition of 'noble'.) As R. Campbell testified: 'The spirit in which we approach Indian questions has been largely influenced by recent investigations upon the language, religion and ancient institutions of the East, proving that the language and mythology, and the types of communal or village organization which belong to the more advanced races of India have a common origin with those of Europe.'[112]

In the first place, these groups had the profoundly important advantage of conforming to European standards of beauty. Speakers at ethnological society meetings testified that some of the purest Aryans in the world were to be found in the northern parts of the continent, and many of these were 'extraordinarily handsome'; tribute was paid to the magnificent good looks of the women of Sind and of the men of Kashmir. Most Jats and Brahmins, in fact, were said to be distinguished by good (elevated or Grecian) features, fine teeth, hair and eyes, and fair colouring – thought of as representing the highest type of Indian mankind – and they possessed the 'noble self-confidence' befitting a conquering race. By contrast, the more primitive tribes of southern India, whom the Aryan invaders had overcome, were seen – in Harry Johnston's words – as 'an inferior type of human being, for the most part dark or black-skinned'. Attention was frequently drawn to their unimpressive stature and ugly, Negroid features and complexion, which Indians themselves were known to despise.[113]

The caste system had divided men, not only according to occupation, but also colour, a fact which seemed to please Victorians not a little. In a famous passage from the *Vedas* the god Indra was praised for having protected the Aryan colour, and the *Rig Veda*, *Ramayana* and *Mahabharata*

[112] *Fortnightly Review*, XXXV (January–June 1884), p. 625.

[113] J.E.S., I (1868–9), p. 134; *Sind Revisited, op. cit.*, I, p. 291, II, p. 256. G. Campbell, *On the Races of India as Traced in Existing Tribes and Castes* (London, 1854), pp. 8–9, *The Ethnology of India* (London, 1872), pp. 18, 22, 29, 31, 57, 81–2; W. W. Hunter, *The Indian Empire, op. cit.*, p. 96; Sir H. Johnston, *Pioneers in India* (London, 1919), pp. 17, 19; Sir George Robertson in T.A.P.S. (1890–6; April 1896), p. 579; C.M.I., I, No. 10 (1865), pp. 294–5.

contained contemptuous descriptions of the Dravidians of the south as black, ape-like, woolly-haired, thick-lipped, and 'noseless' ones.[114] Krishna, the god with a black skin, was thus peculiarly the god of the 'lower orders'.[115] It was pointed out that the lower the caste was, the blacker the colour; a fair skin, especially among females, distinguished the higher classes, a dark skin indicated 'arrested development' (and this admiration for the former was believed to exist even among African Negroes, though to a lesser extent).[116] Ronald Segal, in his *Crisis of India*, reminds us that colour-consciousness still survives in modern India, despite the official abolition of caste, and that African students studying there complain of slights on account of colour, just as they do in Britain.[117] The Victorian colour-consciousness could hardly have failed to reinforce this indigenous prejudice – for did not 'the most scrubby, mean little representative of *la race blanche* . . . regard[s] himself as infinitely superior to the Rajpoot with a genealogy of 1,000 years, or the Mussulman whose ancestors served the early Caliphs'. Or, as the President of the London Ethnological Society baldly stated, speaking for many others, did not 'Beauty and symmetry of person . . . seem to decrease as we proceed from West to East'. While such views prevailed, any Brahmin might be excused for taking pride in the light complexion which reminded his conquerors of their mutual and 'splendid Aryan or Indo-Germanic stock'.[118]

The unfortunate aboriginal tribes did, however, find some defenders, although their lot as helots was accepted without serious protest.[119] We have already seen that they were regarded (being animists and not Hindus) as more receptive to Christianity. They were also of great interest to professional and

[114] W. W. Hunter in *Encyclopaedia Britannica*, XII (1881), p. 776; M. Williams, *Indian Wisdom, or Examples of the Religious, Philosophical, and Ethical Doctrines of the Hindus etc.* (London, 1875), pp. 311, 313.

[115] Williams, *Religious Thought and Life in India, op. cit.*, p. 112.

[116] Burton, *Sindh, op. cit.*, pp. 283, 416; *Sind Revisited, op. cit.*, I, p. 318.

[117] London, 1965, pp. 60, 169.

[118] W. Russell, *Times* correspondent in India, quoted in T.A.P.S., I, No. 10 (October–December 1858), p. 486; Hunter in *Encyclopaedia Britannica*, XII, p. 779; Crawfurd in J.E.S.L., V (1867), p. 60.

[119] See *On the Races of India, op. cit.*, p. 12; Campbell, *The Ethnology of India, op. cit.*, p. 121.

would-be anthropologists. The Khonds, for instance, despite their savagery, were described as hospitable, generous and steadfast; the Kurubars were said to be honest, the Santals quiet, inoffensive, cheerful, industrious and truthful, the Gonds simple and truthful; the skilful adaptation to their environment of the tribes of the central Indian hills was admired, the Todas were the subject of sympathetic study, and H. B. Rowney published in 1882 a judicious survey of *The Wild Tribes of India*.[120] But as far as intellectual attainment was concerned, it was the Aryan (defined as a person with a receptive brain)[121] who once again attracted British admiration.

It was impossible to ignore the fact that he had given evidence of 'immense intellectual energy', had produced a language which was fitly called 'polished' or 'carefully constructed' – namely, Sanskrit – described by Hunter as 'one of the most splendid achievements of human invention and industry'.[122] In addition, he could boast a cultivated literature, particularly some fine epic poetry, and abstruse systems of philosophy and religion, centuries before English existed even in name.[123] It was eminently dangerous, and ultimately impossible, predicted a few observers, to exclude from all share of government a people enlightened over the years by science and education, and possessing organized political, social and domestic institutions. As the Aborigines Protection Society pointed out, there were in India many able natives who, if utilized, might do more for the common advantage of Europeans and Asiatics 'than whole armies of English recruits and foreign mercenaries could

[120] J. Shortt in T.E.S.L., VI (1868), pp. 272–3; William Crooke in J.A.I., XXVIII (1898), p. 223. See evidence of Buchanan, Muir, Sherwell, Champion and others, quoted in C.M.I., II (May 1877), p. 263; W. H. R. Rivers, *The Todas* (London, 1906); Rowney, *The Wild Tribes of India* (London, 1882).

[121] *Spectator*, 1 June 1901, p. 796.

[122] C. Johnston in *Contemporary Review*, LXXIX (January–June 1901), pp. 412–13; Williams, *Religious Thought and Life in India, op. cit.*, p. 4, and Hunter, *The Indian Empire, op. cit.*, pp. 100–1. And see also R. Cust, *A Sketch of the Modern Languages of the East Indies* (London, 1878), p. 149.

[123] C.M.S., *The Bengal Mission, North India* (London, 1892), pp. 19–20, and Williams, *Indian Wisdom, op. cit.*, pp. xvi, 311; Sir Stafford Northcote in P.R.C.I., I (1869), p. 40.

obtain for the one-sided profit of Great Britain alone'.[124] But if, looking to the past, Victorians were impressed by Indian achievements, and admitted that the Hindus were 'a people of more than ordinary capabilities', there was rather less unanimity about prospects for the wide diffusion of knowledge during the second half of the nineteenth century.[125] There were a few sour dissentients, however, even from the general admission of past glories. Thus, John Crawfurd dismissed the absurd notion that Hindu and European were of the same race, for the brain-power of the former was so markedly behind that of the latter. On another occasion, elaborating this theory, Crawfurd maintained that in intellect as in taste, invention, imagination, enterprise and moral sense, the European was greatly superior to the Asiatic; though the latter might be more precocious than the European, from the age of eighteen he was left far behind, as the evidence of mixed schools in India testified.[126]

The scope of English education in India had increased steadily from the 1840s, but the number of students in Government colleges and schools remained small in proportion to population throughout the nineteenth century, while the role of large-scale vernacular schooling was fiercely debated, despite the commitment of 1854, some Victorians regarding it with contempt, others feeling an even greater dislike for the native educated along British lines. (In the same way there was a certain distaste for Indians in European clothes.[127]) The situation was complicated by the opposition of educated Indian opinion to any reduction of Government support for higher education – both for selfish reasons and from a traditional dislike of anything foreign which threatened the existing social order – by the decentralization of the administration of education in 1870, by financial difficulties, and by the difficult position of women and Moslems, the latter for long resentfully opposing English education.

The missionary suspicion of educating merely a small *élite*

---

[124] *Aborigines' Friend*, I, No. viii (1858), p. 327, I, No. vi (April–June 1857), p. 247; and Hunter in *England's Work in India*, op. cit., p. 135; S. Keay, *Nineteenth Century*, XIV (July–December 1883), pp. 11–12.

[125] C.M.I., XIV, No. 12 (1863), p. 271.

[126] T.E.S.L., II (1863), p. 13, and V (1867), p. 60.

[127] See C. T. Buckland, *op. cit.*, pp. 14, 40.

would seem a natural outcome of the notion that missions were most successful among the unresisting poor – the aboriginal peoples of the south, in whom survival-seeking anthropologists were so interested. (In fact, however, missionary work in India aimed first at the higher castes, as the most influential sector of the population.[128] But after about 1870, with the rapid rise in the number of Christian converts, and as a result of Government directives in 1870 and 1883, emphasis was placed upon instructing the rural masses.) Hence a year before the Mutiny an Indian correspondent of the C.M.I. was complaining of the small educated class, which, though smooth and courtly in manner and lively in youth, was overwhelmingly mercenary during the middle years and 'carnalized and stupefied' in old age.[129] The value of Aryan achievements was felt to be diminished when few Hindus were able to comprehend the *Talmud* or the *Vedas*, and these had to be translated by European scholars.[130] The Brahmins could not be relied upon to subsidize the education of Gladstone's 'dumb millions', it was argued, since ignorant people were more easily ruled, and certainly more easily imposed upon, while, according to Mr Samuel John, in Madras, they themselves resisted missionary instruction out of a pride in their wealth, influence, learning and superior caste position. There was, accordingly, growing support for extensive vernacular teaching, concern for the 'crass ignorance' of the underprivileged – some 14 million children of school age were estimated to be unprovided for in 1877 – and the majority of the entire population was pityingly described as illiterate and a-political. In fact, the 'ocean of Indian thought has been for ages stagnant', according to Western exponents of progress, while the rudimentary state of British elementary education, even in 1870, was not generally acknowledged.

There was also a strong dislike and contempt, strengthened by the reports in Parliamentary Blue Books of the mid-1870s and the findings of Lord Lytton, Lord Ripon and others, for the sort of institution which produced so many aspirants for the law and public service that there was unemployment among the nation's *élite*. The literary endeavours (or 'tumid

[128] Bartle Frere, *Indian Missions, op. cit.*, pp. 229–30.
[129] C.M.I., VII, No. 12 (1856), pp. 280–2.
[130] *Ibid.*, VIII (October 1872), pp. 290–1; and Frere, *op. cit.*, p. 43.

declamations', as the C.M.I. preferred to put it) of these scholars came in for a good deal of now-familiar ridicule.[131] Apart from the unfair contempt shown by those whose linguistic achievements were often limited – for instance, in Bengal, on Campbell's evidence[132] – we see here a reflection of the concern shown by the 1882 Government Commission about the over-literary syllabuses in all educational establishments, and the desire for increased technical training. This proposed shift of emphasis was opposed in India as discriminatory, intended to limit the role of educated natives in Government, and is another indication of the problem which Britons had debated with regard to the best educational programme for the freedmen of America and Jamaica.[133] We have already seen that the Indian missionary opposed the secular teaching which was favoured in Government establishments for higher education, on the grounds that this produced a 'gross materialism and rank socialism', hence the 'necessity for suppressing the outspoken sentiments of the vernacular Press', and would ultimately produce a revolt 'in comparison with which the Mutiny was a mere brawl'.[134] By the end of the century the Government itself, under Curzon, was clearly of the mind that the educated minority was indeed dangerous unless its power could be counterbalanced by the extension of British influence over the masses.

The case for vernacular instruction – and, incidentally, greater study of these languages on the part of Britons – as well as ridicule of Indian educational achievements featured prominently in the observations of laymen. Burton, as one would expect, given his flair for languages, took the sensible view that knowledge was power; Orientals despised the ignorant, he believed, so that 'A knowledge of language and manners is all powerful in the East, and the civilized Englishman is called Jangli [i.e. wild man] on account of his neglect of or contempt for the only way to impress his fellow subjects with a feeling

---

[131] C.M.I., VII (January 1882), p. 13, III (December 1878), p. 751, III (March 1878), pp. 144–8, XV (October 1890), p. 661, XII (November 1887), p. 649.

[132] *Memoirs of My Indian Career* (London, 1893, 2 vols.), II, p. 308.

[133] See above, pp. 70–1, 101–2.

[134] Dr C. Macnamara, quoted in C.M.I., VII (January 1882), pp. 15–16.

of respect.' His first study of Sind consequently contained a language appendix, and a tribute to the high standard of vernacular poetry, though most prose works, Burton felt, were of indifferent calibre.[135] Campbell, who was fairly critical of missionaries' work in India (on the grounds that the majority were ill-equipped for their tasks, were over-ambitious, had no social facilities for receiving converts, who hence became rootless outcasts, and insisted on transplanting to India the needless paraphernalia of established churches and elaborate dogma), none the less agreed with them that there was too much emphasis on English and literary training. Homer, he said, might benefit the Englishman, but Milton was of no use whatever to a Hindu. His own preference was for a more practical and scientific type of education, with Hindustani as the main language taught. The European who could not understand any Indian tongues was in many essential matters a blind man, likely to form an unjustly low estimate of native character, to remain ignorant of native education and culture and convinced that the educated Indians were those who spoke bad English.[136] Monier Williams was strongly of the same persuasion, and Robert Cust maintained that a knowledge of the vernaculars could strengthen European rule infinitely more than the use of force.[137]

The British Press, though more concerned about Indian finances and government than anything else, occasionally displayed the typically mocking or patronizing attitude of the late Victorians towards the 'educated native' – as when the *Saturday Review* commented on an article by a Bombay lawyer, whose style 'would not discredit a well-educated Englishman', and the *Spectator* upon the 'dialectic instincts' of the articulate Hindu, which were stronger than in any human being except an Irishman or an English theologian.[138] The *Review* did, however, acknowledge that there was no shortage of Indians clever enough to obtain entry into the

[135] *Sindh, op. cit.*, pp. 58–80, 166.
[136] *India As It May Be, op. cit.*, pp. xvii–xviii, 395–9, 402–3, 406–9.
[137] See letter to *Times*, 7 November 1877; Cust, *A Sketch of the Modern Languages of the East Indies, op. cit.*, pp. 155–6.
[138] *Saturday Review*, 8 September 1866, p. 296; *Spectator*, 14 July 1866, p. 771.

Civil Service, even while suggesting that they might not be honourable enough for such positions.[139] And writers in the *Nineteenth Century* and the *Fortnightly Review* deplored the attempt by Anglo-Indians, when they returned home, still to disparage the native races as corrupt and utterly incompetent to manage their affairs, arguing that in fact the native mind was quick, lucid and eminently judicious, without the supposedly universal tendency to bombast, while for conversation of a political character there were 'few races in the world which can equal those of India'.[140]

Even so the notion of the examination-fixated, incompetent and pompous native official persisted, though Anglo-Indians were for the most part also able to ridicule themselves, and were the subject of ridicule by visiting Britons. Captain Sir Francis Ford's *Neilgherry Letters* offer a sardonic picture of the sort of life an officer on sick leave in the region might expect, while Sir H. S. Cunningham offered a more general but equally mocking account of British life in India in *Chronicles of Dustypore*, complete with dashing military hero adored by his men, a wayward English-rose heroine, a 'competition wallah', patient Army wives, skirmishes in the hills, and a round of social gaiety at its peak between twelve and two, midday.[141] Tom Taylor's popular comedy, *The Overland Route*, ridiculed Indian diplomacy ('a farce very ill acted, and very well paid for'), and boasted a doctor whose chequered career had included the editorship of a newspaper called 'The Mild Hindoo' – before the Mutiny – and a military gentleman who had spent thirty years in India of 'hard work – cold weather and hot – kutchery and jungle – hunting-field and up-country station; not dozing and dangling in lazy, luxurious native courts like some people, with nothing harder to do than nod at a nautch or to take the air on an elephant houdah'.[142] Bengal civil servant C. T. Buckland, in his *Sketches of Social Life in India*, had some wry comments to make on Indian bureaucracy, the ideal official

[139] 20 March 1869, p. 373.

[140] Respectively XV (January–June 1884), p. 559, and XXXVI (July–December 1884), p. 445.

[141] Bombay, 1851, and London, 2 vols., 1875, I, pp. 1, 3, 16–35, 74–100, 199, 277–9, II, pp. 27, 109–10, 285.

[142] Manchester, 1878, pp. 8, 10.

('he should be an Argus and a Briareus. He is often a little sickly-looking man in spectacles'), and the inanities of Anglo-Indian social pastimes, while on the last theme Burton offered an entertaining introduction to the delights of the Bombay season:[143]

> You went to a ball [he predicted] and found it dull; to a concert – duller; to the barn-theatre – dullest. You were invited to a Government House 'garden-party', and saw fifty decently clad people promenading sadly as convicts up and down their strip of jail-ground. You attended a dinner given by the normal 'gentlemanly nonentity', as the lieges say, who governs but who does not rule, and you found it fearfully long, hot, and slow. You walked, umbrella-less, in the mid-day sun, to Malabar Point, and pronounced it cool. You put in an appearance at the races and the steeplechase, and discovered almost all the horses to be half-bred Persians, and the native 'jocks' a race created to lose races. Lastly, you hurried to see a regatta, and you saw nothing.[144]

The Anglo-Indian was, in short, more English than the English; idealizing his homeland because of long absences, his patriotism became somewhat musty – 'it would have been more in place a century ago, when self-glorification was a national failing'.[145]

The writings of Kipling probably present us with the most complete picture of the limitations and vices of Anglo-Indian society, at the same time as he accepts many of the ideas supporting British imperialism. He also accurately sums up the irritation which Anglo-Indians felt for those Englishmen – the 'travelled idiots who duly misgovern the land' – who, though visiting India only briefly, returned home considering themselves experts on the affairs of that great continent.[146] The experiences of Pagett, M.P., on a tour of India (under the impression that it 'would enable him to sweep a larger lyre and address himself to the problems of Imperial administration with a firmer hand') stand as a warning to all such worthies.

[143] *Op. cit.*, pp. 35–6, 45, 57–76, 107.
[144] *Sind Revisited*, *op. cit.*, I, p. 4.
[145] *Spectator*, 1 September 1866, pp. 966–7.
[146] 'Pagett, M.P.', in *Departmental Ditties*, etc. (London and New York, 1925 ed.), p. 48; see also Francis G. Hutchins, *The Illusion of Permanence. British Imperialism in India* (Princeton, 1967), p. 134, for a contemptuous comment on Monier Williams as just such a 'travelled idiot', by J. F. Stephen.

Full of Liberal notions and anxious to hear about the National Congress movement, Pagett offends or misunderstands everyone he meets and is reduced to the gloomy conclusions that the ballot is not a universal panacea, and that India is 'a very curious place'. His host and old friend, Orde, emerges by contrast as tolerant, cynical and well-informed – the epitome of Anglo-Indian virtues.[147]

An early work, *Departmental Ditties*, published in 1886 and well received on Kipling's own testimony, exposed some less sterling qualities, and was based upon the proposition that

> 'As it was in the beginning
> Is to-day official sinning,
> And shall be for evermore!'[148]

Unfair promotions, official pomposity, the guile of the careerist and the futility of criticising 'the authorities', marital dilemmas in a closed community – these are the author's subject matter here and in many other verses and stories.[149] As far as social matters are concerned, however, Kipling's tone is often ambivalent. In several accounts of informal sexual liaisons between Indian women and English men, the latter's callous indifference to their responsibilities is well brought out, but John Holden in *Without Benefit of Clergy* is an honourable if unfortunate exception.[150] Kipling also pays tribute to the wifely skills and devotion of the ill-used Indian women he describes, even while subscribing to the view that 'A man should, whatever happens, keep to his own caste, race and breed. Let the White go to the White and the Black to the Black'.[151] The difficulties

[147] 'Enlightenments of Pagett, M.P.', *In Black and White* (New York, 1899), pp. 340–86, especially 342, 386. See also 'A Friend's Friend', in *Plain Tales from the Hills* (New York, 1899), pp. 288–9.

[148] See *Something of Myself. For My Friends Known and Unknown* (New York, 1937), p. 73, and 'General Summary', *Departmental Ditties, op. cit.*, p. 8.

[149] *In Black and White, op. cit.*, pp. 101–38.

[150] See, for instance, *Wressley of the Foreign Office*, pp. 322–6, and *Thrown Away*, p. 19 in *Plain Tales, op. cit.*

[151] 'Beyond the Pale', p. 189, in *Plain Tales from the Hills, op. cit.*; see also 'Georgie Porgie', *In Black and White, op. cit.*, pp. 233–46; 'Lispeth' in *Plain Tales, op. cit.*, especially pp. 2, 4, 5, 7; and 'Yoked with an Unbeliever', in *ibid.*, pp. 48–54.

of meeting native prejudices with understanding are fully recognized – for instance in *Tod's Amendment* and *The Judgement of Dungara*, although due praise is given to perceptive Anglo-Indian administrators such as Gallio and Yardley-Orde, featured in the last named story and *The Head of the District*.[152] At one point the author frankly acknowledges the fact that 'native and English stare at each other hopelessly across great gulfs of miscomprehension.'[153] A tale like *Moti Guy – Mutineer* depicting a shiftless, drunken elephant driver, given to lies and self-indulgence, follows the tribute to native dignity, courage and unselfishness revealed by the narrator of *In Flood Time*, in Kipling's volume, *In Black and White*.[154]

According to Francis Hutchins, the years after the Mutiny saw an increased interest in Orientalism on the part of Anglo-Indians – something I have earlier denied.[155] However, it is further acknowledged that this interest implied an appreciation of only those things Indian that were relevant to the practice of British Government. (Thus, as we have seen, strong rule was lauded as being in British interests, as well as acceptable to those they ruled.) The late nineteenth-century Orientalist, in other words, believed that British principles should be applied in India, but so disguised as to coincide with, or become acceptable to Indian notions of what was proper. 'Going Native' was not now envisaged, since we have here an explicit assumption that Indian civilisation and character were to be easily understood, at least through the superior perceptions of the Anglo-Indian. Kipling's Kim is perhaps the most famous fictional illustration of such assumptions.[156] The combination of knowledgeable interest in Indian life, humourous self-knowledge of British foibles, and assumptions of racial superiority which characterize Hutchins' Orientalist can be seen to characterize the writing of Kipling, even though in his treatment of race he is often a critic rather than a representative of his age.

[152] See *Plain Tales, op. cit.,* pp. 217–26; *In Black and White, op. cit.,* pp. 46–59; and *Life's Handicap* (London, 1914), pp. 184–211.

[153] *Op. cit.,* p. vii.

[154] *Op. cit.,* pp. 75–100.

[155] See above, p. 179.

[156] Hutchins, *op. cit.,* pp. 153–4, 156–8, 171–4, 194–5.

However, it is clear that even such observations are as much a reflection upon the general shortcomings inherent in a life of exile, beyond the pale of civilization and in the midst of ignorant or ludicrous foreigners, as a repudiation of Britons' insular values. Victorians enjoyed writing about themselves in this way, dissecting the British character, determining its virtues, deciding upon a few shortcomings, generally not too heinous. Thus we know that while anthropologists condemned the British tendency to ignore racial differences and idiosyncrasies, they firmly upheld the superiority of Western – including British – languages, intellect, character and appearance. Similarly, while a critical journal like the *Spectator* might admit that the Englishman at his worst was unamiable, melancholy, contradictory, obstinate, a worshipper of success, even dull of intellect, it was also careful to point out that on the credit side Britons displayed an imaginative vitality, tolerance and sympathy which were 'partly responsible for the Imperial idea', and largely responsible for the philanthropic impulse which enabled them 'to do among those with whom they are in no personal sympathy arduous and often repulsive work, whose failure they continually see and of whose success they are seldom sure'.[157] Likewise, Walter Bagehot was prepared to recognize the inadequacy of British rule in India, but explained that a highly civilized race might fail in rapidly producing an excellent effect on a less civilized race 'because it is too good and too different. The two are not *en rapport* together. . . . The higher being is not and cannot be a model for the lower; he could not mould himself on it if he would, and would not if he could.'[158]

In comparison certainly with the Negro inhabitants of Africa, the Indian was redeemed in British eyes, not only by his appearance and cultural heritage, but by his 'industrial energy', though a widespread belief in Oriental apathy and the daunting, 'all but invisible resistance of the East' to progress, sometimes gave credence to the analogy presented in Thomson's 'Castle of Indolence':

[157] 12 February 1898, p. 232, 1 June 1901, p. 798.
[158] *Physics and Politics* (London, 1872), p. 145.

And oftentimes, how long I fear to say,
Where apple-trees in blossom make a bower,
Retired in that sunshiny shade he lay;
And, like a naked Indian, slept himself away.[159]

Crawfurd predictably maintained that the Hindu was inferior in the useful arts to the Chinese, believing that the latter would earn, in the same market, fully three times the wages of the former, and were at present performing work in the Australian and Californian gold-fields for which Hindus were 'no more fit than they are to perform the labour of English navigators'. Since Crawfurd believed that Europeans could endure the Indian climate, it was inevitable that he would pin his hopes for that continent on British immigration and labour.[160]

The comparison of other races with the Chinese when questions of labour arose was in fact very popular among Victorians, who were agreed that the key characteristic of that race was diligence. Henry Guppy, a Fellow of the London Anthropological Society, during the Society's debates on the Negro in the 1860s, voiced the common opinion that Chinese and Indian coolies, but especially the former, were far superior in diligence and thrift.[161] As far as Africa was concerned, missionary C. T. Wilson described the Baganda as the Chinese of Africa, because of their shrewdness and skill as craftsmen; while Captain Galton, in a letter to *The Times* in 1873, deplored the laziness of the East Coast natives he had encountered and made out a case for Chinese immigration (the Hindu was not seen as so hard-working or strong.)[162] However, as one might anticipate, even this race had its drawbacks – appearance and 'Oriental' depravity being those most usually singled out. H. B. Evans, for instance, opposed the introduction of Chinese labourers in the West Indies, because, while hard-working, they were 'cunning, selfish, cowardly, and treacherous', and if there was any truth in physiognomy or phrenology 'what good thing can come out of that narrow forehead, depressed face, flat nose, small eyes, high cheek bones, without hair, and those

---

[159] *Saturday Review*, 20 October 1877, p. 474; *Spectator*, 21 August 1868, p. 1,058, and 11 December 1880, p. 1,582.
[160] T.E.S.L., I (1861), pp. 77, 88–9, 160, 162.
[161] A.R., II (1864), p. ccxi.
[162] C.M.I., III (August 1878), p. 483; *Times*, 5 June 1873.

long ears?'[163] In the same suspicious mood, New Zealand settler J. C. Firth argued that although 'John Chinaman' was industrious, expert, obedient, inoffensive and thrifty, 'his social habits and certain nameless vices render him altogether unfit to form a portion of any Anglo-Saxon community'. Opium-smoking was mentioned by Firth, and was not one of the nameless vices; even though it was taboo to whites in India, as V. G. Kiernan has pointed out, since Britain fought a war to compel the Chinese to smoke Indian-grown opium, one could scarcely expect this to be so for natives.[164] It is clear that fears about excessive fertility also played a part in forming Victorian notions about the Chinese – although in global terms, as G. M. Trevelyan noted at the turn of the century, the yellow peril was not so terrible as the white – while the Chinese character and culture presented some problems, inscrutability being particularly resented, as it was in the Hindu.[165] Even when the romantic and humanitarian versions of the Negro temperament had been drastically revised, Victorians appear to have felt more confident in their understanding of the latter.

However, when attention was directed to matters they could immediately appreciate, the verdict on the Indians and the Chinese was favourable. Accordingly, a writer in the *Contemporary Review* suggested that in India and China alike the yellow races were 'amongst the most skilful agriculturalists in the world', and the *Spectator* rated the Indian, Tuscan and Irish peasants equally as the most economical of mankind. Such a view was strongly entertained by, among others, Sir George Campbell, who also favoured colonizing the surplus population of India in other British dependencies, which might then benefit from its docility, intelligence and industry. The Jats and Rajputs were particularly lauded for these qualities (notwithstanding that the womenfolk of the latter were often secluded and hence lost to agriculture), and even the

[163] *Op. cit.*, p. 31.
[164] *Our Kin Across the Sea* (London, 1888), pp. 181–2; Kiernan, *The Lords of Human Kind* (London, 1969), pp. 96–7, and see also pp. 146–72 on British attitudes to China.
[165] Firth, *op. cit.*, p. 183; *Nineteenth Century*, L (July–December 1901), p. 1,054; H. Johnston in *Fortnightly Review*, XLVIII (July–December 1890), p. 705; see also B. Johnson, *Letters from John Chinaman* (London, 1901).

inhabitants of southern India received their share of praise.[166] Achievement in this sphere was especially creditable, bearing in mind the poverty and indebtedness of much of the peasantry.

These attitudes were supplemented by both major interpretations of the Indian character, which we have already considered, and which accorded a cautious respect to the astute and intriguing Hindu trader. The antithesis of the Indian, in such respects, was the North American Indian, rated by Victorians as inferior even to the Negro. The reasons for their contempt were the same as the reasons put forward by Americans for depriving the Indians of their land.[167] Cooper and other romantics notwithstanding, the Indians were seen as barbarous and indolent people, who preferred eking out a miserable existence wandering over the great plains, murdering and pilfering, 'rather than accept in peace and good faith the guardianship and protection' which the United States Government had always extended.[168] In other words they would not cultivate and develop their land (unlike the Maoris); hence the men were idle, the women mere domestic drudges, and they were destined to be dispossessed, though one British cynic did describe the theory of manifest destiny as simply 'American for robbery'.[169]

It is clear, after 1857, that the romance of India did vanish for many of the Britons who visited or settled there, and that this contributed to the development of harsher racial attitudes. However, the old thirst for the picturesque was not entirely lacking in Britain itself. Take, for example, this comment from the *Church Missionary Intelligencer* in 1871:

[166] *Contemporary Review*, LXXIX (January–June 1901), p. 410; *Spectator*, 11 December 1880, p. 1,577; Campbell, *White and Black*, op. cit., p. 119; and *The Ethnology of India*, op. cit., pp. 77, 86–7; *On the Races of India*, op. cit., pp. 13–14.

[167] A. K. Weinberg, *Manifest Destiny, a Study of Nationalist Expansionism in American History* (Baltimore, 1935), pp. 72–92.

[168] M. C. Fisher in J.E.S., I (1868–9), pp. 275, 279–82, and J. Crawfurd, T.E.S.L., I (1861), p. 78, and II (1863), p. 7.

[169] General Thompson, M.P., in *Aborigines' Friend*, I, No. vii (July–October 1857), p. 294.

Who can describe the India of the untravelled popular mind? The days of romantic, jewelled visions of the East are past indeed, but there still remains enough to bewilder – the car of Juggernaut, the hideous idol, the sacred river, murderous Thugs, shrivelled fakirs, crafty Brahmins, bigoted Mussulmans, the gibberish of heathen tongues, the seething mass of complicated and horrible superstitions, all illumined by the flames of the Mutiny which cannot be forgotten.[170]

Descriptions of a type supposedly vanished, full of allusions to palm trees, acacias, airy palaces, golden temples, tempting bazaars displaying barbaric jewels and precious ornaments, to pilgrims, holy mendicants and nautch-girls, are to be found in J. Moore's *The Queen's Empire, or Ind and Her Pearl*, published in 1892.[171] Even after the Mutiny the *Spectator* suggested that most Englishmen derived their knowledge of the Orient from the Bible and *A Thousand and One Nights*, and acknowledged the glamour of an Asian climate (the smouldering days and balmy nights), while Bartle Frere noted that the popular picture of a Mohammedan was compounded from Bluebeard and the Crusades.[172] But a change had taken place, as witness the small degree of interest in India on the part of amateur and professional artists alike, and the determined modelling of buildings constructed in the second half of the century on purely European styles.

Many observers recorded the widening gulf between rulers and ruled to which such developments contributed. The Anglo-Indian came in for a large share of blame. Whereas once officials had taken pains to understand the Indian people, made themselves accessible, occasionally married local women, and looked upon India as a semi-permanent home, receiving love, respect and good service in return, in time better transport, easier vacations, and the coming of more Britons and their wives had put an end to the contracting of native habits and native ties. Officers and bureaucrats coming back from furlough brought with them a renewed stock of Western prejudices, were more mercenary, less well-informed and of an inferior

[170] C.M.I., VII, No. 1 (1871), p. 28.
[171] Published, Philadelphia.
[172] 14 July 1866, p. 770, 12 November 1898, p. 694; Frere, *Indian Missions, op. cit.*, p. 54.

class, but none the less sought to 'lord it' (the competitive Civil Service was said to be at fault here). English women were seen as particularly prejudiced on matters of race. This naturally made social mixing difficult, since the women scorned it, their husbands had come to favour it less, while the Indian was indignantly aware that 'your ladies look upon me as something of a wild beast, and you yourself perhaps grow a little brutal after your third glass of sherry'. There was general agreement that Englishmen and Indians were so different that they could not amalgamate, no matter how beneficial this might be to the latter. The consciousness of belonging to a conquering race, of possessing a white skin and European dress (however unsuited to the climate), and memories of the Mutiny all served to support the racial arrogance of the Anglo-Indian clique, which 'neither loves India nor has been able to command its love'.[173]

Nor were the prospects of this group's being called to account by public opinion at home particularly encouraging. Ethnologists complained that the improved data at their disposal was not widely disseminated.[174] Journalists and others deplored the lack of Parliamentary interest in Indian affairs, which was reflected at a wider level.[175] The Fellows of the Royal Colonial Institute frequently deprecated the extraordinary and apparently insuperable ignorance that existed in Britain in regard to colonial matters, and among the various colonies with regard to each other.[176]

This is largely to be explained by the phenomenon we have already noted – namely, the widening of the gulf between the races after 1858, in spite of the growing body of literature on Indian affairs, and even though the growing numbers of whites might have been expected to swell the total of Victorians

[173] *Fortnightly Review*, XXV (January–June 1884), pp. 447–58; *Saturday Review*, 8 September 1866, p. 297; *Spectator*, 11 August 1866, pp. 882–3; Campbell, *India as It May Be, op. cit.*, pp. 422–3; Williams, *Modern India, op. cit.*, pp. 111–13, 189; Bryce, *Studies in History and Jurisprudence, op. cit.*, I, pp. 61, 75–6.

[174] See H. Risley, Bengal, J.A.I., XX (1890–1), p. 235.

[175] See, for instance, *Saturday Review*, 2 February 1867, p. 129, 16 June 1877, pp. 722–3, 17 August 1867, p. 201; *Spectator*, 12 March 1898, p. 365.

[176] P.R.C.I., I (1869), p. 9, Marquis of Normandy, p. 10, Baillie Cochrane, M.P., p. 49, Sir Charles Nicholson; VI (1874–5), p. 61, George Campbell.

informed on Indian affairs, and it might have been anticipated that improved communications between India and Britain, and throughout India itself, would have secured the same effect. For there was not even the same terror of disease which had once kept the European away from Africa, though cholera and malaria were considerable hazards until the end of the century, and there remained those who believed that the 'eastern longitudes' and 'southern latitudes' together produced 'certain climatic effects which are absolutely fatal and inimical to our Anglo-Saxon race', so that only the middle years, with safety, could be spent in India.[177]

Apparently, however, neither lack of interest at home nor lack of understanding in India inhibited the British will to retain India (as is illustrated simply by the continued growth of the Anglo-Indian community). As in Africa, enjoyment of the sense of a heroic exile, desire for social advancement, for physical adventure, the missionary impulse, and a sense of destiny and moral responsibility all strengthened a desire at least to sustain what Britain already held. Whilst educated Indians (and Englishmen) might complain of the arrogant British manner which 'creates ill-feeling and distrust, excites recrimination, and engenders a war of races', the main tendency of Victorian thinking – rooted in the sorts of racial attitude we have been examining – was to support a despotic administration conducted on strictly Western principles, and to approve the cultural and class barriers which existed between Indian and Briton.[178] As Sir Richard Temple put it in 1880, if he lived in India the latter, whatever his means, must live like the gentleman he was. The ex-Governor of Bengal went on to assert that the Indian population was very contented with its lot, and, believing the continent belonged to Indians and English alike, argued that they should 'run a race which is to be the swiftest . . . [a] battle of emulation in which the victory will go to the strongest – not the strongest physically, but the strongest intellectually and

[177] For the view that the climate was not a real barrier see C.M.I., I, No. 11 (1865), p. 324; for a contrary view, Sir Richard Temple, one-time Governor of Bombay, P.R.C.I., XII (1880–1), pp. 60–1, and H. Clarke, Agent for Darjeeling, *The English Stations in the Hill Regions of India: Their Value and Importance, With Some Statistics of Their Products and Trade* (London, 1881), pp. 39, 41–2.

[178] Professor Dadabhai Naoroji in T.E.S.L., V (1867), p. 127.

morally'. He was in little doubt as to the outcome.[179] These attitudes were well summed up by James Bryce, writing at the turn of the century:[180]

> Three things [he suggested] the career of the English in India has proved. One is, that it is possible for a European race to rule a subject race on principles of strict justice, restraining the natural propensity of the stronger to abuse their power. . . . The second is that a relatively small body of European civilians, supported by a relatively small armed force, can maintain peace and order in an immense population standing on a lower plane of civilization. . . . The third fact is that the existence of a system securing these benefits is compatible with an absolute separation between the rulers and the ruled.

[179] P.R.C.I., XII (1880–1), p. 71.
[180] *Studies in History and Jurisprudence, op. cit.*, I, pp. 79–80.

VI

⬦⬦⬦⬦⬦⬦⬦⬦⬦⬦⬦⬦⬦⬦⬦⬦⬦⬦⬦⬦⬦⬦⬦⬦⬦⬦⬦⬦⬦⬦⬦⬦⬦⬦

Conclusion

⬦⬦⬦⬦⬦⬦⬦⬦⬦⬦⬦⬦⬦⬦⬦⬦⬦⬦⬦⬦⬦⬦⬦⬦⬦⬦⬦⬦⬦⬦⬦⬦⬦⬦

> The conflicts of Governments are nothing, it is
> the conflicts of races and peoples that must in
> the end determine the march of events.
> *The Mining Magazine*[1]

JAMES BRYCE once accurately remarked that 'No branches of historical inquiry have suffered more from fanciful speculation than those which relate to the origin and attributes of the races of men . . . Hypotheses are tempting because, though it may be impossible to verify them, it is, in the paucity of data, almost impossible to refute them.'[2] Although Victorians agreed upon the importance of racial theories and conflicts, there was a vagueness as to the exact meaning of the word 'race' which brought, as we have seen, a dangerous confusion between biological and cultural concepts. Nor was 'racism' a much more precise term. (The modern dictionary definition, a 'tendency to racial feeling', an 'antagonism between different races of men', only states the obvious. O. Mannoni's verdict that 'racism' is 'simply a rather poor rationalization of our feelings of indignation' is more helpful.[3] It is not, however, and never has been, merely a matter of black and white. The race question of South Africa at the beginning of the twentieth century was essentially

---

[1] Comment shortly after the turn of the century, quoted in H. Mantsch, *Leopold Graf Berchtold* (Verlag Styria, Gratz, 1963), I, p. 231.

[2] J. Bryce, *Race Sentiment as a Factor in History* (London, 1915), p. 3.

[3] *The Concise Oxford Dictionary of Current English* (ed. H. W. and F. G. Fowler, 4th ed., Oxford, 1951), p. 994, and Mannoni, *op. cit.*, p. 117.

the friction existing between two opposed groups of white men. Not until the nineteenth century did racism begin to acquire its popular association with colour prejudice.

It was also during this century that race became the subject of serious scientific investigation in Britain, as ethnological and anthropological societies extended their activities, and these disciplines were taken up by the British Association and at the universities. Although at the close of the century anthropology had developed enormously in scope and detachment from its beginnings in the 1840s, and had become, according to Edward Freeman, a more popular subject for study than philosophy, some of its early and more controversial findings had undoubtedly exercised an adverse influence on British racial attitudes.[4]

The theory of polygenesis, or separate origins for the different races of man, had been in circulation for hundreds of years when Darwinian discoveries gave it a new importance in scientific circles. (For although Darwin disclaimed any wish to attack religion, his work undermined the Christian and philanthropic defence of monogenesis – or a single, Adamite creation – still further.) In particular, the doctrine of natural selection, as simplified by Spencer, was used by anthropologists to underline the differences between human groups, and to support the theory of the survival of the fittest. Thus, in Spencer's words, it became possible to maintain that 'The poverty of the incapable, the distress that comes upon the imprudent, the starvation of the idle, and those shoulderings aside of the weak by the strong, which leave so many in "shallows and miseries", are the decrees of a large, far-seeing benevolence'.[5] And hence it was feasible to explain as a respectable phenomenon the decline of aboriginal tribes in New Zealand, South Africa and the Americas. With a large degree of wishful thinking, some Victorians maintained that if the survival-of-the-fittest principle operated as it should, the Negro population of North America and the West Indies might soon follow these tribes towards extinction, though such hopes could scarcely be entertained about the bulk of the population of Africa or India.

In this context it should also be noted that, to the

[4] Freeman in *Contemporary Review*, XXIX (December 1876–May 1877), p. 718.
[5] *Social Statics* (London, 1850), p. 323.

polygenesists, though the mixing of widely different races might benefit the inferior, it damaged the superior race, producing a contemptible and infertile hybrid. It is not too difficult to see in these theories the foundation for the racial interpretations of history which are an essential part of imperialism, as well as a theoretical justification for the strict separation of white and non-white which was to become such a feature of society in South Africa, India and the American South. The vanity of the European, and especially the Anglo-Saxon, was increased still further by the testimony of ethnologists as to the superiority of Aryan or inflectional languages over the agglutinative or isolating types, generally confined to Africa and Asia. (Language diversity was also used as an argument for polygenesis, though less frequently in England than in France.) Dubious experiments to establish variations in skull measurements, facial angle, and the dimensions of the brain among different peoples also seemed to confirm the intellectual superiority of Western man, physical structure being seen as determining mental and moral characteristics. Almost all methods of classifying the human species, in fact, whether by language, brain, physical features or colour resulted in the European coming out on top.

Although evolutionary theory was accepted and popularized by the anthropological societies which were founded in Paris, London, Florence, Berlin, Vienna, Moscow and New York between 1859 and 1870, it should, however, be remembered that not all British anthropologists equated evolution with the inevitability of British progress, just as not all Victorians admired the popular definition of progress and civilization as consisting of 'the political economist, the sanitary reformer, the engineer . . . the spinning jenny and the railroad, Cunard's liners and the electric telegraph.'[6] (Today we would accept, in fact, that, far from opposing progress, as all non-Europeans were said to do by reason of race, Africans and Asians are manifestly not lacking in that questioning attitude of mind which produces change.)

This study has been concerned to show the different ways in which Victorian writers looked at Indian and African peoples.

[6] Charles Kingsley, quoted in W. E. Houghton, *The Victorian Frame of Mind, 1830–1870* (London, 1957), pp. 43–4.

It seems clear that the latter have always provoked far more animosity, and that the reasons for this are important.

Cultural arrogance and the ignorance of African history which prevailed until very recently allowed Europeans to assume that the Negro *had* no history (and most Victorians saw Africa as exclusively populated by Negroes). Accordingly, it was stated that 'No full-blooded Negro has ever been distinguished as a man of science, a poet, or an artist, and the fundamental equality claimed for him by ignorant philanthropists is belied by the whole history of the race throughout the historic period'.[7] Political institutions were rudimentary among Negroes, they had no religion worthy of the name, they had never exploited the rich continent they occupied, so the theory went; they were strong, but lacked brain-power, slaves to their own passions and the natural slaves of other races. Children of Nature, the Negroes apparently had no natural rights. Such rights, it came to be believed, depended entirely upon the nature of the possessor, not of the right. These characteristics were thought to belong as much to the Negroes in America and the West Indies as to the black African; indeed, the former were frequently referred to and condemned as Africans throughout the nineteenth century, in spite of the fact that many had no memory of their place of origin, and most had accommodated themselves to their new homes over fundamental questions like religion, dress and language. (This fact would seem to suggest that while race and culture were often confused, it was fundamental biological factors like colour and physical appearance which mattered most in producing prejudice.) Enough was known and thought of India's ancient civilization, however, to make criticisms along these lines impossible.

A crucial point of difference between all black peoples and the Indian races, according to Victorian opinion, was the greater savagery of the former, as demonstrated, for instance, in the South African Wars and the Jamaica revolt of 1865. The Indian Mutiny and Afghan campaigns could not, of course, be explained away, and it must be admitted that the more martial tribes of both Africa and India won respect, but the myth of the soft, effete Hindu persisted, and its overtones were not unfriendly. The Mutiny was not felt to be a product of the peculiar savagery

[7] *Encyclopaedia Britannica*, XVII (1884), p. 318.

of the Sepoy, in spite of the immediate Press outcry along these lines. When the dust had settled, the inefficiency and insensitivity of British rule in certain areas was admitted, at least as a partial extenuation.

It is a telling indication of the degree of Victorian prejudice against the Negro that after 1857 the word 'nigger', as a term of abuse, gained some currency in India among the white community, particularly in military circles. And nothing, even during that year, could match the tone of writers on the Jamaica rebellion (cited by the *Church Times* to illustrate the change in public sentiment on matters of race), who rejoiced that the philanthropist had had his day: 'Gentlemen of Exeter Hall, the game is entirely up! Ladies, given to "presiding" over weak tea and tooth-endangering currant loaves, your ebony friend has fallen from his high estate and swings, by representation, for the delectation of the turkey buzzards of the Gulf of Mexico! It was high time.'[8]

The question of colour was also vitally important in determining British attitudes, but never in the same way, with regard to India, as it was in Africa. This was because large sections of the Indian population – the so-called Aryans of the north – measured up to European standards of beauty, and the higher castes gave evidence of the sort of aversion to a black complexion and Negroid features that was to be found in Britain. In India, furthermore, colour prejudice was not reinforced with class consciousness to anything like the degree it was in Africa, America and the West Indies, where poverty and consequent low status made the coloured population inevitable targets of contempt for whites accustomed to despise uneducated working men of their own race. This is not to say that class was not an issue in India, of course, but it became so plainly only in the closing decades of the nineteenth century, when the challenge of Indian nationalism produced fear, bitterness, and the insistent implementation by the British of every possible barrier between the races, to maintain the necessary myth of white superiority.

Religion and caste were at the outset far greater obstacles to racial harmony in India. Although the acceptance for centuries of alien rule laid the inhabitants of that continent open to contempt in the climate of the nineteenth century, they, like

[8] 25 November 1865.

210

the Chinese, were not thought to be lacking in 'industrial energy' – in marked contrast to the proverbially indolent Negro. In addition, if we are to attach any importance to Mannoni's 'Prospero complex' as affecting the white colonist – a malady which was frequently diagnosed, though not so defined, by Victorians themselves – the Indian middle class apparently showed its 'gratitude' for British rule by an initial acceptance of English education and the English language. Even by the end of the century there were comparatively few parts of Africa where this could be said to be true.

The enslavement of the African since the sixteenth century, which had disturbed and sometimes destroyed indigenous cultures, was also crucial in accounting for his low estimation in Western eyes, and we have seen that not even British abolitionists and missionaries were free from the cultural arrogance and colour prejudice to which knowledge of this fact and of Britain's commercial and technical preeminence in the world naturally inclined them. (There is no Indian counterpart of the 'poor deluded African' beloved by Exeter Hall, just as there are no Indian equivalents of such offensive epithets as 'Sambo' and 'Quashee'. The constantly conquered deserved more respect, in the Victorian world, than the constantly enslaved.) The early anthropologists, because they generally had little patience with the philanthropist, went far to discredit the doctrines of human equality which the latter had at least publicly advanced. But it was infinitely preferable, in my view, to argue such doctrines from Christian conviction, notwithstanding frequent ignorance of African conditions and private prejudices, than to argue against equality in a scholarly fashion, on the grounds that African religious beliefs or cultural achievements were inferior or non-existent. (Such were the reasons put forward by James Hunt and his followers for maintaining that the Negro was the lowest form of man, and the link, so far as could be determined, between human and anthropoid life.)

The Negro likewise suffered even more than the Indian from the traditional attempts, still popular in Victorian times, to explain the main racial divisions of the world in terms of Biblical history, particularly regarding Noah and his three sons. An anonymous American pamphlet published in 1860, a last justification of the South's 'peculiar institution' in the face of Lincoln's election, maintained that the world's population was divided into three principal groups, descended from Shem, Japheth and Canaan. According to its author, 'Ethnology, as well as Scripture, testifies that Ham peopled Egypt. The native name for Egypt is Chami, the black. The race of Ham includes Egypt and all the black tribes beyond. In the North Caucasian regions the [white] race of Japheth spread widely; and in central Asia the [brown] race of Shem.' The whole Negro population of Africa, he then went on to insist, 'manifest in their low animal propensities, the same utter lack of reverence for duty, the disregard of decency, and the insensibility to shame', which characterized the conduct of Ham towards his father, Noah. These assertions were supported with reference to Blumenbach, Morton, Cuvier, Bunsen and Pritchard. The Indian descendants of Shem fared a little better, but the writer felt that the Hindu could not be compared with the Anglo-Saxon: 'As well compare the lordly lion with the creeping jackal, the war-horse, "his neck clothed with thunder", with the servile ass, "crouching down between two burdens".'[9]

Such notions were supported, around the same time, by the English cleric Dr J. Cumming, who stated flatly that Shem represented the Asiatic, Japheth the European, and Canaan the African, while at present both the offspring of Canaan and of Ham were 'bondsmen', as predicted. Hence 'the African is a slave still', and England was 'the mistress of all India; the most magnificent of the tents of Shem'. (On the grounds of Noah's curse, Cumming in fact argued that England would not lose India, 'for the prediction is that it is to be hers'.)[10]

But if, in some important respects, British attitudes to Indian and African peoples varied considerably, there were certain ways in which they were similarly viewed. Both were regarded as potential recipients of the Christian message, since Christianity was thought to be as superior to Islam, Buddhism or Hinduism, as it was to the 'mere fetishism' of the Negro, and its fortunate adherents bound to undertake proselytism on as wide

[9] *The Governing Race: a Book for the Time, and for All Times*, by H.O.R. (Washington, 1860), pp. 8–9, 39, 62.
[10] Cumming, *The Destiny of Nations, op. cit.*, p. 172; *The Great Tribulation, op. cit.*, pp. 283–4.

a front as possible. As a clergyman speaking at an Ethnological Society meeting in 1863 remarked, nations which had adopted Christianity were those, like Britain, 'that had been raised to the highest conditions of superiority; and wherever the Christian nations set foot they will not degenerate'; but it was equally clear that racial superiority was given by God 'for the accomplishment of some good work on this earth'.[11]

It has been argued that missionary enterprise came to be an essential part of imperialism; this assumption, though containing a strong element of truth, has been debated by some scholars, and in any event is an over simplification.[12] We have noticed the hostile criticism levied against foreign missions by sections of the Victorian Press, by anthropologists, and by travellers critical of their methods. The C.M.S. complained in 1850 that while all matters connected with the overseas extension of trade and commerce and the prosecution of scientific research aroused public interest, 'Missionary labours, except so far as details of geographical discovery are interwoven with them, continue to be undervalued and despised'.[13]

The position had improved considerably by the end of the century, and missionary periodicals and lives had a large readership in Britain (as did all other similar records of personal adventure and national achievement). During the 1890s the *Spectator* carried a series of letters devoted to the proposition that the progressive and imperialistic nations of the world were all Protestant – Protestantism had produced in Britain 'a more robust and virile type of national character' – and purporting to show that it was 'possible to be a Christian and yet a conqueror'.[14] But though the missionary might be caught up in the extension of British rule in Africa, and while his support for 'legitimate' commerce as an aid to Christian civilization and attack on one vital aspect of African culture might seem to

[11] Rev. Brymer Belcher in T.E.S.L., II (1863), p. 21.

[12] For a denial of missionary pressure for imperial take-overs see R. Oliver, *The Missionary Factor in East Africa* (London, 1952); for the opposite view see K. S. Latourette, *The Great Century in Europe and the United States of America, A.D. 1800–A.D. 1914* (London, 1941), p. 52.

[13] C.M.I., I (1850), No. 10, p. 219.

[14] 29 October 1898, p. 591, 22 October 1898, p. 558, 8 October 1898, p. 488.

invite this extension, as we have seen, the evangelist could also find himself in conflict with the trader and official, assuming the role of defender of people he had come to convert.

Elsewhere it is even less easy to make a definite connection between missionary and imperialist attitudes. In America and Jamaica during the period under review the question does not, of course, arise. In India it is apparent that missionary efforts were greatly stepped up after the assumption of control by Britain in 1858, and received covert Government aid. But during the years of British penetration the founding of missions had been strongly opposed, an indication of the Victorians' greater respect for Eastern religions, as well as of a shrewd self-interest on the part of the East India Company.

Another area in which both Indian and African suffered from British prejudice was colour, as we have seen. The degree of colour-consciousness to be found among Victorians seems peculiar to the Anglo-Saxon. Strictly representative of its tone was the reaction of a writer who, when approached for a donation to missionary funds, declined to help 'a lot of woolly-headed, thick-lipped monsters of ugliness'.[15] This prejudice was freely acknowledged in Britain, and was strengthened by the connotations which the word 'black' had come to acquire in English by the nineteenth century, and with reference to scientific arguments about the undesirability of interbreeding between superior and inferior races. Writing in 1902, James Bryce concluded that nothing arrested racial fusion except physical repulsion, and that 'physical repulsion exists only where there is a marked difference in physical aspect, and especially colour'. Not all white races, he believed, were averse to intermarriage with races far different from themselves: the Arabs, the Turks and the southern Europeans were not; the red and yellow races showed only slight reluctance; the English, however, totally opposed amalgamation with the non-whites they ruled.[16] This may have been the result of regarding the latter, to use Michael Banton's terminology, as archetypal strangers, both in appearance and behaviour. For in Britain xenophobia was recognized as the norm even in Victorian times – as Goldwin Smith admitted in 1878, the 'insular arrogance of

[15] Quoted in P.M.A., I (1866), p. 20.
[16] *Race Sentiment as a Factor in History* (London, 1915), pp. 18–20.

the English character is a commonplace joke. . . . For an imperial people it is a very unlucky peculiarity, since it precludes not only fusion, but sympathy and almost intercourse with the subject races.'[17] (This hypothesis is not necessarily incompatible with the colour-class interpretation of Kenneth Little already noted; my own researches would support the findings of Sheila Patterson – namely, that most Britons entertained preconceptions about both the strangeness *and* low status of coloured peoples.[18])

British notions with regard to the wisdom of strong government over 'uncivilized' peoples, and their own destiny and moral responsibility to provide such leadership and bestow civilization, are also predictable, notwithstanding the apparent indifference to the extension of formal empire in the 1860s and 1870s, whether the area under review is Jamaica, Africa or India. The preference for strong rule sprang from unflattering notions about the savagery, infantilism, and general incompetence of the non-white inhabitants of the British Empire. The expansion of the British race was justified by allusion to the inexorable laws of progress and natural selection, and was held to be 'as certain in its operation as the force of water'. That the United States had been compelled 'to take up their share of the white man's burden against their most cherished principles, shows there is no escape from Nature's benevolent despotism'. In general, this process was looked upon as desirable.

Missionary supporters reported that the 'humanitarian spirit undoubtedly gathers increasing force and energy'.[19] The British campaign against slavery and the slave trade – described as 'the emanations of a pure philanthropy' – seemed to confirm this, in spite of the commercial interests involved, which we have noticed.[20] V. L. Cameron saw Britain's operations in the Sudan as involving no less than the defence of

---

[17] *Contemporary Review*, XXXIV (December 1878–March 1879), p. 6.

[18] *Dark Strangers: A Sociological Study of a Recent West Indian Migrant Group in Brixton, South London* (London, 1963), p. 23.

[19] *Contemporary Review*, LXXIV (July–December 1898), p. 296; LXXX (July–December 1901), p. 397, and LXXIII (January–June 1898), p. 826.

[20] C.M.I., V (1869), p. 119; and for similar proud defence of British actions in this area see *Sheffield and Rotherham Independent*, 11 September 1872, 13 October 1875 and 17 February 1876.

Christian and Western civilization.[21] Under the direction of Britons, it seemed, even a despotism – such as Edward Dicey advocated for Egypt – could be just, law-abiding and progressive.[22]

The responsibilities of governing diverse peoples – for instance, in India – helped to save the English mind from parochialism, it was believed, and turned 'a nation of . . . industrials, into a race of governing men.' It was unworthy of Britain to shirk her responsibilities, in Tennyson's line, 'through craven fears of being great'; the extension of the Empire and civilization should rather be seen as a trust to be accepted, a duty to be fulfilled. A three-point programme laid down by the *Spectator* to foster this course maintained that the 'dark races' committed to British care were, by that very reason alone, not fitted for self-government, and accordingly the latter were 'to govern, to guide, to train, . . . to rule, as completely and with as little repentance as if we were angels appointed to that task'. Non-whites were to be subject to the rule of law, but denied political rights, and governed by an administration answerable solely to Britain, acting in important matters through white agency alone.[23]

In all historical periods there will be exceptions to popular trends, and the existence of critics – both white and black – of imperial attitudes such as these is too well known to require elaboration here. Though one might notice the wry comment of an American Negro preacher, Sella Martin, in 1866 that 'If the history of civilization is to be like the history of the Anglo-Saxon race with respect to . . . [Indians and Negroes], then . . . either God has made a mistake in making the Anglo-Saxon race, or the Anglo-Saxon race is on the wrong track'; or take heed of the warning of a native of Antigua that Africans came to Britain, read British newspapers, received British education and would one day seek to avenge the insults and oppression

21 *Contemporary Review*, XLVIII (July–December 1885), p. 572.

22 *Nineteenth Century*, XV (January–June 1884).

23 *Spectator*, 15 October 1864, p. 1,179, 30 July 1868, p. 137, 5 March 1898, p. 331; see also Sir George Grey in *Aborigines' Friend*, I (1855), pp. 7–8, for similar sense of mission.

they experienced.[24] It is necessary to admit, however, particularly in view of my own criticism of the racial theories upon which these attitudes depend, that peace, stability, the extension of commerce and political and social horizons were not negligible by-products of imperialism.

It may fairly be asked whether such theories were confined to Victorians, and, of course, they were not, being in wide circulation among Europeans and Anglo-Saxons alike during the nineteenth century. Nor can it be claimed that racism was a novel phenomenon. The 'race-lust for dominance', the campaign of civilization against barbarism, have influenced many other empires than the British, for, as Trollope expressed it, 'Those who are educated and civilized and powerful will always, in one sense, despise those who are not'.[25] But in the ancient world, according to Arnold, 'Distinctions of race were not of that odious and fantastic character which they have been in modern times'.[26] During the Victorian epoch, with the advance of world trade and the improvements in world communications, as literacy increased, and travellers, geographers, settlers and anthropologists enlarged the sum of knowledge about distant peoples, there was a unique degree of popular interest in race and racial theories. This interest was in turn significant because of the importance of public opinion in Britain.

The precise influence of opinion on government policy can never be determined (though the *Spectator* in 1901 complained that British Governments should recognize the importance of guiding it in matters of foreign policy, rather than allowing opinion to form itself 'and then be regarded with a kind of idolatrous reverence'[27]). However, it seems that, with the exception of the slave-trade issue, popular attitudes were less

[24] *Aborigines' Friend*, II (1866), p. 23; T.A.P.S. (1889), p. 567. For typical white protests against British aggression and unease about British rule see *Aborigines' Friend*, I, No. iii (1856), p. 108, No. 5 (1857), pp. 213, 219; II (January–December 1862), pp. 321–2 (January–December 1866), pp. 568, 573; T.A.P.S. (1880), pp. 252–3.

[25] J. A. Hobson, *Contemporary Review*, LXXVII (January–June 1900), p. 16; Trollope, *op. cit.*, p. 75.

[26] Quoted in Bagehot, *op. cit.*, pp. 39–40; see also Bryce, *Race Sentiment, op. cit.*, pp. 25, 28.

[27] 6 April 1901, p. 487.

significant in shaping policy than providing a perfect rationale for imperialist ventures once undertaken, and fashioning a 'colonial mentality' to which the establishment of colonial governments merely put the final seal.

Although the 'armchair philanthropists' and the British Press were frequently critical of settler harshness or bias towards colonized peoples – as in South Africa – they were also frequently even more prejudiced and more complaisant. These domestic opinions are peculiarly important because, however much the settler's opinions might be shaped by his practical experience of an alien race, he came to it with a set of assumptions acquired in Britain, and reinforced during every period of home leave. (And once returned to Britain, of course, the ex-colonial in turn reinforced the prejudices of his untravelled fellow countrymen.)

This study has been concerned with the racial attitudes of the nineteenth century, but it should be emphasized, in conclusion, that a great many of these have survived to disturb the present. A pamphlet published in 1961 on *Race, Heredity and Civilization*, written by W. C. George, Professor of Histology and Embryology at the University of North Carolina, contains this statement: 'The Caucasian race, in spite of all its frailties . . . has demonstrated a capacity for creative genius that has produced most of the civilizations of history. On the other hand, whatever its other virtues may be, the Negro race has never produced any civilization anywhere at any time.'[28] The work of an American anthropologist, Calvin Kephart, which appeared the same year, may also be noticed. In his book, *The Races of Mankind*, Kephart accepts the old tripartite division of man; his division is according to colour: the black race he calls Indafrican, the yellow and red races Turanian, the brown-white race Aryan. Frankly accepting the existence of innately superior and inferior races, Kephart claims the Aryans as 'the most energetic and capable of all races, the . . . Turanian . . . and . . . Indafrican races, in that order, . . . [as] the most backward'.[29] South African born Dr J. C. Carothers, writing in the *Journal of Mental Science* for 1951 and for the World Health

[28] London, 1961, pp. 8–9.
[29] London, 1961, pp. 71–2, 89–90, 233.

Organization in 1953, presents a picture of the African 'child of Nature', which, though without deliberate malice, is seized upon as proof of their views by Kephart and George, and would have been acceptable to the average middle-class reader of 100 years ago.[30]

Among the most common myths still surviving about race, as Jean Fraser has shown, we find these theories: that purity of blood should be preserved by the avoidance of racial mixing; that brain size has proved the superiority of Europeans over Negroes (evidence to the contrary notwithstanding); and that intelligence tests have established the inferior capacity of the Negro. Audrey Shuey's massive work, published in 1958, sought to demonstrate just this.[31] However, Dr Otto Klineburg's lifelong researches in this field seem to show that no intelligence tests so far devised have enabled us to differentiate safely between what is due to innate capacity and what is the result of environmental influences, training and education.[32] Where, however, reasonably accurate allowances have been made for differences in environmental opportunities, tests have shown essential similarity in mental characters among all human groups, or failed to prove the existence of fundamental differences in intelligence between different races.[33]

The findings of a team of U.N.E.S.C.O. experts on science and the race question, reported in the 1950s, were that no modern national or religious group is, scientifically viewed, a race; that there is no evidence that racial crossing has harmful biological effects; and that the term 'race' is less a biological fact than a social myth.[34] As Michael Banton has pointed out in his book, *White and Coloured*, men do not react simply to the physical characters of strangers, but according to the social significance that is placed on these characters.[35]

Some of the old shibboleths of the nineteenth century have been destroyed. We now accept that man is *one* species and

[30] Quoted in *ibid.*, p. 87.

[31] *Colour Prejudice* (London, 1960), pp. 16, 19; A. Shuey, *The Testing of Negro Intelligence* (London, 1958); and see above, p. 15.

[32] See, for instance, O. Klineberg, *Negro Intelligence and Selective Migration* (New York, 1935).

[33] See P. Mason (ed.), *Man, Race and Darwin* (London, 1960), p. 63.

[34] Fraser, *op. cit.*, p. 17. For details of titles see Bibliography.

[35] *White and Coloured, op. cit.*, p. 39.

believe in the fertility of hybrids. We still accept, however, the threefold division of man into Mongolian, Negro, and—here we still have difficulties—Caucasian; one hesitates to use this emotive term, but the common alternative is 'white', which puts the stress, as of old, on colour.

The doctrine of the survival of the fittest no longer exerts its old fascination, though other ramifications of evolutionary theory are still important. The elucidation of the mode of genetic transmission in the twentieth century has not solved finally the question of racial classification, because there are relatively few physiological features that can be linked unequivocally with particular genes. Work on the sickle cell gene in the 1950s – the transmission of which may secure protection from malaria among certain groups of Africans – was a step in this direction, but the majority of geneticists today (with the exception of writers like the American, George) would accept that the most important feature of man is his ability to pass on information from one generation to the next through the process of social learning. In other words, the course of evolution has come to depend more and more on the transmission of behavioural instructions by learning instead of by genetic inheritance. It is thus possible to explain physical characteristics in biological terms and mental characteristics in cultural terms. Race and culture undoubtedly interact, but scientists have at last managed to explode the theory that race determines culture or culture determines physical type. This theory is still entertained by the uninformed.[36]

Racism now, as Ronald Segal's disturbing book, *The Race War*, makes clear, has taken on a new aspect. Although he sees the circumstances provoking today's race war as essentially rooted in the past, in the sort of theories and events I have been describing, Segal suggests that the fact that the non-whites are the world's poor is at present all-important, since, given the dispersion of the mass media, for the first time they cannot be unaware of their position. Racial antagonism, hitherto the spur of nationalism in newly independent countries, will, Segal predicts, ultimately bring about a world-wide alliance of the poor non-whites against the rich whites. The strategy of guerrilla warfare has already been employed effectively by the

[36] See M. Banton, *Race Relations* (London, 1967), pp. 52–4.

underprivileged against the rich nations in this nuclear age in Cuba, China and Vietnam.[37]

Segal, rather disquietingly, seems much more prepared to condone animosity between coloured races – for instance, between Negro and Arab Africans in the Sudan, Negro and Indian in Guyana, Chinese and Malay in Singapore and Malaysia – perhaps because this falls outside his definition of racism. And, of course, the phenomenon is not, and probably never will be, as destructive as the black-white conflict, though it was certainly a sour additional element during the recent troubles in Kenya. For instance, it is true, as Philip Mason points out in *Christianity and Race*, that much as one might deplore the Victorian treatment of Lobengula, King of the Matabele, the Matabele had first persistently stolen land from and enslaved the Mashona. But it is the memory of white offences which rankles most and is most dangerous in today's world, as in the nineteenth century. On the whole the Mashona preferred the uncertain threat of the Matabele to the constant presence of new white masters.[38] The whites expected gratitude, but found none.

It would be dangerous, however, to over-simplify. Racial problems have not been the same the world over, as we have seen. Thus, for example, things have generally been easier in West Africa where, in the absence of a large white settler group, no colour bar has developed, than in South and Central Africa, where substantial tracts of land were once almost uninhabited and certainly undeveloped until the coming of the Europeans, where whites have consequently felt they have earned a stake in the country and wished to stay permanently. In India the British sense of being strangers was never entirely lost, but neither was exclusiveness ever one-sided. If the nineteenth-century Englishman despised the Hindu, the high-caste Hindu felt polluted by, say, eating a meal with a European. Although we are told today that West Indian problems are political and economic, that a search for identity preoccupies the articulate, but that race prejudice is not a problem, perhaps for this very reason Jamaicans – and West Indians generally – in Britain have proved particularly sensitive to discrimination on account

[37] *Op. cit.*, pp. 1–31, 411–46.
[38] London, 1956, p. 130.

of colour. The weakness of British rule in India was the absence of any archetypal appeal – on religious or other grounds; only the Army provided something in this direction.[39] In the West Indies, with a permanent white planter class and the widespread ministrations of British missionaries, a very different relationship was established between the races.

Similar differences are reflected in Britain today. As the studies of Kenneth Little, Ruth Glass, Michael Banton, Sheila Patterson, A. H. Richmond and R. B. Davison have shown, the Indian or Pakistani visitor is more acceptable because his stay is often only temporary, he demands little of his host, and accepts his role as 'archetypal stranger'; the West Indian, on the other hand, has higher expectations, a shared language and religion, demands equality and refuses to play his expected role. These studies bring out the fact that the solidarity of the coloured group has its only foundation in the affirmation of opposition to the white group – otherwise in Britain the Jamaicans, Nigerians and others have little in common.[40]

Books such as these also reveal the extent to which primitive superstitions about race still persist. We read of the obsession with colour, recognize the old cultural arrogance, are reminded of the alleged fecklessness and excessive sexual potency of Negroes. We see the 'Prospero complex' in outrage that decolonization has not been better received in the non-white world. It is not sufficiently recognized that the more we have tried to divest ourselves of the wrongs of the past, the more subconscious remains of old racial attitudes have come out, in provisions to guard against black rule or criticism of the governments of newly independent nations. Class fears still underpin racial prejudice. We find it excessively difficult to realize that there *is* no fundamental difference between animosity arising from language, religious and social-class

[39] *Ibid.*, pp. 123 f., and *Prospero's Magic. Some Thoughts on Class and Race* (London, 1962), pp. 13, 38–9, 108. See also Mason's *Race Relations in Africa* (London, 1960).

[40] Banton, Patterson and Little, *op. cit.*; M. Banton, *The Coloured Quarter* (London, 1955); R. Glass, *Newcomers. The West Indians in London* (London, 1960); A. H. Richmond, *Colour Prejudice in Britain. A Study of West Indian Workers in Liverpool, 1941–51* (London, 1954); R. B. Davison, *Black British* (London, 1966).

differences and those that spring from racial differences. Notwithstanding the encouraging findings of the Rose survey published in 1969, there is still a desperate need for common sense about race.[41]

[41] See P. Mason's book, *Common Sense About Race Relations* (London, 1961).

Q

Appendix

Some Notes on Abolitionist Attitudes to Race

These attitudes have been dealt with only indirectly, with regard to the freedmen's aid societies, mainly because this study begins in the 1850s, when the anti-slavery movement proper was declining both in prestige and influence. However, some further notice is due to the abolitionists since many of their ideas were accepted, if modified, by missionaries who constituted the more numerous and vocal expression of British humanitarianism by the end of the nineteenth century.

There are difficulties involved in estimating the opinions of abolitionists on questions of race. For much of the first half of the century, and especially after 1833, they were held fairly high in popular esteem, and their reputations have remained high among historians. The early trials, well documented by Thomas Clarkson, William Wilberforce, Thomas Fowell Buxton and others do not normally include the violent persecutions which American abolitionists met with in the 1830s and 1840s. Hence there were fewer pressures on the British opponents of slavery to make them pander to contemporary prejudices or reveal their own suppressed racial bias, where this existed. Examination of private letters and published sources produces comparatively little on this score that might be called incriminating.

Edward Abdy, for instance, after visiting the United States, later wrote to Maria Weston Chapman that the European abolitionist was no more free of colour prejudice than the American, but the racist he quoted to prove his point was French not English, and the American abolitionist Samuel J. May was at pains to stress in his memoirs that Abdy was personally lacking in prejudice. May's protestations are, ironically, indicative rather of his own innocent sense of superiority: 'the last time I saw Mr Abdy it was a sight to be remembered – he, an accomplished English gentleman, a Fellow of Oxford or Cambridge University, riding on the driver's box of a stage-coach side by side with an American slave-woman, that he might learn more of her history and character'.

The fact that British anti-salvery campaigners were frequently charged with insincerity, however, demonstrates that their motives were not regarded as unimpeachable. The usual argument of contemporary critics was that charity should begin at home, and that the humanitarians were only concerned about misery when it occurred overseas, cheerfully accepting wage slavery at home as an indispensable part of British prosperity. Such accusations may also imply, of course, an indifference to the plight of Negro slaves on the part of the British labour leaders and conservatives who normally voiced them. Typical was the complaint of a Jamaica newspaper in 1823 that abolitionists were 'canting, hypocritical rascals', who simply desired, for political and economic reasons, the downfall of the West Indian planters; but the journal was the mouthpiece of the latter, and scarcely above suspicion.

Opinions from two contemporary groups who did not usually hesitate to criticize white philanthropists may be briefly noted before examining the comments on race of the British abolitionists themselves: namely, the black American abolitionists who visited England from the 1830s onwards, and the ethnologists and anthropologists who were developing their disciplines during the same period.

The latter, as we have seen, initially spent much time denouncing the British humanitarians as 'nigger-worshippers' and victims of a misguided 'rights-of-man mania', while the former generally testified to the favourable reception accorded them by their British co-workers. The Negro teacher, William G. Allen, forced out of America in 1853 because of his marriage to a white student, Mary King, wrote to William Lloyd Garrison contrasting his treatment in England with the patronizing attitude Negroes encountered in the United States, even among abolitionists. Professor Benjamin Quarles has argued that all blacks visiting Britain were well received by eminent individuals and large audiences alike, explaining this as follows: 'Small in number and transients for the most part, they posed no threat to the labouring man or to the purity of the national blood stream. Hence they received that heartiest of welcomes that comes from a love of virtue combined with an absence of apprehension.' There were additional factors of importance. Since black people in Britain were rare at the same time as they were found to attract the biggest crowds at anti-slavery meetings, the black abolitionist was an exotic, valued for his emotional appeal as a fund raiser, and therefore to be treated with respect. Also, visiting Negroes often hoped to benefit from, or take some of the funds they raised back to America, so circumspection on their part might be anticipated. (However, the approving comments were not, it seems, modified once the black evangelists were safely home.)

The English abolitionists did not – unlike their missionary successors – specifically crusade against the scientific racism which developed as they declined. Rather, like their fellows in America, they asserted in general terms the equality of races, using the Bible, history, simple observation *and* science to vindicate the attainments and character of black peoples in the Americas, Africa and the West Indies. In particular, the abolitionist urged that unfavourable environmental conditions caused degradation and backwardness, when it occurred, rather than innate biological or cultural inferiority.

In his *Letter on the Abolition of the Slave Trade*, William Wilberforce emphasized the environmentalist argument, even while he acknowledged that the British, in contrast to the unhappy inhabitants of Africa, were 'the most free, enlightened, and happy people that ever existed upon earth'. For this reason, because of the merits of British civilization, Wilberforce argued, it was particularly disgraceful to 'prolong in Africa the reign of ignorance and superstition'. The explorers Parke and Golberry were quoted to show the attractive moral qualities, the intelligence, industry and courage of the Mandingoes, Foulahs and Jaloffs. Unlike many of his contemporaries Wilberforce was detached enough to see as encouraging the characteristics of the central African tribes, and to point out that the cultural attainments of Europe were of very recent origin. The departed glories of African civilizations were acknowledged, though the presently desolating effects of Mohammedan conquests and European invasions were noted and deplored. Even more unusual, the fundamental differences between African and white-imposed systems of slavery was grasped, and a vast body of material accumulated to demonstrate that while the American or West Indian slave was indeed degraded – was immoral, indolent and unintelligent, by Victorian standards – it was the system alone which made him so.

Thomas Fowell Buxton reveals many attitudes characteristic of British abolitionism in personal reminiscences and writings on the African slave trade. Some of these are not attractive to the modern reader. In relation to the slave trade Buxton displayed the missionary's assumptions of cultural superiority, departing from Wilberforce's refreshing attempts at cultural relativism, when he described the inhabitants of the 'kingdom of darkness' as 'bound in the chains of the grossest ignorance', and 'a prey to the most savage superstition'. He later emphasized that 'the African is not wanting in those qualities which accompany civilization', even though, with the paternalism which accompanies much humanitarianism, he believed that 'a right direction [had] to be given to his industry and intelligence to qualify him for intercourse with the more refined European'. This guidance, of course, the latter was to provide.

Throughout his reminiscences, however, Buxton appears in a more appealing light, upholding the basic equality and brotherhood of all men, acknowledging his imperative religious duty to fight for freedom, even to the point of losing friends and wrecking his health. Here the degradation of the slaves is accepted, but the environmentalist defence is urged; furthermore Buxton has dropped his early support for apprenticeship on the grounds of planter determination to turn this into a disguised form of slavery, and is persuaded of the piety, diligence and eagerness for education of the West Indian slaves freed in 1833. He also praised the absence of violence on the islands. 'The negroes,' he declared, accepting popular stereotype here at least, 'are a very affectionate and docile race.' (If we object to this it is well to recall that the Victorian public was inconsistent in its admiration of martial qualities: when these aggressive drives produced native revolts, as in Jamaica in 1865 and India in 1857, the press was full of the 'innate savagery' of the black races.)

Most of the leading British abolitionists could not draw upon any sustained, first-hand experience of Negroes. Religious principle drove them on, and often there was something overly pious and sentimental in their commitment, from today's viewpoint, as witness Priscilla Gurney's dying exhortation to remember 'The poor, dear slaves!' But such inexperienced idealists were often far ahead of their time. One such was Leeds Quaker and abolitionist Wilson Armistead, the author of a number of remarkable books on the Negro, anticipating much twentieth century scholarship as well as complementing the work of contemporary black abolitionists such as William Wells Brown in his attempt to prove that Africans had long contributed to the civilization and progress of the world.

Thomas Clarkson, though he met a group of Negro representatives from Santo Domingo in France, and later conducted an unusual correspondence with the island's dictator Henry Christophe, by comparison with American abolitionists had seen very few black people, much less had any social intercourse with them. His long campaign against the slave trade was, none the less, prompted not only by a sense of Christian duty, and revulsion in the face of cruelty and wrong, but by an appreciation of African attainments in the arts. On board a vessel engaged in trade with Africa he was 'shown one or two pieces of the cloth made by the natives, and from their own cotton. . . . Here new feelings arose . . . when I considered that persons of so much apparent ingenuity, and capable of such beautiful work as the Africans, should be made slaves, and reduced to a level with the brute creation.' During his first meeting with William Pitt, Clarkson reported that the Prime Minister doubted statements purporting to prove the 'genius and abilities' of the African peoples. By producing the artefacts that he had collected, Clarkson was able to convince Pitt of their truth. He also took care during the post-emancipation period to defend the diligence of the West Indian freed-men, and to point out that 'the deficiency in point of profit to the planters, is owing to their *mismanagement of their estates*'.

Clarkson, as did Buxton, damaged his health in the long crusade, regarding himself as a 'slave to the Slave', though those who dislike the martyr temperament in abolitionist or missionary may explain such excesses with reference to selfish motives. Also like Buxton, and like the missionary, Clarkson took for granted the desirability of supplanting native religions with Christianity, wherever possible, in Africa or the West Indies. But his approach to race questions was still advanced for Victorian England, as is shown by the reception he and his wife gave to the family of Henry Christophe, during their visit to England after the chief's death. Madame Christophe and her two daughters stayed with the Clarksons for several months, a situation which their friends, including the Wordsworths, treated as something of a joke. Clarkson was not amused, later confiding to Benjamin Haydon that when he and Wilberforce introduced the refugees to their circle 'there was a sort of shrink at admitting them into high society'. This revulsion, in two of Britain's leading aboli-tionists at least, was apparently quite absent.

Selected Bibliography

Manuscript Material

Goldwin Smith Papers, Cornell University Library, Ithaca, New York.
Anti-Slavery Papers, Cornell University Library, Ithaca, New York.
English Manuscripts, John Rylands Library, Manchester.
Rathbone Papers, Liverpool Public Library.
Anti-Slavery Papers, Rhodes House, Oxford.
Foreign Office Records F.O. 5, Public Record Office, London.
Reform League Letterbooks, Bishopsgate Institute, London.
Abolitionist pamphlets and notebooks in Glasgow Public Library.
Birmingham Public Library and John Rylands Library.
Minute Books, Gloucester and Nailsworth Monthly Meeting of the Society of Friends.

Newspapers, Periodicals and Official Series

Hansard's Parliamentary Debates.
Encyclopaedia Britannica.
Church Missionary Intelligencer, a Monthly Journal of Missionary Information.
London Missionary Society Chronicle.
Journal of the Anthropological Institute of Great Britain and Ireland.
Anthropological Review.
Journal of the Anthropological Society of London.
Transactions of the Ethnological Society of London.
Memoirs Read Before the Anthropological Society of London.

Journal of the Ethnological Society of London.
Popular Magazine of Anthropology.
Extracts from the Minutes and Proceedings of the London Yearly
  Meetings of the Society of Friends.
Journal of the Society of Arts.
Proceedings of the Royal Geographical Society.
The Geographical Journal.
Proceedings of the Royal Colonial Institute.
Proceedings of the Aborigines Protection Society.

Good Words
Reynold's Weekly
Saturday Review
Economist
Spectator
Macmillan's Magazine
North American Review
Encounter
Folk Lore

Freedmen's Aid Reporter
Freed-Man
Friend
Aborigines' Friend
Contemporary Review
Fortnightly Review
Macmillan's Magazine
Fraser's Magazine
Nineteenth Century

Daily Telegraph
Daily News
Times
Pall Mall Gazette
Bee-Hive
Morning Post
Manchester Courier

Manchester Guardian
Manchester Examiner and Times
Sheffield and Rotherham
  Independent
Birmingham Daily Gazette
Rochdale Spectator

Bolton Chronicle
Preston Guardian
Irish Times
Dublin Evening Mail
Freeman's Journal
Northern Wing

Banner of Ulster
Scotsman
North British Daily Mail
Edinburgh Evening Courant
Glasgow Daily Herald

Miscellaneous Pamphlets

Sixty Years Against Slavery . . . By the British and Foreign Anti-
  Slavery Society (London, 1900).
Anti-Slavery Jubilee, August 1st, 1884, Meeting of the British and
  Foreign Anti-Slavery Society, in the Guildhall of the City of
  London, Under the Presidency of His Royal Highness the Prince
  of Wales (London, 1884).

232

An Epitome of Anti-Slavery Information, or A Condensed View of Slavery and the Slave Trade, etc (London, 1842).

First and Second Annual Reports of the Ladies' London Emancipation Society (London, 1864, 1865).

Twenty-Fourth Annual Report of the British and Foreign Anti-Slavery Society (London, 1863).

Annual Reports of the Edinburgh Ladies' Emancipation Society, and Sketch of . . . the Condition of the Freedmen During the Years Ending . . . 1866 and 1867 (Edinburgh, 1866 and 1867).

Jamaica Papers No. 5. Martial Law. Six Letters to *The Daily News* (London, 1867).

The Outbreak in Jamaica. A Speech by the Rev. William Arthur, M.A., Delivered at the Anniversary of the Folkestone Auxiliary to the Wesleyan Missionary Society, November 21st, 1865 (London, 1865).

Jamaica; Who is to Blame? (London, 1866).

Jamaica: Its State and Prospects. With an Exposure of the Proceedings of the Freed-Man's Aid Society, and the Baptist Missionary Society (London, 1867).

The West India Labour Question, etc. (London, 1858).

Emancipation In the West Indies. Two Addresses by E. B. Underhill, Esq., and the Rev. J. T. Brown, etc. (London, 1861).

H. B. Evans – Our West Indian Colonies. Jamaica, a Source of National Wealth and Honour (London, 1855).

E. Thompson, W. Smith, W. Girod – Statement of Facts Relative to the Island of Jamaica (London, 1852).

C. Roundell – England and Her Subject-Races with Special Reference to Jamaica (London, 1866).

A. Lindo – Dr Underhill's Testimony on the Wrongs of the Negro in Jamaica (London, 1866).

The Success of Missions in India (London, 1872).

The Indian Crisis. Memorial to the Queen from the London Missionary Society, on the Religious Policy of the Government of India. With an Explanatory Statement on the Policy of the Indian Government in Respect to Religion, and the Education of the Natives (London, 1858).

C.M.S. Godda District Report. Santal Mission (Pokhuria, Manbhoom, 1898).

A Brief View of Slavery in British India (London, 1841).

The Hill Tribes of India. An Account of the Church Missionary Society's Work Among the Santals, Paharis, Gonds, Kors, Bheels, and Hill Arrians (London, 1891).

Papers Referring to the Educational Operations of The Church Missionary Society in North India (London, 1864).

Address Delivered at the Geographical Section of the British Association, Newcastle On Tyne, Descriptive of the State, Progress, and Prospects of the Various Surveys, and Other Scientific Enquiries, Instituted by the East India Company Throughout Asia; With a Prefatory Sketch of the Principles and of Geography. By Major T. B. Jervis (Torquay, n.d.).

W. St Clair Tisdall – Dieux Li Vuelt! It is the Will of God! A Plea For a Great Extension of Mission Work in Muhammadan Lands (London, 1891).

Report of the Centenary Conference on the Protestant Missions of the World (London, 1889, 2 vols.).

Rev. J. Rooker – A Missionary Criticized by an Outsider (London, 1891).

A Native Church For the Natives of India; Giving an Account of the Formation of a Native Church Council, for the Punjab Missions of the Church Missionary Society, and of the Proceedings at Their First Meeting, at Umritsur, 31st March to 2nd April 1877 (Lahore, 1877).

A Tribute of Affectionate Respect to the Memory and Founders of the London Missionary Society. A Sermon Delivered in Surrey Chapel, Wednesday Morning, May 9th, 1849. By J. A. James (London, 1849).

A Debate on India in the English Parliament, By M. Le Comte De Montalembert (London, 1858).

Special Winter Mission to India and Ceylon (London, 1888).

On the British Colonization of New Zealand. By the Committee of the Aborigines' Protection Society (London, 1846).

The New Zealand Government and the Maori War of 1863–4, With Especial Reference to the Confiscation of Native Lands, and the Colonial Ministry's Defence of Their War Policy (London, 1864).

G. Campbell – On the Races of India as Traced in Existing Tribes and Castes (London, 1854).

Special Appeal for India (London, 1857).

The Governing Race: a Book for the Time, and for all Times, by H.O.R. (Washington, 1860).

Contemporary Works

H. G. ADAMS (ed.), God's Image in Ebony: Being a Series of Sketches, Facts, Anecdotes, etc., Demonstrative of the Mental Powers and Intellectual Capacities of the Negro Race (London, 1854).

Anthropological Essays Presented to Edward Burnett Tylor in Honour of his 75th Birthday, October 2nd, 1907 (London, 1907).

George Douglas, Eighth Duke of Argyll . . . 1823–1900. Autobio-

graphy and Memoirs (ed. Dowager Duchess of Argyll, London, 1906, 2 vols.).

W. ARMISTEAD (ed.), *A Tribute for the Negro: being a vindication of the moral, intellectual, and religious capabilities of the coloured portion of mankind, etc.* (Manchester, 1848).

W. BAGEHOT, *Physics and Politics or, Thoughts on the Application of the Principles of 'Natural Selection' and 'Inheritance' to Political Society* (London, 1872).

T. BAINES, *The Victoria Falls* (London, 1865).

The Northern Goldfield Diaries of Thomas Baines (ed. J. P. R. Wallis, London, 1946, 3 vols.).

S. BAKER, *The Albert Nyanza, Great Basin of the Nile, and Explorations of the Nile Sources* (London, 1866, 2 vols.).

The Nile Tributaries of Abyssinia and the Sword Hunters of the Hamram Arabs (London, 1867).

Ismailia, A Narrative of the Expedition to Central Africa for the Suppression of the Slave Trade, Organised by Ismail, Khedive of Egypt (London, 1874, 2 vols.).

E. W. BICKLEY, *The Central African Mission at Urambo and Lake Tanganyika* (London, 1894).

L. BLANC, *Letters on England* (trans. J. Hutton and L. J. Trotter, 2nd Series, London, 1867, 2 vols.).

Speeches of John Bright . . . In Birmingham . . . 1868 (London, 1868).

W. H. BROWN, *On the South African Frontier* (London, 1899).

J. BRYCE, *The Relations of the Advanced and Backward Nations of Mankind* (London, 1902).

Studies in History and Jurisprudence (Oxford, 1901, 2 vols.).

The American Commonwealth (London, 1895, 2 vols.).

Impressions of South Africa (London, 1897).

Race Sentiment as a Factor in History (London, 1915).

C. T. BUCKLAND, *Sketches of Social Life in India* (London, 1884).

R. BURTON, *Sindh, and the Races That Inhabit the Valley of the Indus; With Notices of the Topography and History of the Province* (London, 1851).

Sind Revisited: With Notices of the Anglo-Indian Army; Railroads; Past, Present, and Future, etc. (London, 1877, 2 vols.).

A Mission to Galele, King of Dahome. With Notices of the So Called 'Amazons', the Grand Customs, the Yearly Customs, the Human Sacrifices, the Present State of the Slave Trade, and the Negro's Place in Nature (London, 1864, 2 vols.).

The Lake Regions of Central Africa (London, 1860, 2 vols.).

Notes on the Dahoman (London, 1865).

Wanderings in West Africa (London, 1863, 2 vols.).

Two Trips to Gorilla Land and the Cataracts of the Congo (London, 1876, 2 vols.).

Selected Papers on Anthropology, Travel and Exploration (ed. N. M. Penzer, London, 1924).

Zanzibar: City, Island and Coast (London, 1872, 2 vols.).

T. BUXTON, *The African Slave Trade and Its Remedy* (London, 1967 ed.).

A. CALDECOTT, *The Church in The West Indies* (London, 1898).

G. CAMPBELL, *The Ethnology of India* (London, 1872).

India as It May Be: an Outline of a Proposed Government and Policy (London, 1853).

The British Empire (London, 1887).

Memoirs of My Indian Career (London, 1893, 2 vols.).

White and Black. The Outcome of a Visit to the United States (London, 1879).

Modern India: a Sketch of the System of Civil Government. To Which is Prefixed, Some Account of the Natives and Native Institutions (London, 1852).

T. CARLYLE, *Occasional Discourse Upon the Nigger Question* (London, 1853).

Shooting Niagara: and After? (London, 1867).

J. CHAPMAN, *Travels in the Interior of South Africa* (London, 1888, 2 vols.).

J. CLARK, W. DENDY, J. M. PHILLIPPO, *The Voice of Jubilee; a Narrative of the Baptist Mission, Jamaica, From its Commencement; With Notices of its Fathers and Founders* (London, 1865).

H. CLARKE, *The English Stations in the Hill Regions of India: Their Value and Importance, With Some Statistics of Their Products and Trade* (London, 1881).

E. CLODD, *The Story of 'Primitive' Man* (London, 1885).

M. D. CONWAY, *Autobiography. Memories and Experiences of Moncure D. Conway* (London, 1904, 2 vols.).

Testimonies Concerning Slavery (London, 1864).

W. D. COOLEY, *A Memoir on the Lake Regions of East Africa* (London, 1864).

H. S. CUNNINGHAM, *Chronicles of Dustypore* (London, 1875, 2 vols.).

J. CUMMING, *The Great Tribulation; or, the Things Coming on Earth* (London, 1859).

The Destiny of Nations (London, 1864).

R. N. CUST, *Africa Rediviva. Or the Occupation of Africa by Christian Missionaries of Europe and North Africa* (London, 1891).

A Sketch of the Modern Languages of Africa (London, 1883, 2 vols.).

Pictures of Indian Life Sketch With the Pen From 1852 to 1881 (London, 1881).

236

A Sketch of the Modern Languages of the East Indies (London, 1878).

C. DARWIN, *The Origin of the Species* (London, 1859).

The Descent of Man, and Selection in Relation to Sex (London, 1871, 2 vols.).

C. DILKE, *Greater Britain* (London, 1868, 2 vols.).

W. H. DIXON, *The White Conquest* (London, 1876, 2 vols.).

New America (London, 1869).

H. DRUMMOND, *Tropical Africa* (London, 1888).

D. J. EAST, *Western Africa* (London, 1844).

M. E. EGERTON, *A Short History of British Colonial Policy, 1606–1909* (London, 1897).

R. W. EMERSON, *English Traits* (London, 1856).

F. W. FARRAR, *Chapters on Language* (London, 1865).

H. FIELDING, *Tom Jones* (Philadelphia and Toronto, 1948).

J. C. FIRTH, *Our Kin Across the Sea* (London, 1888).

F. FORD, *Neilgherry Letters* (Bombay, 1851).

R. A. FREEMAN, *Travels and Life in Ashanti and Jaman* (London, 1898).

B. FRERE, *Indian Missions* (London, 1873).

J. A. FROUDE, *The English in the West Indies* (London, 1888).

Oceana, or England and Her Colonies (London, 1886).

F. GALTON, *Inquiries into Human Faculty and Its Development* (London, 1883).

A. DE GOBINEAU, *The Inequality of Human Races* (London, 1915 ed.).

G. L. GOMME, *Ethnology in Folklore* (London, 1892).

A. HADDON, *History of Anthropology* (London, 1910).

The Study of Man (London, 1898).

R. B. HONE (ed.), *Seventeen Years in the Yoruba Country. Memorials of Anna Hinderer* (London, 1872).

J. HUNT, *Introductory Address on the Study of Anthropology Delivered Before the Anthropological Society of London, February 24th, 1863, by James Hunt* (London, 1863).

Anniversary Address Delivered Before the Anthropological Society of London, January 5th, by James Hunt (London, 1864).

Farewell Address, Delivered at the Fourth Anniversary of the Anthropological Society of London, January 1st, 1867, by James Hunt (London, 1867).

W. W. HUNTER, *The Indian Empire: Its People, History, and Products* (London, 1886).

England's Work in India (London, 1881).

The Indian Musalmans: Are they bound in Conscience to Rebel Against the Queen? (London, 1871).

T. HUXLEY, *Evolution and Ethics* (London, 1893).

W. L. JAMES, *The Wild Tribes of the Soudan* (London, 1884).

237

B. JOHNSON, *Letters from John Chinaman* (London, 1901).

H. JOHNSTON, *The Story of My Life* (London, 1923).

British Central Africa (London, 1897).

The Uganda Protectorate (London, 1902, 2 vols.).

The River Congo, etc. (London, 1895).

Pioneers in India (London, 1919).

A. H. KEANE, *Africa* (London, 1895).

Ethnology (London, 1896).

The World's Peoples. A Popular Account of Their Bodily and Mental Characters, Beliefs, Traditions, Political and Social Institutions (London, 1908).

J. KENNAWAY, *On Sherman's Track: or, the South After the War* (London, 1867).

R. KIPLING, *Departmental Ditties, etc.* (London and New York, 1925 ed.).

In Black and White (London, 1914).

Plain Tales from the Hills (New York, 1899).

Something of Myself. For My Friends Known and Unknown (New York, 1937 ed.).

Life's Handicap (New York, 1899).

Kim (New York, 1901).

R. KNOX, *Races of Man: a Fragment* (London, 1862 ed.).

S. W. KOELLE, *Polyglotta Africana, etc.* (London, 1854).

A. LANG, *Custom and Myth* (London, 1884).

Myth, Ritual and Religion (London, 1887).

G. R. LATHAM, *Natural History of the Varieties of Man* (London, 1850).

H. LATHAM, *Black and White: a Journal of a Three Months' Tour in the United States* (London, 1867).

W. E. H. LECKY, *The Empire: Its Value and its Growth* (London, 1893).

F. B. LEIGH, *Ten Years on a Georgia Plantation Since the War* (London, 1883).

D. LIVINGSTONE, *The Last Journals of David Livingstone in Central Africa, From 1865 to His Death* (London, 1874, 2 vols.).

Missionary Travels and Researches in South Africa, etc. (London, 1857).

MARQUIS OF LORNE, *A Trip to the Tropics, and Home Through America* (London, 1867).

R. LOVETT, *The History of the London Missionary Society* (London, 1899, 2 vols.).

J. LUBBOCK, *The Origin of Civilisation and the Primitive Condition of Man. Mental and Social Conditions of Savages* (London, 1870).

F. D. LUGARD, *The Rise of Our East African Empire* (London, 1893, 2 vols.).

Diaries (ed. M. Perham, 4 vols., London, 1959).

238

A. LYALL, *Asiatic Studies. Religious and Social* (London, 1882).

R. M. MACBRIAR, *Africans at Home* (London, 1861).

A. M. MACKAY, *Pioneer Missionary of the Church Missionary Society* (by his Sister, London, 1898).

D. MACRAE, *The Americans at Home* (Edinburgh, 1870, 2 vols.).

H. MARTINEAU, *British Rule in India* (London, 1857).

J. MCQUEEN, *The Nile Basin* (London, 1864).

H. MERIVALE, *Lectures on Colonization and Colonies Delivered Before the University of Oxford in 1839, 1840 and 1841* (1861 ed., London).

The Letters of John Stuart Mill (London, 1910, 2 vols.).

J. S. MILL, *Autobiography* (London, 1908).

Memorandum of the Improvements in the Administration of India During the Last Thirty Years (London, 1858).

J. MOORE, *The Queen's Empire, or Ind and Her Pearl* (Philadelphia 1892).

C. NEW, *Life, Wanderings, and Labours in Eastern Africa* (London, 1874).

J. C. NOTT and G. R. GLIDDON, *Types of Mankind* (London, 1871 ed.).

L. OLIPHANT, *On the Present State of Political Parties in America* (Edinburgh and London, 1866).

S. M. PETO, *Resources and Prospects of America* (London, 1866).

A. L. F. PITT-RIVERS, *The Evolution of Culture and Other Essays* (Oxford, 1906).

Proceedings of the Massachusetts Historical Society, 1912–13, Vol. XLVI.

C. READE, *Put Yourself in His Place* (London, 1922).

W. READE, *The Outcast* (London, 1875).

The Martyrdom of Man (London, 1872).

Savage Africa (London, 1863).

The African Sketch Book (London, 1873, 2 vols.).

The Story of the Ashantee Campaign (London, 1874).

J. E. RECLUS, *Africa and Its Inhabitants* (ed. A. H. Keane, London, 1899).

H. RICHARD, *Memoirs of Joseph Sturge* (London, 1864).

J. C. RICKETT, *The Quickening of Caliban* (London, 1893).

W. RIPLEY, *The Races of Europe* (London, 1900).

W. H. R. RIVERS, *The Todas* (London, 1906).

M. ROBERTS, *Son of Empire* (London, 1899).

J. G. ROMANES, *Mental Evolution in Man – Origin of Human Faculty* (London, 1888).

Darwin, and After Darwin. An Exposition of the Darwinian Theory and a Discussion of Post-Darwinian Questions (London, 1892, 3 vols.).

G. ROSE, *The Great Country, or Impressions of America* (London, 1868).

H. B. ROWNEY, *The Wild Tribes of India* (London, 1882).

Letters of John Ruskin to Charles Eliot Norton (Boston, 1905, 2 vols.).

G. SALA, *America Revisited* (London, 1882, 2 vols.).

W. SAUNDERS, *Through the Light Continent, or the United States in 1877–8* (London, 1879).

A. H. SAYCE, *Introduction to the Science of Language* (London, 1880, 2 vols.).

J. R. SEELEY, *The Expansion of England* (London, 1926 ed.).

N. W. SENIOR, *American Slavery* (London, 1856).

W. SEWELL, *The Ordeal of Free Labour in the West Indies* (New York, 1861).

M. A. SHERRING, *History of Christianity in India; With Its Prospects. A Sketch* (Madras, 1895).

A. F. SIM, *Life and Letters of Arthur Fraser Sim* (London, 1896).

B. SMITH, *Mohammed and Mohammedanism* (London, 1889).

G. SMITH, *The Moral Crusader, William Lloyd Garrison: a Biographical Essay* (Toronto, 1892).

R. SOMERS, *The Southern States Since the War, 1870–1* (London, 1871).

H. SPENCER, *Social Statics* (London, 1850).

V. H. SPEKE, *What led to the Discovery of the Source of the Nile* (London, 1864).

F. R. STATHAM, *Blacks, Boers and English. A Three-Cornered Problem* (London, 1881).

South Africa as It Is (London, 1897).

E. STOCK, *The History of the Church Missionary Society* (London, 1899, 3 vols.).

J. STRACHEY, *India* (London, 1888).

T. TAYLOR, *The Overland Route* (Manchester, 1878).

J. C. THOMSON, *Our Medical Workers and Their Work* (London, 1894).

G. O. TREVELYAN, *Competition Wallah* (London, 1866).

A. TROLLOPE, *The West Indies and the Spanish Main* (London, 1859).

E. B. TYLOR, *Anthropology: An Introduction to the Study of Man and Civilization* (London, 1881).

E. B. UNDERHILL, *Life of James Mursell Phillippo, Missionary in Jamaica* (London, 1881).

J. F. WATSON and J. W. KAYE (eds.), *The People of India* (London, 1868–75).

B. WEBB, *My Apprenticeship* (London, 1946 ed.).

J. P. WEBSTER, *The Oracle of Baal* (London, 1896).

ARCHBISHOP WHATELY, *Introductory Lectures on Political-Economy, Delivered at Oxford, etc.* (London, 1855).

M. WILLIAMS, *Modern India and the Indians: Being a Series of Impressions, Notes, and Essays* (London, 1878).

Religious Thought and Life in India (London, 1883).

240

Indian Wisdom, or Examples of the Religious, Philosophical, and Ethical Doctrines of the Hindus, etc. (London, 1875).
F. YOUNGHUSBAND, *South Africa of To-Day* (London, 1898).
F. B. ZINCKE, *Last Winter in the United States* (London, 1868).

Secondary Works

E. D. ADAMS, *Great Britain and the American Civil War* (Longmans, 1925, 2 vols.).
J. F. AJAYI, *Christian Missions in Nigeria, 1841–91: the Making of a New Elite* (Longmans, 1965).
R. ANSTEY, *Britain and the Congo in the Nineteenth Century* (Clarendon Press, 1962).
H. APTHEKER, *A Documentary History of the Negro People in the United States* (New York Citadel, 1951, 2 vols.).
H. ARENDT, *The Origins of Totalitarianism* (Harcourt, Brace and World, 1964).
E. AXELSON (ed.), *South African Explorers* (London, 1964).
E. AYANDELE, *The Missionary Impact on Modern Nigeria, 1842–1914: a Social and Political Analysis* (Longmans, 1966).
M. AYEARST, *The British West Indies: The Search for Self-Government* (Allen & Unwin, 1960).
M. BANTON, *Race Relations* (Tavistock Publications, 1967).
   White and Coloured. The Behaviour of British People towards Coloured Immigrants (Jonathan Cape, 1959).
   The Coloured Quarter. Negro Immigrants in an English City (Jonathan Cape, 1955).
J. BARZUN, *Race: a Study in Superstition* (Harper, 1965).
G. D. BEARCE, *British Attitudes Towards India, 1784–1858* (Clarendon Press, 1961).
R. BENEDICT, *Race and Racism* (London, 1959).
G. R. BENTLEY, *A History of the Freedmen's Bureau* (University of Pennsylvania Press, 1955).
E. BERWANGER, *The Frontier Against Slavery* (University of Illinois, 1967).
B. BETTELHEIM and M. JANOWITZ, *Dynamics of Prejudice* (Harper, 1950).
F. BOAS, *Race and Democratic Society* (J. J. Augustin, 1945).
M. L. BONHAM, *The British Consuls in the Confederacy* (Columbia University Press, 1911).
W. C. BOYD, *Genetics, and the Races of Man* (Oxford, 1950).
W. L. BURN, *The British West Indies* (Hutchinson, 1951).
   Emancipation and Apprenticeship in the British West Indies (Cape, 1937).

241

SELECTED BIBLIOGRAPHY

J. W. BURROW, *Evolution and Society. A Study in Victorian Social Theory* (Cambridge U.P., 1966).

H. A. CAIRNS, *Prelude to Imperialism* (Oxford University Press, 1965).

O. CHADWICK, *Mackenzie's Grave* (Hodder & Stoughton, 1959).

J. COMAS, *Racial Myths* (Paris, 1953, U.N.E.S.C.O.).

E. M. COULTER, *The South During Reconstruction, 1865–77* (Louisiana State University Press, 1947).

R. COUPLAND, *The British Anti-Slavery Movement* (T. Butterworth, 1933).

R. CRUDEN, *The Negro During Reconstruction* (Prentice-Hall, 1969).

J. CUMMING (ed.), *Revealing India's Past* (India Society, 1939).

P. D. CURTIN, *Two Jamaicas, 1830–65* (Harvard U.P., 1955).
The Image of Africa (Macmillan, 1965).

B. DAVISON, *The Lost Cities of Africa* (Little, 1959).
Black Mother: Africa, The Years of Trial (Gollancz, 1961).
Africa. History of a Continent (Weidenfeld & Nicolson, 1966).

D. B. DAVIS, *The Problem of Slavery in Western Culture* (Cornell University Press, 1966).

R. B. DAVIDSON, *Black British* (Oxford University Press, 1966).

H. DONALD, *The Negro Freedman* (Schunan, 1952).

M. DUBERMAN (ed.), *The Anti-Slavery Vanguard* (Princeton University Press, 1965).

W. E. B. DUBOIS, *Black Reconstruction: An Essay Toward a History of the Part which Black Folk played in the Attempt to Reconstruct Democracy in America 1860–80* (Harcourt, Brace & Co., 1935).

L. C. DUNN, *Race and Biology* (Paris, 1952, U.N.E.S.C.O.).

W. H. DUNN, *James Anthony Froude. A Biography* (Oxford University Press, 1961–3, 2 vols.).

E. B. DYKES, *The Negro in English Romantic Thought* (Associated Publishers, 1942).

M. EDWARDES, *British India, 1772–1947* (Sidgwick & Jackson, 1967).
High Noon of Empire: India Under Curzon (Eyre & Spottiswoode, 1965).

G. F. EDWARDS (ed.), *On Race Relations* (Chicago, 1968).

H. D. FAIRCHILD, *The Noble Savage. A Study in Romantic Naturalism* (Columbia University Press, 1961).

F. FANON, *The Wretched of the Earth* (Grove Press, 1968).

J. FINOT, *Race Prejudice* (Dutton, 1907).

J. H. FRANKLIN, *Reconstruction. After the Civil War* (Chicago University Press, 1961).

J. FRASER, *Colour Prejudice* (Edinburgh House Press, 1960).

F. FRAZIER, *The Negro in the United States* (Macmillan, 1957).

W. C. GEORGE, *Race, Heredity and Civilization* (Bartons Publishing, 1961).

242

E. GENOVESE, *The Political Economy of Slavery* (MacGibbon & Kee, 1967, and Pantheon, 1965).

R. GLASS, *Newcomers. The West Indians in London* (Allen & Unwin, 1960).

S. GOPAL, *British Policy in India, 1858–1905* (Cambridge University Press, 1965).

T. F. GOSSETT, *Race. The History of an Idea in America* (Schocker, 1965).

C. P. GROVES, *The Planting of Christianity in Africa* (Lutterworth Press, 1948–59, 4 vols.).

D. HALL, *Free Jamaica, 1838–65. An Economic History* (Yale University Press, 1959).

J. HARRIS, *A Century of Emancipation* (Dent, 1933).

R. HARRISON, *Before the Socialists: Studies in Labour and Politics, 1861–1881* (Routledge & Kegan Paul Ltd., 1965).

C. F. HARROLD and W. D. TEMPLEMAN, *English Prose of the Victorian Era* (London, 1938).

L. J. HENKIN, *Darwinianism in the English Novel, 1860–1910* (Russell, 1940).

M. J. HERSKOVITS, *Myth of the Negro Past* (Harper, 1941).

J. G. HIBBEN, *A Defence of Prejudice and Other Essays* (New York, 1921).

T. HODGKIN (ed.), *Nigerian Perspectives* (Oxford University Press, 1960).

W. E. HOUGHTON, *The Victorian Frame of Mind, 1830–1870* (Oxford University Press, 1957).

C. HOWARD (ed.), *West African Explorers* (London, 1951).

F. G. HUTCHINS, *The Illusion of Permanence* (Princeton University Press, 1967).

M. V. JACKSON, *European Powers and South-East Africa* (Longmans, 1942).

R. JENKINS, *Sir Charles Dilke. A Victorian Tragedy* (W. Collins, 1958).

W. JORDAN, *White Over Black. American Attitudes Toward the Negro, 1550–1812* (University of North Carolina Press, 1968).

A. G. KELLER, *Colonization* (London, 1908).

C. KEPHART, *The Races of Mankind* (P. Owen, 1961).

V. G. KIERNAN, *The Lords of Human Kind* (Weidenfeld & Nicolson, 1969).

O. KLINEBERG, *Negro Intelligence and Selective Migration* (Columbia University Press, 1935).

Race and Psychology (Paris, 1953, U.N.E.S.C.O.).

F. J. KLINGBERG and A. H. ABEL, *A Side-Light on Anglo-American Relations, 1839–58* (Association for the Study of Negro Life and History Inc., Lancaster, Penna., 1927).

243

W. L. LANGER, *The Diplomacy of Imperialism, 1890–1902* (Knopf, 1935, 2 vols.).

K. S. LATOURETTE, *The Great Century in Europe and the United States of America, A.D. 1800–A.D. 1914* (Eyre & Spottiswoode, 1941).

M. LEIRIS, *Race and Culture* (Paris, 1952, U.N.E.S.C.O.).

C. LEVI-STRAUSS, *Race and History* (Paris, 1952, U.N.E.S.C.O.).

A. W. LEWIS, *Labour in the West Indies* (London, 1939).

G. D. LILLIBRIDGE, *Beacon of Freedom* (New York, 1961).

K. LITTLE, *Negroes in Britain* (Routledge & Kegan Paul, 1948).
Race and Society (Paris, 1953, U.N.E.S.C.O.).

E. LONN, *Foreigners in The Confederacy* (University of North Carolina Press, 1940).

A. O. LOVEJOY, *The Great Chain of Being* (Harvard University Press, 1936).

R. H. LOWIE, *The History of Ethnological Theory* (Harrap, 1937).

I. D. MACCRONE, *Race Attitudes in South Africa. Historical, Experimental and Psychological Studies* (Witwatersrand University Press, 1965).

J. M. MCPHERSON, *The Struggle for Equality: Abolitionists and the Negro in the Civil War and Reconstruction* (Princeton University Press, 1964).

D. P. MANNIX and M. COWLEY, *Black Cargoes* (Viking, 1965).

O. MANNONI, *Prospero and Caliban. The Psychology of Colonization* (transl. P. Powesland, Praeger, 1964).

H. MANTSCH, *Leopold Graf Berchtold* (Verlag Styria, Gratz, 1963).

P. MASON (ed.), *Man, Race and Darwin* (Royal Anthropological Institute & Institute of Race Relations, Oxford University Press, 1960).
Christianity and Race (Lutterworth Press, 1956).
Prospero's Magic. Some Thoughts on Class and Race (Oxford University Press, 1962).
Race Relations in Africa (S.C.M. Press, 1960).
Common Sense about Race Relations (Gollancz, 1961).

W. L. MATHIESON, *British Slave Emancipation, 1838–49* (Longmans, 1932).
The Sugar Colonies and Governor Eyre, 1849–1866 (Longmans, 1936).

R. MAUNIER, *Great Britain and the Slave Trade, 1839–65* (London, 1929).
The Sociology of Colonies (Routledge & Kegan Paul, 1949, 2 vols. transl. E. Lorimer).

G. R. MELLOR, *British Imperial Trusteeship, 1783–1850* (Faber, 1951).

T. R. METCALF, *Aftermath of Revolt. India 1857–1870* (Princeton University Press, 1964).

244

SELECTED BIBLIOGRAPHY

H. MILLER, *Races, Nations and Classes* (Philadelphia, 1924).
Race Conflict in New Zealand, 1814–65 (Tri-Ocean, 1966).

A. MONTAGU, *Man's Most Dangerous Myth: the Fallacy of Race* (Columbia University Press, 1947).

S. NEILL, *A History of Christian Missions* (Hodder & Stoughton, 1964).

E. A. OGDEN, *A Sketch of Anglo-Indian Literature* (London, 1908).

R. OLIVER, *The Missionary Factor in East Africa* (Longmans, 1952).

R. OLIVER and G. MATHEW (eds.), *History of East Africa* (Oxford University Press, 1963).

S. OLIVIER, *Jamaica, the Blessed Isle* (Faber, 1937).
The Myth of Governor Eyre (Hogarth Press, 1933).

G. OSEI, *The Forgotten Great Africans* (Osei, 1965).

Papers on Inter-Racial Problems Communicated to the First Universal Races Congress Held at the University of London, July 26–29, 1911 (London, 1911).

R. E. PARK, *Race and Culture* (Glencoe Free Press, 1950).

O. PATTERSON, *The Sociology of Slavery* (MacGibbon & Kee, Ltd., 1967).

S. PATTERSON, *Dark Strangers: A Sociological Study of a Recent West Indian Migrant Group in Brixton, South London* (Penguin, 1963).

T. K. PENNIMAN, *A Hundred Years of Anthropology* (G. Duckworth, 1952).

L. RICHARDS and J. PLACE (eds.), *East African Explorers* (London, 1960).

A. H. RICHMOND, *Colour Prejudice in Britain. A Study of West Indian Workers in Liverpool, 1941–51* (Routledge & Kegan Paul, 1954).

G. ROBERTS, *The Population of Jamaica* (Cambridge University Press, 1957).

R. ROBINSON, J. GALLAGHER and A. DENNY, *Africa and the Victorians, the Official Mind of Imperialism* (Macmillan, 1961).

J. A. ROGERS, *One Hundred Amazing Facts About the Negro* (New York, 1934).
Real Facts About Ethiopia (New York, 1936).
Sex and Race (New York, 1941–4).

A. M. ROSE, *The Roots of Prejudice* (Paris, 1952, U.N.E.S.C.O.).

A. and C. B. ROSE (eds.), *Minority Problems* (Harper, 1965).

A. G. RUSSELL, *Colour, Race and Empire* (Gollancz, 1944).

R. SEGAL, *The Race War* (Cape, 1967).

B. SEMMEL, *The Governor Eyre Controversy* (MacGibbon & Kee, 1962).

H. L. SHAPIRO, *Race Mixture* (Paris, 1953, U.N.E.S.C.O.).

P. SHERLOCK, *West Indies* (Thames & Hudson, Ltd., 1966).

A. SHUEY, *The Testing of Negro Intelligence* (London, 1958).

245

M. G. SMITH, *The Plural Society in the British West Indies* (University of California Press, 1965).

E. D. SOPER, *Racism. A World Issue* (Abingdon-Cokesbury Press, 1947).

T. G. SPEAR, *A History of India* (Penguin, 1966).
Oxford History of Modern India, 1740–1947 (Oxford University Press, 1965).

K. STAMPP, *The Peculiar Institution. Negro Slavery in the American South* (Eyre & Spottiswoode, 1964).

W. R. STANTON, *The Leopard's Spots. Scientific Attitudes Towards Race in America, 1815–59* (Chicago University Press, 1960).

E. STOKES, *The Political Ideas of English Imperialism* (Oxford University Press, 1960).
The English Utilitarians and India (Oxford University Press, 1959).

H. L. SWINT, *The Northern Teacher in the South, 1862–70* (Nashville, 1941).

F. THISTLETHWAITE, *The Anglo-American Connection in the Early Nineteenth Century* (University of Pennsylvania Press, 1959).

E. T. THOMPSON and E. C. HUGHES, *Race: Individual and Collective Behaviour* (Free Press, Glencoe, 1958).

A. P. THORNTON, *The Imperial Idea and Its Enemies* (Macmillan, 1959).

A. K. WEINBERG, *Manifest Destiny, a Study of Nationalist Expansionism in American History* (John Hopkins Press, 1935).

E. WILLIAMS, *Capitalism and Slavery* (University of North Carolina Press, 1947).
British Historians and the West Indies (Deutsch, 1966).
The Negro in the Caribbean (New York, 1942).

G. WINT, *The British in Asia* (Faber, 1947).

Thesis

M. JONES, *Lancashire and the American Civil War*, London Ph.D., 1969.

Index

251